THE
EVERYTHING®
SALES
BOOK

Dear Reader,

My first sales job was more than four decades ago. Was I ever nervous! I had taken sales courses, but was not ready for the reality of selling things to others. I knew the steps, the theories, and the motivational phrases, but the first sales call—and first "No"—was devastating. I almost quit right there.

Somehow, I didn't. I persevered. I learned how to help others buy what they need. I discovered inner strengths that professional salespeople develop. I've even been able to apply some of these skills to other aspects of my life.

Since my first day in sales, I've sold in retail stores; sold advertising for newspapers, shoppers, and radio; sold business software systems; houses and businesses; and a wide variety of other products and services, garnering sales awards and a good income. One of my sales jobs took me to England, Germany, Holland, Belgium, France, and Indonesia—and my bosses were happy to pay all of my expenses.

I wish I knew then what I know now about the profession of sales. It is a satisfying and rewarding career that contributes to the lives of others. And it doesn't have to be cutthroat. You don't have to be deceptive or greedy to be successful. There are plenty of opportunities for those who sincerely care about their customers and how they serve others. I'm honored to be able to share these proven techniques with you in this book.

Wherever you are in your sales career—starting out or burning out—this book will guide you in developing a fulfilling and rewarding career as a Golden Rule Seller.

Best wishes,

Dan Ramsey

Welcome to the EVERYTHING® Series!

These handy, accessible books give you all you need to tackle a difficult project, gain a new hobby, comprehend a fascinating topic, prepare for an exam, or even brush up on something you learned back in school but have since forgotten.

You can choose to read an *Everything*® book from cover to cover or just pick out the information you want from our four useful boxes: e-questions, e-facts, e-alerts, and e-ssentials.

We give you everything you need to know on the subject, but throw in a lot of fun stuff along the way, too.

We now have more than 400 *Everything*® books in print, spanning such wide-ranging categories as weddings, pregnancy, cooking, music instruction, foreign language, crafts, pets, New Age, and so much more. When you're done reading them all, you can finally say you know *Everything*®!

QUESTION?

Answers to
common questions

FACTS

Important snippets
of information

ALERTS!

Urgent
warnings

ESSENTIALS

Quick
handy tips

PUBLISHER Karen Cooper

DIRECTOR OF ACQUISITIONS AND INNOVATION Paula Munier

MANAGING EDITOR, EVERYTHING SERIES Lisa Laing

COPY CHIEF Casey Ebert

ACQUISITIONS EDITOR Lisa Laing

SENIOR DEVELOPMENT EDITOR Brett Palana-Shanahan

EDITORIAL ASSISTANT Hillary Thompson

Visit the entire Everything® series at *www.everything.com*

THE
EVERYTHING®
SALES
BOOK

Proven techniques guaranteed to get results

Dan Ramsey

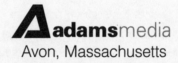

Avon, Massachusetts

To your Golden Rule career in sales.

An Everything® Series Book.
Everything® and everything.com® are registered trademarks of F+W Media, Inc.

Published by Adams Media, a division of F+W Media
57 Littlefield Street, Avon, MA 02322 U.S.A.
www.adamsmedia.com

ISBN 10: 1-59869-638-6
ISBN 13: 978-1-59869-638-7

Printed in the United States of America.

J   I   H   G   F   E   D   C   B   A

Library of Congress Cataloging-in-Publication Data
is available from the publisher.

This publication is designed to provide accurate and authoritative information with regard to the subject matter covered. It is sold with the understanding that the publisher is not engaged in rendering legal, accounting, or other professional advice. If legal advice or other expert assistance is required, the services of a competent professional person should be sought.

—From a *Declaration of Principles* jointly adopted by a Committee of the American Bar Association and a Committee of Publishers and Associations

Many of the designations used by manufacturers and sellers to distinguish their products are claimed as trademarks. Where those designations appear in this book and Adams Media was aware of a trademark claim, the designations have been printed with initial capital letters.

This book is available at quantity discounts for bulk purchases.
For information, please call 1-800-289-0963.

Contents

Acknowledgments

Literally thousands of people have taught me about the profession of sales. They include customers, prospects, employers, competitors, and—especially— other salespeople. In addition, I've been fortunate to learn from Zig Ziglar and Tom Hopkins, two of the world's greatest salespeople. Zig is a consummate Golden Rule Seller. Tom is a leading inspiration in the sales profession. Thanks also go to the U.S. Bureau of Labor Statistics for compiling employment statistics on people in the occupation of sales.

I also thank editors Lisa Laing and Brett Palana-Shanahan, and agent Bob Diforio for making this book possible—and my family for making it necessary.

Top Ten Things You'll Learn After Reading This Book

1. **Features and Benefits:** Buyers purchase features and benefits, not products and services.

2. **Selling Against Your Competition:** Make sure that you know your competition better than your buyers do.

3. **Selling on Price:** Instead of selling on price, help your buyers undestand the greater value of what you offer.

4. **The Soft Sell:** Use suggestion and gentle persuasion to help your buyers make decisions.

5. **The Hard Sell:** Most buyers today have too many other choices than to be sold using fear and intimidation.

6. **Good-Friends Selling:** Buyers don't want the good-friends approach; they prefer friendly assistance.

7. **Selling on Reputation:** If your buyers trust you to be honest and accurate, they will buy more from you.

8. **Problem-Solution Selling:** Buyers have a problem that you can solve. By asking relevant questions and listening to answers, you can help them buy.

9. **Consultive Selling:** Once you've earned a position of authority and trust with your buyers, you can consult with them toward the best solution.

10. **Value-Added Selling:** Adding real or perceived value to transactions can improve your sales income.

Introduction

▶ NOTHING HAPPENS UNTIL something IS SOLD. Take a look around you. Everything you see—from beans to buildings—has been sold by someone to someone. Our modern economy rolls forward on the wheels of sales. Without sales, factories and stores would close worldwide, trucks would park, airplanes would be grounded, and virtually everyone would be unemployed.

Fortunately, selling is alive and well. It contributes significantly to our economy and offers us jobs as well as something to spend our earnings on. It keeps trillions of dollars in motion and benefits everyone.

Unfortunately, the profession of sales has been damaged by an unscrupulous few who will say or do just about anything to get a buyer's dollars. They are the minority. Most of the *14 million* people who sell are honest. They recognize that selling is an honorable and necessary profession. Many also recognize that they could do a better job if they knew how.

The Everything® Sales Book is written for people who are considering their first or twenty-first job in sales. It offers practical and proven advice gleaned from decades of experience and dozens of experts. It isn't a textbook; it's a guide. It's about selling in the real world.

The majority of salespeople are employed in retail sales. They are the clerks and cashiers that are paid to help customers buy. Many of them migrate from other jobs, not fully prepared to sell. A few hours of orientation, if any, and they are put out on the sales floor. The intuitive ones learn on their own; the others get frustrated and quit. They miss the opportunity to discover how rewarding a sales career can be.

Experienced salespeople are discouraged in their efforts to succeed. They begin disbelieving in themselves and their products or services. They become disheartened. A sales guru comes up with another "foolproof" selling method and they try it. Many learn that it just doesn't work for them. It's not real. It uses high-pressure tactics or unproven psychology to do what should be easy: help buyers make good choices.

The Everything® Sales Book is based on common sense: Sell as you want to be sold. That's Golden Rule Selling. It builds your sales career from where you are right now and it shows you how you can build a future with it. No hypes. No gimmicks. Just common sense. It begins by clearly answering the question, "What is selling?" and explains how and why Golden Rule Selling is productive without being pushy. *The Everything® Sales Book* then guides you through your career, beginning with elementary retail sales and moving into professional business-to-business sales with high salaries. You'll learn how to find buyers, make successful presentations, solve their problems, and keep them satisfied. You'll discover how to get your first or next satisfying job in sales. In addition, this book focuses on how you can work smarter rather than harder by using the numerous technology tools to find and manage customers.

The Everything® Sales Book is written for people who want to find success in sales. They want to contribute to the lives of others as they build their own. They want to feel good about being in one of the world's most valuable professions: sales.

Life is selling. Enjoy both.

CHAPTER 1

What Is Selling?

The good news is: You've got a job. The bad news is: It's in sales. Or maybe you've been in sales for some time, but you're struggling. Or you're doing okay, but having trouble sleeping at night because of ethical pressures. This first chapter starts at square one: What is selling? It offers a practical look at what sales is about, explains how it is actually a noble profession, and helps you to understand your primary role as a salesperson. This chapter offers you a solid foundation from which to start or renew your sales career—and to enjoy what you do.

It's Not What You Might Think

Many people's view of salespeople comes from images of Willy Loman in Arthur Miller's play *Death of a Salesman*. Willy earned a good living for forty years as a seller by setting aside his principles. He finally sells himself on the fact that he is a better salesperson than he really is. As customers walk away and his income recedes, Willy is forced to borrow from neighbors to pay bills, making him angry and bitter. Only a few relatives show up at his funeral. Willy dies without money, friends, or prestige.

Other fictional characters strengthen the perception that salespeople are sleazy and will do nearly anything to make a sale. Unfortunately, a few real-life salespeople reinforce the stereotype. Even so, the sales profession is actually populated by millions of people with varying skill levels who ethically help others make purchases. They offer a genuine service to others, building the economy and contributing to the lives of their customers and employers, and to society. This is the type of seller that most people want to emulate.

The Sales Profession

The U.S. Bureau of Labor Statistics reports that nearly 11 percent of the work force is employed in the sales profession. That's more than 14 million people. Of these, nearly a third are retail sellers and another 25 percent are transaction cashiers. They don't use the advanced sales techniques of other sales jobs, but they should know the basics to make their jobs easier and more secure. Their jobs can lead them into professional sales positions—and more money.

When most people think of salespeople they think of insurance sales, real estate sales, travel agents, manufacturing representatives, financial services, advertising sales, sales engineers, and door-to-door sales. These are the people who offer the greatest services to the economy, as they bridge the span between producer and consumer in a thousand ways. Some earn impressive salaries, while others are paid in part or in full by a commission, a percentage of their sales. That puts some professional salespeople among the highest-paid employees. It also gives a few an opportunity to be self-employed as independent salespeople.

Selling 101

So, what is selling? A *sale* is an exchange of goods or services, typically for money. Anyone involved in the transaction with the customer is in the sales profession, a salesperson, a seller. On the retail level, that includes the counter person who helped the customer select the product and the cashier who made the transfer and suggested that they "come again." In technical sales, the sale is the transfer of real property, stocks or mutual funds, insurance, travel tickets, or any one of hundreds of other products or services that require extensive product knowledge and, in some cases, licensing.

Selling is informing the customer of the features and benefits of the product or service and, as needed, persuading the customer to make the purchase. *Persuasion* is the skill of guiding people toward making a decision. The job of a *seller*, then, is to inform and persuade. That's it.

FACT

The adage that nothing happens until a sale is made is true. Without a transaction—the exchange of goods, services, ideas, promises, or funds—the economy would come to a standstill. Fortunately, billions of sales are made each day at all levels of commerce and society. That makes everyone a seller. The best salespeople make the most money and have the potential for better lives.

What does it take to become a good seller?

- Product knowledge
- Knowledge of competitive products
- Knowledge of product features
- Knowledge of benefits to customers
- Communication skills
- Listening skills
- Persuasion skills
- Professional skills (presentation skills, recordkeeping, etc.)

Ethics

Ethics is moral conduct and judgment. It is choosing products to represent, the facts that you present to customers, and the persuasion techniques you use. It is the missing ingredient from Willy Loman salesmanship. This book will guide you in developing ethical sales skills, focusing on the practices and benefits of Golden Rule Selling (Chapter 2).

Selling Is Helping

"Can I get some help here?"

It sometimes seems like all of the sales clerks are on break and that customers are on their own when trying to make a selection or find a product. It often occurs in big-box stores, where the clerk's position is underpaid and underappreciated. That's why many customers prefer to shop in independent retail stores where help typically is easier to get—sometimes by the owner herself. It's just too difficult—and frustrating—to find help in many stores and from many services. What's the problem?

The Problem

Originally, retail stores were smaller, franchises were nonexistent, and assistance was expected. Then came the self-service stores that put products on the shelf and expected customers to follow the signs and find them. Product labeling made it a little easier to find and buy what was needed. The self-service stores grew for one reason: they cut costs. Retail stores got away from helping their customers and depended on product selection to make up for any sales losses.

The lack of assistance in purchasing has moved to the technical sales fields. People can now buy financial stock or cars without any help or advice from knowledgeable salespeople. They save money, but they don't always make the best decisions because they don't have a professional and ethical advisor to help them with the purchase. It often seems like it's hard to find good help.

The Solution

The decline in assistive selling can work to your benefit. As a seller, you can focus on helping *your* customers make good buying decisions. With expanded product knowledge, an understanding of features and benefits, good communication skills, a working knowledge of persuasion, and your ethical judgment, you can stand out as a helpful salesperson.

Two men were being chased by a bear. One took off his shoes and threw them away. The other man said, "Taking off your shoes won't help you outrun that bear!" The shoeless man responded, "I don't have to outrun the bear. I only have to outrun you!" Sometimes a little extra effort can put you at the front of the pack.

The extra effort to offer genuine service to customers can help your sales career in many ways. In an entry-level sales position, it will show your employers that you are willing to work a little harder to help customers—the source of business profits. In a technical sales position with commissions, it will earn you more sales and more income. It also will earn you repeat and referral customers, the sources of your future sales. Higher-than-average sales can help you land a better job. In addition, the extra effort will help you build satisfying relationships with your customers. Assistive selling is win-win.

Everyone Sells Something

In truth, everyone is a seller. Everyone has knowledge, a product, or a service that he or she offers to others and, in many cases, attempts to persuade others to acquire. Need some examples?

- A job interview
- A marriage proposal
- A friendly smile to another driver, asking to allow you into his traffic lane

- "If you do your chores, you can go to the football game."
- "I think you'll like that movie. The star is gorgeous!"
- "Can you be here by ten? I need to leave by eleven."

Sales is persuasion. Everyone sells something every day, and often many times a day. The techniques that you use to inform and persuade others are extensively developed in professional salespeople, but everyone can use them.

Persuasion 101

As defined earlier in this chapter, *persuasion* is the skill of guiding people toward making a decision. Whether you are a real estate salesperson, a retail clerk, or a rather nervous suitor, persuasion can help you get your message across and, possibly, accepted by another—a transaction. You can persuade others by appealing to their reasoning, their emotions, or both. Besides verbal persuasion, there are other ways to help get your point across.

Appeal to Reason

Reason is a description or explanation. It's the facts. When buying a product or service, purchasers want to know what it is, how it works, and what benefits they will derive. You, as a customer, want to know this. Your customers do, too. Depending on what you are selling—a simple product, a complex service, or a concept—you can appeal to others by using various types of reasoning, such as logic, rhetoric, and proof. Following are some examples to illustrate.

- **Logic:** "You want something that will clean stubborn stains on enamel and XYZ has been proven in scientific tests to clean enamel easier and better than any other stain cleaner."
- **Rhetoric:** "XYZ is the best stain fighter available."
- **Proof:** "Let's test XYZ on this stubborn stain."

These simple examples offer three ways that you can appeal to a person's reasoning to help you convince them of the validity of your facts. You probably recognize these phrasings from the thousands of ads that bombard you daily. That's because advertising, too, uses persuasion.

The crafts of persuasion and reasoning are a lifelong study. If you are interested in a technical sales career, consider taking college-level courses in these topics or self-studying books that can give you more insight into the powers of reasoning and persuasion.

Appeal to Emotion

Emotion is a strong human feeling, such as love, hate, anger, fear, and compassion. Salespeople and other persuaders often use emotional appeals to help make a sale. Should they? That depends on what is being sold. Selling real estate, for example, involves the buyer's reasoning, of course, but it also is an emotional purchase. So it's appropriate to use emotional appeals to help sell a home. It isn't an appropriate tactic for selling industrial control valves.

Emotional appeals are frequently used in advertising, religion, propaganda, and sex. For example:

- "Imagine living in the nicest home on the block."
- "Find full acceptance at our church."
- "Immigrants are taking over our jobs."
- "Buy me a drink?"

Many consumers still consider appeals to their emotions as primary elements in their decisions to buy. However, a growing number of educated consumers expect salespeople to only use emotional appeals when they are appropriate to the product or service, and they will stop buying if the appeal is inappropriate.

Aids to Persuasion

The art of persuasion is highly developed and utilizes a variety of tools to make the sale. Voice control is one of the most important to the seller. The voice can be used to help persuade customers with reason as well as with emotion. Voice is a primary tool in telephone sales, so it is covered more thoroughly in Chapter 6. Body language, too, is invaluable as a persuasive sales tool. Chapter 7 offers proven methods of improving your people skills including the basics of body language.

You'll also need to understand common personality types and how to persuade them. The variety of customers and other people you will encounter in your sales career are described further in Chapter 7.

Whatever type of customer you serve and whatever type of sales job you have, the art of appropriate persuasion will be one of your greatest sales tools.

QUESTION?

How can I find out more about the art of persuasion?
There are many classic textbooks. A popular title is *Persuasion: Messages, Receivers, and Contexts by William Rogers*. Online, visit Changing Minds *(www.changingminds.org),* a resource explaining in layperson's terms how people think, believe, feel, and do. It includes hundreds of articles with explanations and examples.

The Accidental Seller

The majority of working salespeople came into their jobs from other directions. That is, they didn't have formal training in sales before accepting the job. That includes many technical, retail, and telephone salespeople.

There are about 3 million technical salespeople in the United States, ranging from wholesale sales representatives (wholesale reps) to sales engineers and financial service agents. In addition, there are more than 9 million retail clerks and cashiers who work in the broadly defined sales field. The majority of these are accidental salespeople; they didn't plan on getting into sales. It just happened.

Technical Sales

For many, sales jobs evolve from technical jobs. For example, sales engineers sell technical products: computer systems, industrial chemicals, heavy equipment, and so on. Most sales engineers were first trained engineers who, for various reasons, accepted jobs selling what they know. Many are promoted from engineering positions and taught the basic skills of selling.

Other technical salespeople have some experience within the field, but require additional technical and sales training before they can begin selling. Real estate sales is a good example. Many real estate salespeople have knowledge of housing as a homeowner, contractor, or from the financial trades, but need additional training in real estate law and financing. They take courses in real estate sales or complete courses such as the Graduate Realtor Institute (GRI) training.

Technical salespeople are hired because they know their product and they have the people skills to help others buy their product. Often, they then must learn the basics of how to sell.

Retail Sales

Most people who serve in retail sales, too, never planned a career in this trade. They often are people of diverse skills with some basic knowledge of what they sell or how to help customers buy. At the entry level, retail clerks may not know more than their customers about the products and services offered. They are hired more to keep inventory on the shelves and answer basic questions about product and location and are paid accordingly.

Eventually, retail salespeople select a specialty or two that will earn them higher wages or possibly a commission on sales. For example, an experienced retail clerk may ask for an assignment to the discount store's jewelry department and then learn the product sufficiently to move on to an independent jewelry store. An experienced cashier may apply for a position with more sales opportunities and a higher wage.

In retail sales, new employees soon discover that the more they know about product and the buying process, the more income they can make. Knowledge and experience pay off. Chapter 5 offers further training in retail sales and how to advance your career—and income—in retail.

Telephone Sales

Another entry-level sales job is telephone sales, which, like other sales jobs, has been tarnished by unethical salespeople. However, the telephone is a dynamic sales tool that can reduce sales costs and make salespeople more productive. Chapter 6 shows you how to make an honest living in telephone sales.

How much do technical salespeople make?
The answer depends on what level of technical knowledge is required in selling the product. It also depends on the price of the product or package that is sold. Many industrial sales engineers earn over $100,000 a year in salary, commissions, and bonuses. Commercial aircraft manufacturers pay their salespeople many hundreds of thousands of dollars for a sale; however, they may not have a sale for a year or two. There currently are about 75,000 sales engineers in the United States.

Sales Writing

Another job that many accidentally enter is sales writing. People with writing skills discover that the craft of persuasive writing can pay off well. They take jobs writing advertising copy, promotional materials, sales literature, and other sales collateral. They often support sales and marketing people in communicating their messages to prospective buyers.

The Sales Professional

On the other end of the sales marketplace are the pros. These are highly trained, motivated, professional salespeople who know their product, their customers, and how to bring them together. In most sales fields, the pros earn the top 20 percent in income. Many of them began as accidental salespeople and then went back to school for the education and training to become pros. Others decided early to develop a professional sales career and spent their time and money on advanced sales training. They can sell cars, condos, or convention events equally well. Most sales professionals require state licensing or other certification to develop required credentials and customer trust.

Chapters 8 through 14 cover the basics of what sales professionals do to make a sale. It's a process with many proven steps and great rewards. These are the components and techniques required to make large sales that involve thousands and even millions of dollars.

All salespeople, from the retail clerk to the securities agent can expand their income by learning and using professional sales techniques. Some of the steps don't apply to retail selling, but you can still learn from them and apply general principles to enhance your sales career at any level.

As the sales process and profession becomes more developed, you can learn from the advanced techniques offered in Chapters 15 through 19. These include developing sales proposals, selling to multiple buyers, self-management, and setting and achieving sales goals.

Chapters 20 and 21 can help you develop your sales career by showing you how to apply sales techniques to marketing yourself and getting the best sales jobs.

QUESTION?

How much do top-level sales professionals make?
How high can you count? Leading sales professionals, especially in the technical trades, can earn $1 million or more in a year. They are selling things like huge construction projects, defense contracts, extensive computer systems, and other big-ticket items. They frequently hold numerous engineering degrees and have spent many years learning and developing advanced sales techniques. They also have large support staffs that do the detail work for them.

Your Sales Career

"I've been in sales for six months now and have sold lots of things: my house, my car, my boat . . ."

Selling is a difficult profession that will challenge your feelings of self-worth, your relationships, and your bank account—especially if some or all of your income is derived from commissions.

If you are considering a job in sales, think of it as the beginning of a career—a long-term progression of jobs that will take you to your personal and financial goals. As you develop your sales career, you will develop the things, listed previously, that make a good seller.

ALERT!

Don't fall for the job ads that promise unrealistic incomes in sales. Though they may be possible, 99 percent of the applicants will never earn them. Instead, they will work for little or no money selling a few products—often to friends and family—with little cost to the employer. If it's too good to be true, it's too good to be true.

Where to Start Your Career

Many sales careers begin in areas of prior training or personal interest. Following are some examples.

- Computer programmers can sell software programs wholesale or retail.
- Well-traveled people can sell travel services.
- Banking and financial employees can sell financial services.
- Health care professionals can sell medical supplies, pharma-ceuticals, health insurance, or other health-related products and services.
- People with economic or business degrees can sell financial prod-ucts or services.
- Construction trades people can sell real estate, building materials, tools and equipment, or related services.
- Auto mechanics can sell tools, parts, or auto repair services.
- Experienced retail clerks can sell to wholesale accounts.

You get the picture. Use your own training, experience, and interests to map out a career in sales that offers progressively more opportunities to help people buy. Many people start their sales career at the retail level to determine if they have the desire and personal skills to be successful. If they don't, they either go out and get them or they choose another career. Sales isn't for everyone.

Life Is Sales

Everyone can benefit from understanding the sales process and how things are sold. Consumers can make better buying decisions by understanding the approaches that sellers use. Basic sales techniques, inherently understood by most people, can be useful in relationships and even in other careers. Simplified sales methods can be used to help children accept household rules or to explain your political positions to friends. In addition, many other professions use the principles of persuasion and sales in their fields. Actors are persuaders. So are waiters, doctors, mechanics, and many others who don't officially work in the sales trade. They all can benefit from learning the basics of sales.

What is selling? It's a noble profession that helps buyers and sellers solve their problems. With your current knowledge, the ability to learn new skills, and diligence, you can proudly tell others that you are "in sales."

CHAPTER 2

Golden Rule Selling

Sales has developed such a negative image that many consumers feel they could never consider a career in sales. It's almost akin to a life of crime. They think, "Why should I force people to buy things they don't want or need?" The reality is that selling things can be an ethical and rewarding job of helping others. What's the difference in viewpoints? It's all in how you approach the job and what you expect from it. This chapter offers an increasingly popular method of selling that offers valuable rewards to you and to those you serve.

The Golden Rule of Sales

Everyone's heard of the Golden Rule, but what is it really? And how can it be applied to the job of selling? Isn't the term "Golden Rule Selling" an oxymoron? Isn't it contradictory?

You might be surprised at how many salespeople use Golden Rule techniques in their work. They typically aren't the plaid-suited fellows with shiny shoes and a constant grin. They are the quieter salespeople who actually consider what *you* want first. They sincerely desire to help you. Of course, they aren't totally selfless, but they usually are trustworthy. They need to make a living, too. But most will not do so dishonestly. They understand that the rewards of Golden Rule Selling are greater than those of Do-Whatever-It-Takes Selling.

Golden Rule 101

The Golden Rule is a universal law, advocated by all of the major religions and belief systems around the world. They include Hinduism, Buddhism, Confucianism, Jainism, Judaism, Christianity, Islam, Baha'i, and others. Basically, it says "However you want others to treat you, treat them likewise."

The Golden Rule is also known as the ethic of reciprocity. It is a fundamental moral principle. It is a global ethic. It is a human right. Imagine how the world would change for the better if all practiced the Golden Rule and treated others as they want to be treated.

FACT

Confucianism and Judaism, among others, have an opposite rule; Confucians call it the Silver Rule. Paraphrased, it says "However you don't want others to treat you, don't so treat them."

The problem is that the Golden Rule can be difficult to apply. Your job as a wage earner is to consider yourself and your needs first and foremost. If there's some left over, you'll consider sharing. That's human nature. The internal struggle, then, is between human rights and human nature. You versus them.

What Do You Want as a Buyer?

So, how can the Golden Rule be applied to sales? Rephrased, the Golden Rule of Sales is: Sell as you want to be sold. It means sell things to others as you would like them to sell to you. What does that actually suggest?

First, answer the question: How *do* you want to be sold? That's easier to define. As a typical consumer, a buyer, you probably want purchasing transactions to involve:

- Trust
- Honesty
- Helpful attitude
- Acknowledgment as an individual
- Listening to your needs
- Accurate information
- Options
- Clear explanations

Imagine buying a car, for example, with the help of a seller that you totally trust to be honest, accurate, and helpful, and who listens to your needs before offering options and clear explanations. Isn't that what *you*, as a buyer, want in a sales transaction? Of course, you may ask a question that the seller cannot answer, but an honest seller will tell you so rather than make something up. There's one more quality that you, as a buyer, want in your seller: Assistance with the decision. You want the seller to recognize the stages of the sales process and help you through them. You want them to honestly answer your unstated question, "Now what?" You want them to be your guide in the buying process—not pulling or pushing you through it. You want to be sold through the application of the Golden Rule.

How Can You Sell by the Golden Rule?

Now that you know what you want from a seller, you can better define the type of seller that you can be. The characteristics you want to have include:

- Trust
- Honesty
- Helpful attitude
- Acknowledgment as an individual
- Listening to the buyer's needs
- Accurate information
- Options
- Clear explanations
- Guidance through the buying process

Is this definition of a Golden Rule Seller realistic? Is it attainable? Again, there are many successful salespeople working right now who strive to apply Golden Rule Selling in all of their transactions. You can join them.

Don't depend just on your own perceptions of what buyers want. Ask them. Find prospective buyers for what you want to sell and ask them how they make their buying decisions. What do they consider? What do they want from the seller? How could their current sales source be improved? Your job is to listen to buyers; start now.

Building Trust

Trust is "assured reliance on the character, ability, strength, or truth of someone or something." To trust someone is to not question what that person says or does. Trust is built by not giving people a reason to disbelieve you.

Unfortunately, once you are identified as a "seller," trust often goes into negative numbers. That's why many salespeople refer to themselves as "associates" or "buyer consultants." But a title in itself won't convince many people to trust you.

FACT

Trust is an invaluable asset in all transactions. Trust is the belief that others will not take advantage of your position, needs, vulnerabilities, or openness. It is offering personal information to others and expecting them not to abuse it. It is believing that what someone tells you is true. It is acting upon the knowledge of others. Unfortunately, the perception of trust can be forged. That's why many people withhold individual trust until they test it. As a seller, your job is to initiate and build mutual trust with your customers.

How can you, as a seller, build trust? There are many ways, expanded upon throughout this book. In short, building trust begins with acting in a trustworthy manner. For example, if you walk up to a retail buyer and start acting like a pushy "seller," it won't work. Instead, approach buyers neutrally. By coming up to them wearing a name tag and/or uniform, you've already identified yourself as a representative of the store. If they don't respond to you, leave them alone. If they do, be as helpful as possible. If they attempt to end the conversation with a "thank you," respond with, "Please ask me if you have any other questions. Thank you." Then step away. Sell as you want to be sold.

Honesty

Honesty is adherence to the facts. It is a refusal to lie, cheat, or steal. It is knowing as much as possible about the product or service that you sell—and not making things up if you don't know. It's how you want to be sold.

For example, a real estate salesperson may respond to your question about financing with "You should have no problem getting a loan on this home." Unless the person already knows the specifics of your financial condition (called "prequalification"), the statement may or may not be true. It's not honest. An honest response would be "I'd have to know more about your financial qualifications to answer that question."

Unfortunately, too many salespeople feel that if they answer all questions honestly, they will lose the sale. They feel they can't afford the personal loss, so they make up an answer they believe the buyer will accept. The right answer is the honest answer, even if it is "I don't know, but I can attempt to find out." Most buyers will accept this answer and also respect the honesty of the seller. Most can easily spot a made-up answer and dock you points in the "honesty" column.

Helpful Attitude

All buyers have purchased products or services from salespeople who weren't very helpful. They needed the product more than they needed the help. However, millions of dollars in products and service have gone unsold because buyers didn't get the help needed to make an informed decision.

How can you apply the Golden Rule of Sales—sell as you want to be sold—to helping buyers? That's an easy one: Think of yourself as the buyer's helpful assistant. In fact, that's what you are. What does the buyer need to make the buying decision? Facts? Examples? A demonstration? A reputable endorsement? Offer these services to your buyer, whether selling shoes, software, sailboats, or samba lessons. Be helpful. But don't be pushy. Some buyers don't want much help in making their decision. Others do.

Acknowledgment

In this world of nearly 7 billion people, it's nice to be acknowledged as an individual—sincerely acknowledged. In some sales situations, names may not be exchanged, but the seller still can acknowledge the individual buyer by looking him or her in the eye and being friendly.

If names are given, they should be remembered and reused appropriately. As the dynamic sales psychologist Dale Carnegie said: "Our name is, to us, the sweetest word in the English language." Remember a person's name, and you will be remembered. It's a major component in Golden Rule Selling.

Listening

If everyone's talking, no one is listening. One of the most neglected rules of selling is "Listen to the customer." Most salespeople would rather "talk" the customer into buying. Unfortunately, many continue talking after the sale is made and keep talking until the sale falls apart. The problem is that gregarious people attracted to sales often think of themselves as born talkers. Instead, they should be born listeners.

But what if the buyers aren't talking much? Then ask. Begin with neutral questions that can be answered positively, then move on to questions that tell more about the buyer's needs and thoughts. Ask both closed-ended and open-ended questions, as appropriate.

- **Closed-ended question:** "Is the red or the blue one better for you?"
- **Open-ended question:** "How would you use this tool in your shop?"

Additional techniques of questioning will be developed in this book. One of the greatest skills of selling is knowing how to ask questions of buyers.

Accuracy

Accuracy is freedom from error. As a buyer, you don't want to base your purchasing decision on erroneous facts. In addition, if you discover an inaccuracy, it will pollute your perception of the product or service and the people who represent it.

Some error comes from honest mistakes. The list of product specifications weren't carefully reviewed before publication. A misleading statement was made or an accurate statement was misunderstood. Mistakes happen. The task of a responsible seller is to immediately correct the mistake or error as soon as it is identified. Doing so in conversation with a buyer can actually enhance your image as a knowledgeable seller. Just don't let it happen twice.

Options

Buying is about choices. Some salespeople believe that offering buyers too many choices will bog down the process and ruin the sale. It may. However, most modern buyers are sophisticated, multitasking people who can make clear decisions among numerous choices.

Your job, as a responsible and helpful seller, is to make sure that the buyer is offered appropriate choices. That doesn't mean you drag out all of your samples, color combinations, accessories, and options. It does mean that you ask appropriate questions to narrow down the options, then present products or services that fit your buyer's agreed-upon needs.

For example, if you are a car buyer, you don't want every model made by every manufacturer to be paraded past you. Instead, you want the seller to ask you relevant questions, then to offer you appropriate choices. That's Golden Rule Selling.

Clear Explanations

Selling isn't a monologue—it's a dialogue. However, to be effective, the conversation must be clearly delivered and clearly received. That means questions, answers, and explanations need to be understandable. Otherwise, the seller is answering irrelevant questions or explaining points that don't need clarification. Time and trust are being wasted.

There are numerous proven techniques for clarifying a buyer's question or comment. One is to rephrase the question and ask if that is what the buyer means. For example, "Are you asking about the length of the warranty?" Another is to ask the buyer to rephrase the question or comment. "Can you tell me what you mean by 'trouble free'?"

On the other side of the dialogue, make sure that you speak clearly and at a moderate pace when explaining features, benefits, or terminology. Remember that some of the words you use may not be clearly defined in the buyer's mind. Watch the buyer for facial and body clues that indicate failure to understand what you are explaining.

Guidance

As you will learn in this book, selling is a process. The process is similar for selling and buying most things. The primary difference is in the detail. The process and detail required to sell a book, for example, is less involved than that for selling a boat. However, each requires a decision. A *decision* is the process that leads to a selection from among variables.

- "Should I go to work today or to the ball game?"
- "Given traffic, which way should I drive to work today?"
- "Should I stop for a donut before going into the office?"
- "Where will I have lunch?"
- "Should I ask for a raise?"
- "Should I leave a little early?"
- "Where am I going to work now that I'm fired?"

Each day is filled with hundreds or thousands of decisions, most of them small and inconsequential. Stopping for one donut probably won't redirect your life. But it still requires a decision. Others can be life changing, such as where to find a new job. The *decision process* includes identification of a need, criteria, research, analysis, and one or more choices. For example:

- **Identification of a need:** You decide that a donut would satisfy both a need for sustenance and a desire for carbohydrates.
- **Criteria:** You want a cake donut rather than a fried donut to minimize calories. You also don't want to travel too far for the donut.
- **Research:** In your mind, you consider the donut shops located on your way to work.
- **Analysis:** You remember that Dunkin' Donuts has more cake donuts than Krispy Kreme does.
- **Choice:** You drive to Dunkin' Donuts and walk in. Uh-oh. More decisions!

Buying a boat is certainly a much more complex decision than buying a donut. However, the process is similar. Identify the need, develop the decision criteria, do the research, analyze the research, and make choices.

There will be dozens of choices involving a variety of criteria: finances, dock location, number of passengers, typical use, speed requirements, and so on. That's where professional guidance comes in.

Your job as a Golden Rule Seller is to help your clients make the best decision for *them* rather than for you and your employer. Why? Because that's how *you* want to be sold.

Lose a sale, but don't lose a customer. A sale may bring you a hundred dollars in income, but a customer, over time, can be a source of thousands of dollars in salary and commissions. For example, if you direct a prospect to a competitive product you may lose the sale, but you probably will gain a customer, one who will trust you for honest and relatively unbiased advice on future purchases. In addition, you probably will earn referrals to the customer's acquaintances.

Silver Rule Selling

Golden Rule Selling isn't necessarily easy. In fact, any selling isn't easy. However, there are proven benefits and rewards to the approach of selling as you want to be sold. You often can reach your own goals by helping others reach theirs. Golden Rule Selling is a proven method for doing so.

The opposite side of assistive selling, mentioned earlier in this chapter, can help you apply Golden Rule Selling. It's Silver Rule Selling. The Silver Rule says, "However you *don't* want others to treat you, *don't* so treat them." Silver Rule Selling, then is: Don't sell as you don't want to be sold. What does that mean?

Most buyers easily recognize and cringe at high-pressure sales tactics. They also don't like salespeople who are self-important and rude. Buyers don't like know-it-alls. They don't want to feel intimidated by others. They also don't like to answer unwelcome personal questions. How can these be usefully applied to Golden Rule Selling?

- Don't use high-pressure sales tactics on buyers.
- Don't attempt to put yourself on a higher status than the buyer.
- Don't be rude and condescending to the buyer.
- Don't pretend that you know everything about anything. No one does.
- Don't use intimidation to coerce buyers.
- Don't ask personal questions unless invited.

There are other don'ts to Golden Rule Selling. The point is that you should not only sell as you want to be sold, but also avoid the negative ways that you know firsthand that buyers dislike.

Benefits of Golden Rule Selling

Selling as you want to be sold is a nice philosophy, but does it work? It's altruistic, but is it practical? Can you build a satisfying sales career on it?

Think again about your experiences as a consumer, a buyer. How do you respond to Golden Rule Selling? Most consumers genuinely appreciate it. They often suffer through egocentric salespeople in hopes that, one day, a genuine Golden Rule Seller will step up and offer their assistance. They yearn for an honest, trustworthy, helpful buying guide who can assist them in making informed decisions. Maybe you do, too.

But is it profitable? Can you make a living applying Golden Rule Selling principles. Definitely, yes. In fact, your career can thrive as you develop resources that many other salespeople don't have:

- Loyal customers
- Referral business
- Buyer's trust
- Genuine self-confidence
- Job satisfaction

No one can truthfully claim that Method A will bring you more sales than Method B. Results depend on application. However, common sense tells you that treating your buyers as you want to be treated can earn trust and enhance your contribution to the lives of others. That's of much greater value than dusty Salesperson-of-the-Month plaques.

What you will discover is that selling as you want to be sold will benefit you in many ways. You will continue to make sales, possibly at a higher level than without these techniques, but you also will feel better about what you do. You'll discover that the slick tricks some salespeople use really don't work for very long. These sellers make a sale, but lose a customer and future referrals. They get caught in an untruth. They pretend to be superconfident but are masking feelings of inferiority.

You may actually earn a few Salesperson-of-the-Month plaques—or you may not. In either case, you will be proud of your role and your rewards in selling.

Problems of Golden Rule Selling

The bad news is that there are problems—euphemistically called "challenges"—that arise when Golden Rule Selling is your chosen sales method. You may have difficulty finding products or services to represent that allow you to sell as you want to be sold. You also may find it complicated to consistently sell by the Golden Rule.

Finding Appropriate Products or Services

It's a good thing that people are diverse. Some genuinely enjoy selling funeral services, while others abhor the job. The same is true for sporting equipment, books, housing, financial services, building materials, furniture, cruise tickets, air conditioners, widgets, and a thousand other products and services that are bought and sold daily.

Unfortunately, some salespeople already are selling things that they don't have an interest in. They aren't buyers and they probably shouldn't be sellers. Subconsciously, many of them make it clear to buyers that they really don't enjoy what they sell or how they sell it. Using coercive sales techniques, they sell anyway. Or they leave the sales profession, dissatisfied and broke.

How can you find products and services that you can represent with Golden Rule Selling? Look to your training and your interests. Consider the jobs you've previously held, the products you've bought and enjoyed, the hobbies and pastimes that have given you pleasure. It is so much easier to sell things that you are passionate about. You can even learn to sell them with sincerity in an environment that isn't pleasing to you. With experience, you can soon move on to a new environment and take your skills of selling what you love with you.

Whether you are currently employed in sales or are looking for your first or next job, take time to make a comprehensive list of the products and services that you would enjoy selling. What are they? In what environment would you prefer to sell them? Do you prefer face-to-face selling or telephone sales? Would you enjoy evangelizing this product or service, finding new prospects—or would selling to existing users be more comfortable for you? Do you like to challenge yourself daily or are you more comfortable with less-frequent challenges? To know what you can sell best, you must first know more about yourself.

QUESTION?

How can I know what I should be selling?
Ask your family and friends. They may know you better than you presume. Ask them what they think you would be good at selling. Of course, some will project their own desires on you. Others may offer ideas that you had not considered. You may be able to combine suggestions from others into the model sales job. In any case, their perspective on you and the world of products and services may help you choose an appropriate job that fits your personality and interests.

Consistency

Another problem of Golden Rule Selling is doing it consistently. It's one thing to believe that you will not apply undue sales pressure on a potential buyer. It's another thing to get into a sale and realize that if you don't make it, you won't make your car payment. What's the right answer?

Before you have to make such a decision, consider the scenarios appropriate to the products or services you sell as well as your own ethics. Hundreds of other decisions have led you to where you must make this decision: the buyer or me.

Of course, it's best not to get into a position where so much is riding on a single sale. Yes, easier said than done. Unexpected bills come up. Solid sales fall through. All it would take is a nudge and this buyer will make the purchase. Should you? Only you can make that decision. Use what you've learned about the decision process: identify the need, develop the criteria, do the research, make the analysis, and make the choice in advance. Consistency pays off in the long run.

The Key to Profitable Sales

Golden Rule Selling is a method of helping buyers make informed purchases based on trustworthy information and an understanding of the decision process. Is that what sales is all about?

Not completely. Actually, the job of a seller is to solve problems. Golden Rule Selling is a satisfying method of doing so. Solve problems? Exactly! Each buyer brings a problem (or more) that must be solved before the sale can be made. For example, the problem could be:

- Replacing a broken DVD player
- Selling a home in preparation for retirement
- Purchasing a trustworthy automobile
- Finding low-risk investment opportunities
- Selecting toothpaste that the whole family can agree upon
- Choosing a wedding gift for an office partner
- Lowering housing costs

The opportunity for the seller comes from helping the buyer identify and solve the problem. In some cases, input from salespeople isn't needed—or even desired—by buyers. For example, the buyer enters the store, heads to the electronics department, looks at the row of six DVD players, scans the price stickers, grabs one of the boxes and heads for the cashier. Not much opportunity for sales there.

FACT

Solution selling is a popular sales method among business and industrial salespeople. Sellers spend extensive time clearly defining the problem before attempting to discover potential solutions. A business problem may be high employee turnover, excessive loss from shoplifting, or poor sales in a specific department. Professional salespeople use questioning techniques to develop a problem statement that the customer agrees is accurate and critical. Only then does the seller offer various solutions.

Even so, a Golden Rule Seller may stand nearby—maybe even straightening stock—and smile at the buyer. If the buyer asks a question, the seller responds, then asks another question, probing for the perceived and additional problems.

"Yeah, my DVD player just went out and I want to watch a movie tonight."

"Would you like to see movies in the new High Definition format?"

"Would you also like a model that plays music CDs? MP3s?"

"Would you prefer a model that has a longer warranty?"

Each question from the seller is aimed at identifying additional problems that the DVD player can solve for the buyer. The seller gently probes to help the buyer determine what is needed. No high pressure. Trust. Honesty. Assistance. The seller sincerely wants to help the buyer solve one or more problems. That's Golden Rule Selling.

CHAPTER 3

Types of Selling

A major mistake made by many new salespeople is selling themselves on the wrong job. They see the dollar signs, hear the claims of great riches, and soon find themselves in a job that doesn't fit their personality, their needs, or their future. Instead, they should become smart job buyers, analyzing their unique needs and skills, researching all opportunities, seeking testimonials, and considering the costs before committing to the job. This chapter offers you an inside look at the sales profession, its primary categories, and their advantages and disadvantages. You'll also get to see how and where sales professionals make a living, which will help you determine if selling is for you.

Business-to-Consumer Selling

The majority of salespeople represent products and services to consumers. It's called business-to-consumer selling, often abbreviated B2C. Salespeople are consumers themselves, so selling to other consumers is easier than selling to industrial clients, for example. New salespeople are more comfortable selling retail merchandise, consumer services, cars, houses, securities, and other items to people just like them.

Because the price of consumer items is less than most sales made to businesses and industry (wholesale inventory, heavy equipment, etc.), income derived from B2C sales initially is lower. However, an experienced seller can, within a few years, develop an income that rivals or exceeds that paid to other professional positions. Income from some sales jobs is open-ended—in both directions.

Retail Sales

Nearly 60 percent of all salespeople work in retail, either as clerks or cashiers. They sell everything from general merchandise to cosmetics, books, music, clothing, auto parts, hardware, and other common commodities. Most are paid an hourly wage, ranging from minimum wage to double the minimum wage.

Depending on how much assistance customers need in selection, some retailers also pay a commission or bonus. A *commission* is a fee based on a percentage of the value of the sale. The commission typically ranges from 3 to 15 percent of the sale total (excluding taxes). To be eligible, commissioned salespeople must accurately track their sales, or the employer must have a trustworthy system for tracking the source of all sales. A *bonus* is based on individual, department, or store sales totals for a period. For example, a retailer may offer a bonus of 5 percent if monthly sales exceed a specified level. Some retailers offer yearly bonuses and split it among all employees based on the number of hours or days they worked.

Unfortunately, some retailers take advantage of commission structures, cutting salaries to a minimum and forcing employees to sell hard to make a living wage. Some employees do. Some don't, and they soon begin looking for another job. In the meantime, the retailer has minimized employee costs. It often puts retail salespeople in a position where they must coerce rather than persuade. Many otherwise good salespeople give up this career because of excessive pressure to sell at any cost. Others find jobs without this pressure and learn that being a seller can be a rewarding career.

A typical retail sales job is as a sales clerk in a specialized store (hardware, electronics, etc.) or in a department of a large store. Many retail salespeople work when consumers shop, often evenings and weekends. Others have nine-to-five jobs. In addition to basic sales skills, clerks typically need knowledge and training in their store's primary product lines. For example, an auto parts clerk must first know the components of cars and how they are purchased. They also must know customer sales and service techniques (see Chapter 5). This includes a practical knowledge of using computers and product databases. Their pay and advancement depends on both product knowledge and customer satisfaction. Specialty clerks often move into retail management or into wholesale sales in their field.

Consumer Services

Consumers need services as well as products. Parents need day care for their children, car owners need auto detail services, homes need cleaning services, wage earners need tax services. In each case, what is sold is a service rather than a tangible product. Selling services to consumers can be a full-time job, or it can be a component of providing the service. In either case, basic selling skills can be invaluable.

Selling services to consumers is similar to selling retail products. The primary difference is that the seller must be adept at helping the buyer understand the intangible benefits. You can't point to the product and tell how it works. You must make promises. This type of sales takes more developed trust and usually more sales skill. If you are personable and enjoy helping others, selling consumer services may be a better fit for you than other types of sales.

Consumer service sales often pay a basic wage and a commission or bonus. Because there often are fewer costs to providing a service than a product, commissions can be higher than in retail product sales. Dedicated consumer service salespeople can earn commissions of 10 to 20 percent. If consumer service sales interest you, focus on the services that you use yourself. You can then help buyers more easily visualize benefits.

For example, there are more than 100,000 travel agents in the United States selling travel services ranging from airplane tickets to cruise excursions to round-the-world packages. Travel agents sell a combination of products and advice. Before the Internet, travel agents handled the majority of travel products for travelers. They now face stiff competition from online services like Expedia and Travelocity that allow consumers to directly book travel with airlines and purchase other travel products. Many travel agents now specialize in selling unique travel packages: two weeks of golf in Scotland, small ship ocean excursions to remote islands, or all-inclusive packages to the Olympic games. Others specialize in last-minute travel sales or cater exclusively to business travel clients. Most travel agents earn a relatively small salary, usually two or three times minimum wage, plus a small commission on sales. In addition, most agents also get complimentary, or "comp," travel from airlines and packagers wishing to promote their services. In fact, the comps are why many people become travel agents.

Vehicles

Though car salespeople often have the lowest consumer rating, the majority are knowledgeable and professional. That's why millions of cars are sold each year. The advantages of selling cars over other consumer products is that (1) nearly everyone loves to look at cars and (2) income is higher for selling cars. What buyers *don't* like is pushy salespeople. Become a Golden Rule Seller (see Chapter 2) and selling cars may be the best job for you.

Car salespeople typically are paid a salary plus a commission and bonuses. The pay structure varies widely depending on whether you are selling new or used cars, the local demand, and the dealership's market position. Selling cars for a living typically earns from two to five times minimum wage. Experienced salespeople offering high-ticket cars, trucks, and SUVs can earn up to ten times minimum wage.

How can you find a car dealership that matches your sales philosophy? By becoming a consumer. Visit area dealerships and analyze how they treat you. Do they attempt to sell you as you want to be sold? Also, ask family, friends, and acquaintances about their local car buying experiences. Can they recommend a dealership or seller? When you're ready, talk with the dealership's sales managers about career opportunities. There's no obligation. Chapter 21 will guide you in getting a job in sales that meets your needs and benefits both your employer and your customers.

FACT

The Internet has dramatically impacted the sales profession. Consumers now can do extensive product research and compare prices on thousands of products and services without leaving home. Knowing this, smart salespeople must offer benefits to buying through them rather than online. They must offer unique knowledge, provide superlative service, and be prepared to negotiate harder. Learn how to use the Internet to advance your sales career (see Chapter 17).

Houses

For many people, their first sales job is in real estate. It also may be their last and only. Real estate sales is a high-turnover career that requires advanced skills for long-term success. In a "hot" market, sales are relatively easy. In a down market, many real estate salespeople either work twice as hard or get out of the business.

Most real estate salespeople don't get a salary or wage. They are paid a commission on the sale of the property. Actually, they share the commission. For example, if the sales commission is 5 percent and the home sells for $400,000, the total commission is $20,000. Typically, it is shared four ways, with one-quarter each going to the seller's broker, seller's agent, buyer's broker, and buyer's agent. In this example, each gets a commission check of $5,000. From that income, sales agents must pay expenses ranging from auto and fuel to office expenses. The actual split depends on the office agreement. Sell three houses a month and you're rich. Sell one house every three months and you can barely pay expenses.

In all states, real estate agents must be licensed to represent property and buyers in a transaction. To be licensed, they must know real estate law sufficient to pass a state test. The test covers property rights, transfers, and financials as well as residential construction basics. In addition, real estate agents acquire ongoing training to keep up with market and financial trends. There currently are about 47,000 real estate brokers and 168,000 agents in the United States. Related jobs include insurance agents, with more than 310,000 agents offering insurance to consumers as well as businesses.

Financial Services

About 280,000 B2C salespeople work in the financial services trade. Actually, this trade serves both consumer and business clients. They sell securities (stock and mutual funds) and commodities (crude oil, soybeans, etc.) to investors. In addition, some sell related services, such as financial planning, tax planning, and other knowledge-based products. They sell financial advice.

Most financial service sales jobs require licensing and advanced training, just as real estate sales jobs do. They often have college degrees in business or finance and additional training in their specialty. They typically work for brokerage houses and other financial service groups. Some work for banks and related financial institutions. Many are self-employed and work from their home or a small professional office.

FACT

More than 120,000 workers involved in sales are demonstrators, product promoters, and models. Their job is to get you interested in the product or service. Someone else will actually make the sale. If you enjoy showing off a product, but aren't yet comfortable asking for the purchase, consider a job showing how to use the product. In most cases, these jobs are part-time; however, they are a vital part of selling products and can be a rewarding way of making a living.

Financial service salespeople are paid well, often among the highest sales incomes. A financial investment person can earn twenty times minimum wage or more. Of course, most entry-level jobs begin at just a few times minimum wage to entice new employees and keep them ambitious. Financial services can be a highly stressful job, especially for the most successful. Hundreds of critical financial decisions are made daily, each capable of dramatically impacting clients' wealth—and your own. A career in financial sales can be extremely rewarding for those with the knowledge, skills, emotions, and stamina required to maintain long-term professionalism.

Business-to-Business Selling

About 20 percent of salespeople sell products and services to other businesses. It's called business-to-business, or B2B, sales. Many of these jobs are technical sales, engineers and other professionals selling complex products and services to business customers. Other jobs require fewer technical skills. The process for B2B selling is different from B2C. Typically, more dollars are involved. In many cases, the sale occurs at the buyer's location rather than the seller's. Many businesses needing a product or service will write a request for proposal (RFP) that outlines their requirements. Other businesses, called suppliers, will bid on the RFP with their own sales proposal (see Chapter 15).

QUESTION?

How can I determine if B2B sales is the better career choice for me?
Talk with B2B salespeople about their own careers. Salespeople love to talk and most don't get a chance to speak about their careers, so many would enjoy answering your questions. Where can you find them? Ask among friends and relatives. You also may know B2B salespeople through your employment. Alternatively, check with a college career counselor who may have volunteers you can contact.

Because the B2B sales process is more complex, getting a job selling to businesses requires more training and experience than the majority of B2C jobs. Many B2B salespeople have college degrees in technical or marketing fields, or both. B2B salespeople earn higher income than many other types of salespeople, depending on what they are selling. B2B commodities and services range from manufacturing equipment to aircraft and everything in between.

Some B2B salespeople work exclusively with small businesses. Their training requirements and income are lower. For example, advertising salespeople sell radio, newspaper, magazine, outdoor, and other types of ads to businesses. Others sell wholesale merchandise to retailers for resale. They have specialized product knowledge but usually don't need advanced degrees or training. There are about 1.5 million nontechnical wholesale sales reps and 160,000 ad reps in the United States. As manufacturing trades are developed overseas, many reps must travel and sell internationally.

Where You Sell

Your sales career will be most productive if you find products, services, and customers that fit your skills, personality, needs, and goals. You will be more prolific if you enjoy what you do. A component of that decision is to determine where you prefer to sell. It can either expand or limit your career.

Where can you sell products and services to consumers or businesses? The right answer is: Wherever the customers are. However, the decision of what to sell also can depend on where you feel most comfortable selling. For example, some people don't like to talk on the telephone, while others prefer it. Some abhor going to a client's office to make a sale, but feel comfortable selling in their own office. Some salespeople do their best in meetings but become nervous when talking with individual buyers, especially reluctant ones.

Many new salespeople quickly become frustrated because they try to sell too far outside of their comfort zone. It can be rewarding to expand your current skills, but going too far beyond them can be exasperating. For example, if you have no experience with selling to major business clients, develop required skills before you do. As needed, apprentice yourself to a professional seller who can help you develop the skills needed to be successful.

Consider your own selling comfort zone. Where do you prefer to sell? Does this limit what you can sell? How can you develop your comfort for selling in other places? Many salespeople are good at what they do, but unhappy because they are selling outside of their comfort zone.

Selling at Your Location

The majority of retail sales are conducted at your employer's location, such as in a mall or downtown shop. For many buyers, this is comfortable; in fact, it can be enjoyable to get out of the house and go "shopping" to see the latest merchandise selection. Salespeople, too, often prefer selling to customers who come to them. Buyers coming into a retail store accept that someone will attempt to assist them in buying. In fact, many welcome the assistance—if done professionally.

Especially if you are new to sales, you may feel more comfortable selling at your employer's store. Of course, because you are not seeking out and developing customers—they are seeking your store out—your pay typically will be lower. However, the majority of new salespeople prefer to sell at their location. It's in their comfort zone.

Selling at the Buyer's Location

As you develop selling skills and understand the process better you will discover that there are more potential buyers in the world than those who visit your employer's place of business. In fact, if you take the initiative and go to the buyers' locations, you will expand your world of potential buyers and probably your sales income. As described earlier in this chapter, the salespeople who sell at the buyer's location typically make more money.

Professionals who sell at the buyer's location include those working in industrial sales, wholesale sales, advertising sales, door-to-door sales, and some insurance sales. They must identify and visit prospective buyers, rather than wait for them to show up at a store or office. They must *prospect*, or identify potential buyers. This process requires additional time, knowledge, and skills (covered in Chapter 11). That's why selling at the buyer's location can be more profitable for you.

Some sales jobs require that you conduct business only at the buyer's location or may discourage buyer visits if the sales office is no more than a few desks and filing cabinets. In some cases the seller may work out of his or her home, car, or delivery truck. Are you comfortable with that?

Selling at Both Locations

There are many ways in which both the buyer's and seller's locations are involved in the sales process. The most common is in real estate sales. The sales process may begin in the real estate office, move to the buyer's or seller's home, continue at homes offered for sale, and culminate at a financial or escrow office. Along the way, the sale process will continue in the agent's car, a coffee shop, and at other locations. Before getting into this and similar careers, make sure that you are comfortable—or can become so—working in these various environments.

Alternatively, you can sell at both your location and that of the buyer by using the telephone as your primary meeting place. Millions of dollars in sales are made daily without any face-to-face contact between the buyer and seller. In the business world, this is called *inside sales*. Wholesale merchandise, for example, is purchased from wholesalers via telephones and the Internet using inside salespeople. They have product knowledge, basic sales and customer service skills, and a desire to help. They typically are paid a salary plus a small commission or bonus and can handle dozens or even hundreds of orders in a business day. For many salespeople, inside sales fits their comfort zone better than any other type. Chapter 6 explains how to sell by phone.

Selling at a Neutral Location

Sales also can occur in places other than where the buyer or seller normally conduct business. That's one of the functions of trade conventions. A convention is a location where sellers can offer their products and services to potential buyers. Some are in exotic locations, but most conventions are held where it is most convenient to the buyers. For example, manufacturing conventions often are located in the eastern or midwestern United States. Pacific trade conventions are usually on the West Coast of the United States or in Pacific Rim countries.

Business centers also serve as neutral locations for buyers and sellers in some industries. Business centers in major metropolitan areas include product showrooms, sales rep offices, and buyer offices in a single location. Nearby businesses support these centers with food, lodging, and entertainment.

Sales is a major profession within industrialized and consumer societies. It involves both business-to-business and business-to-consumer transactions in a variety of locations. As you start or develop your sales career, carefully consider your opportunities, your options, and your unique abilities. Begin where you are most comfortable. For success, expand from your initial comfort zone.

CHAPTER 4

Ten Top Sales Approaches

Golden Rule Selling is your goal: Sell as you want to be sold. But what does that mean? What are the proven approaches and techniques for selling products and services? How can new salespeople develop these techniques or experienced ones add to their repertoire? This chapter presents ten of the most frequently successful sales approaches that all salespeople should know. What is sold and to whom will dictate the most appropriate technique. These ten should be in your sales skill kit.

Features and Benefits

What is it that salespeople offer to buyers? Products and services, yes. But buyers don't purchase products and services. They buy features and benefits. A feature is a characteristic. A primary feature of a car is that it gets you from here to there. It is transportation. A benefit is what that feature gives you. It is safe, reliable, stylish, economical transportation. It makes you look cool parked in traffic.

All products and all services that you will represent as a seller have features and benefits. In most cases, the features are listed by the manufacturer. You won't have to guess. The features of a specific computer might be:

- 22-inch flat panel monitor
- 240 GB hard drive
- 1 GB dual-channel memory
- 2-year warranty

Your job, as a Golden Rule Seller, will be to help specific customers understand how these features relate to benefits they need or want.

- The large flat-panel monitor makes viewing easier, yet it doesn't take up much desk space.
- The large hard drive can store thousands of digital photographs and MP3 music files for you.
- The dual-channel memory makes your computer operate faster and smoother.
- The extended warranty assures you that the manufacturer will take care of any hardware problems for a full two years after purchase so you don't have to worry about it.

As you know from your experience as a buyer, benefits are what you are really shopping for. You have a problem: you want a computer that will efficiently let you manage your photos and music. If you can find a computer that has the features and benefits that solve the problem at a price within your budget, a sale is made.

Some salespeople call benefits the "sizzle." The features are the cooking steak, and benefits are the sizzle that makes it appetizing. A thick steak on the barbeque may make you salivate (unless you're a vegetarian) as you anticipate the taste of it. The red steak in the butcher shop isn't as appetizing without visualizing how it will taste when cooked. That's why professional salespeople help buyers focus on the benefits, the sizzle, of their product or service.

Not sure what features and benefits your products or services have? First, read the packaging; it often lists the most important features, and you can deduce the benefits. Second, check for documentation, if available, within the product packaging; it typically includes specifications. For services, make your own list of what the service is, who needs it, and why. Interview the service providers as needed to learn their process and to identify its benefits to buyers.

Before you sell products or services, make a comprehensive list of its features and a matching list of the benefits of those features to the typical buyer. Then help individual buyers recognize the features and benefits that most apply to their needs and wants. That's Golden Rule Selling.

Selling Against Your Competition

Remember the story in Chapter 1 about the bear chasing two people? The object of the foot race, one person quickly determined, was not to outrun the bear but to outrun the other person. Selling against your competition is like that. Your product or service doesn't have to be the best in the world. It only has to meet the buyer's needs better than your competitors do.

Most products are a standardized commodity. The tube of toothpaste you buy from one store is exactly the same as that available at dozens of other nearby stores. To beat your competitors, the retailers' job may be to offer better service. They make shopping more convenient, are open longer hours, have helpful clerks standing by, are friendly and considerate, and use other service enticements to beat their competitors. Industrial salespeople do, too. They may provide additional services that their competitors don't. They offer spare parts, assistance with installation, toll-free technical help, free shipping—whatever it takes to beat the competition.

Service businesses, especially, need to sell hard against the competition. Their business *is* service. Salespeople must make sure that buyers and prospects clearly understand the benefits that the service business they represent offers. And they must make their service the best available to the buyer. *Every* business has competition for its buyers' dollars.

Who is your competitor? In this electronic age, any business that potentially can serve your buyer is your competitor. How can you compete against these businesses? You can't—unless you know who they are and what they offer. Get on their mailing lists, do online research, and ask your customers about your competitors. Think like a buyer to be a smarter seller.

Selling on Price

The old business maxim is: If all else fails, sell on price. Unfortunately, too many salespeople apply this rule too quickly in the sales process. Instead, they should be helping the buyer understand their product's or service's features and benefits as well as how they better the competition.

Rather than sell on *price*, salespeople are more successful if they sell on *value*. Value is worth. Your product or service costs more because it is worth more. After saying so, you must back it up with facts, then review the unique features and benefits it offers the buyer. If you are selling tires, for example, you can point out that:

- The cost per thousand miles-driven is actually lower than cheaper tires.

- Included in the price is free repair of flats for the life of the tire.
- These tires have the highest safety rating of all consumer tires and safety is important.
- If budget is the issue, these tires can be purchased on a no-interest payment plan.

Unless you are selling a commodity, a widely available product, avoid the temptation to sell primarily on price. It will reduce your employer's profits (where your salary comes from) and encourage the buyer to attempt discounting future purchases from you. If you are authorized to offer price reductions, do so as necessary to make the sale, but don't sell on price alone. Instead, help buyers understand the value of the features and the benefits they will derive. Your buyer will be happier if she or he understands the *value* of what is purchased.

FACT

Whatever you sell, you should know what your competitors charge for it. Put your buyer hat on and visit their business as often as possible, checking prices, service, and other factors that draw buyers. If your buyers also purchase online, check out your online competition as well. What can you as a seller or your employer do to minimize competition?

The Soft Sell

Some products and services don't require selling techniques. The buyer only needs some guidance in making the selection. Many buyers appreciate this approach and prefer to purchase through salespeople who use what's called the soft sell.

Soft sell is the use of suggestion and gentle persuasion to make a sale rather than aggressive pressure. For example, in a sales situation the seller may say:

- "We've sold a number of those widgets in the last week."
- "Is this feature one that you are looking for in a widget?"

- "I bought one for myself and am very happy with it."
- "If you're giving this to children, I'd recommend the model 89 that has brighter colors; it actually costs less."
- "*Consumer Reports* recently rated these highly."

Soft selling uses statements or questions to suggest a conclusion. There is no coercion. You state a relevant fact and give the buyer room to make the decision. Soft selling is especially effective when buyers expect a hard sell (see below). It can be disarming and develop a relationship of trust that salespeople need to help buyers make appropriate purchases.

The Hard Sell

Most buyers don't respond well to the hard sell. Hard sell is an aggressive sales technique that relies on fear and intimidation to push buyers to a pre-selected decision. Common hard-sell tactics include:

- "If you don't buy this today, it will be gone tomorrow and you will have lost it."
- "Don't tell me that you can't afford it; I know you can."
- "I absolutely guarantee that you will be 100 percent satisfied with this product."
- "You don't have to ask your spouse; you can make the decision right now."
- "Look, if I don't sell this unit, they're going to fire me. You don't want that, do you?"

Unfortunately, the hard sell sometimes does work. Some buyers are fearful or intimidated by these pressures and buy something they really don't want. Fortunately, consumers are learning that they don't have to accept hard-sell tactics; they have choices.

Psychology studies show that soft sell wins more sales than hard sell—and the customers typically are happier with their decision. Soft selling says, "Here are some things you should consider in making a decision." Hard sell says, "I've made the decision for you; accept it."

Of course, hard-sell salespeople are easy to spot and just as easy to walk away from. Less obvious are semihard sales tactics used by many salespeople. The tactics are subtler and less confrontational, but often put undue pressure on the buyer to make the purchase. Golden Rule Sellers don't use high-pressure tactics. They prefer to sell as they want to be sold.

Friendly Selling

"Hello, ma'am! That certainly is a beautiful purse. And I'm so glad that you stopped by today. I really want to save you some money. It's your lucky day!"

Everybody wants a friend. Buyers want friendly sellers who will help them make informed decisions about important purchases. However, buyers know that some salespeople will feign friendship to make a sale. Buyers realize that true friendship is built over time and shared experience, and it has no profit motive. They don't want "we're good friends" selling. What they really want is *friendly* selling.

To be friendly is to show kindly interest and goodwill. It certainly isn't hostile or adversarial. How can you be a friendly seller?

- As appropriate, ask and use the buyer's name.
- Ask the buyer relevant purchasing questions.
- Listen to the buyer's responses and ask for clarifications as needed.
- Help the buyer to feel important to you and worthy of your time and efforts.
- Appreciate the buyer's time and efforts to purchase from you.
- Be knowledgeable about the features and benefits of what you sell.
- Be helpful.

In many sales situations, "friendly" is exactly how most people want to be sold. *Friendship* assumes a position that you may not have earned with the buyer yet. *Friendly* help is automatically earned by everyone you meet. Once you have established an ongoing relationship with a buyer, know their needs and wants, and are familiar with their likes and dislikes, you may be on the road to becoming a "good friend." When this occurs, you must be even more careful in how you help make decisions. Meantime, be friendly to all buyers. That's probably how you want to be sold.

Selling on Reputation

Trust is a key to productive transactions. If the buyer gives you a check and you don't trust that the indicated funds are currently deposited in the named bank, you probably won't accept it as payment. Equally, if the buyer doesn't trust you to accurately represent the features and benefits of what is being offered, the buyer won't buy it. As noted in Chapter 2, trust is "assured reliance on the character, ability, strength, or truth of someone or something." Once you build a widely known reputation for trustworthy selling, your job will be significantly easier.

Another name for developing a positive reputation in business is branding. *Branding* is promoting trust in a product or service—or a person. Brands are valuable. Millions of dollars are spent on developing consumer trust in a brand of cars, restaurants, toothpaste, and other items. The majority of products that you will sell have brands. Your employer probably spends advertising and promotional dollars on developing a reputation for selection, service, or price.

FACT

Businesses are built on two of three criteria: selection, service, price. For example, discount stores usually sell on price and selection, but not on service. Luxury cars are often sold on selection and service, but usually not price. A specialty store may sell on service and price, but not selection. Rarely can a business build a reputation on all three criteria. That's because lower prices usually mean less service or less inventory.

How can you develop your sales reputation—your "brand"?

- Sell as you want to be sold.
- Only sell products and services that you can honestly represent to buyers.

- Be accurate and truthful in your transactions.
- Encourage appreciative buyers to tell others about their experiences with you.
- If appropriate, give out your business card to build name recognition.

One of the greatest assets you can have as a seller is a reputation for honest and accurate dealings with others. It will gain you repeat and referral customers and help you develop an income level above those who rely on naive buyers for their sales.

Problem-Solution Selling

As noted in Chapter 2, one of the major tasks of salespeople is to help buyers solve specific problems. Following are some problems that Golden Rule Sellers can help solve:

- Buyer needs to purchase an economical car for commuting to a new job.
- Buyer wants wholesale merchandise that will sell faster and more profitably in his store.
- Buyer needs a new cell phone contract that will allow them to travel farther without roaming charges.
- Buyer would like a unique gift that will be memorable to a new friend.
- Buyer must have a new chronograph watch immediately—for less than $50.
- Buyers want an unforgettable wedding event planned for them.

The key to problem-solution selling is clearly defining the problem. How can you, as a seller, do that? By asking relevant questions and listening to the answers. Salespeople have a tendency to talk more than listen, so it's not as easy as it sounds. As much as possible, ask a question for every one that you answer.

"Does this widget come in blue?"

"Yes, it does. Would you like to take a blue one with you today?"

QUESTION?

How can I know what questions to ask buyers?
What tips do buyers give you as you listen to them? How do their responses relate to the features and benefits of your products? What knowledge can you share with them, in question form, to help them clarify their needs? Will careful questioning to identify the problem help them make a better buying decision? Questions work.

Remember that each person to whom you sell has a problem they want solved. You can't help them until you clearly understand the problem—and get them to agree on it. Then the solution becomes much easier. In addition, each feature and benefit of your product can be restated as a possible solution to the agreed-upon problem. Using questions to define the problem not only gathers the information you need, it also illustrates your personal interest in striving to find an acceptable solution for the buyer as you listen to what they have to say. That's the way that most people want to be sold.

Consultive Selling

Consultive or consultative selling combines other Golden Rule selling techniques. It's based on reputation and uses problem-solution techniques to help the buyer make informed decisions. The primary difference is that consultive selling requires more time to develop the authority and trust needed to offer the buyer valued advice. Consultive selling is more common in selling technical products and services to businesses and industry. The seller, usually one with extensive technical training or an advanced degree in the field, builds a relationship of trust with the buyer before analyzing specific problems and offering appropriate solutions.

For example, a sales engineer meets with an industrial plant supervisor who is concerned about an increase in maintenance costs. The sales engineer may spend a day or more asking relevant questions about operations and visually inspecting the plant. Only when all needed information is gathered will the sales engineer—now a trusted consultant—make a specific recommendation on the solution.

Consultive sales techniques can be used in some retail sales as well. For example, a clerk in a high-end jewelry store will present himself or herself as a knowledgeable expert. Buyers can be confident that the information they receive is trustworthy. The industry motto is: If you don't know jewelry, know your jeweler.

Another consultive sales career is in real estate. Agents and brokers are licensed by their state and usually complete additional training to make them more knowledgeable in their field. They work to develop a reputation for being an expert in real estate matters. They strive to develop professional trust from buyers, sellers, and other participants in real estate transactions.

Consultive selling is an advanced technique that requires additional experience and training. However, it can be rewarded by greater sales and higher incomes than many salespeople earn.

Value-Added Selling

A value-added product is one that has something extra added to it in production, processing, or selling. For example, a retailer may offer free batteries with the sale of a battery-operated device. Or the retailer can offer free gift wrapping for purchases. A manufacturer may offer 10 percent more product for the same price.

A value-added service, likewise, is one that becomes more valuable to the purchaser by the addition of other services. For example, an accountant may offer a discount on tax services to existing clients. A real estate agent can offer the use of a moving truck at no charge to their buyers or sellers.

How can salespeople add value to help make a sale? Many sales managers make value-additions available to salespeople. For example, a car seller may be authorized to offer specific upgrades to buyers in order to close a sale. To minimize the giveaways, the sales manager may reduce the seller's commission or withhold some bonuses on sales that involve these free upgrades. Otherwise, the seller will not see the value of defending the price to make the sale.

Another way that salespeople can add value to the sale is to offer their time at no additional cost. "Buy this bicycle today and I'll set it up for you myself at no extra charge." In retail, stores offer free gift wrapping, free shipping, assistance carrying merchandise to the car, and other value-added services that help buyers make a decision.

Also, remember that value-added is a perception. That is, if your buyer sees that the value of purchasing an item from you is greater than buying the same one from your competitor, that's a value added. Extra value can be derived by meeting the buyer at her or his place of business, making transactions easier, offering faster delivery, and in many other ways. Sell as you wish to be sold.

CHAPTER 5

Retail Selling

About 3.3 percent of the U.S. work force is employed as retail salespeople. Another 2.6 percent are cashiers and other transaction workers who often use retail sales techniques in their job. That's nearly 8 million people involved directly or indirectly in retail sales. Unfortunately, many of them don't see their jobs as career opportunities. They don't understand basic sales skills. They don't understand the importance of their jobs to others and to their own career. This chapter outlines these skills to help you derive the greatest income and satisfaction from helping others in retail transactions.

Your First Retail Job

For many people, their first job is in retail. They are clerks, cashiers, stockers, or workers performing related tasks in stores large and small across the country. Some move to other professions, but many stay in retailing or shift to other sales jobs in wholesaling, manufacturing, or the service industries. Retailing is a good place to start—or restart—a sales career.

Once the domain of the young, retail sales is now a new-career entry point for thousands of retired people who work to supplement retirement income and to continue participating in commerce. They choose a product or service that they enjoy buying and offer their developed knowledge and skills to employers and customers.

If you are considering making retail sales your first or your twenty-first job, this chapter will give you a better look at what you will be doing. It may be for you, or it may not. However, knowing what's involved in retail sales not only can help you decide whether to seek employment in the field, it also can help you choose a product line and employer that matches your goals.

What Retail Salespeople Do

You've probably used their services hundreds of times, but maybe not considered what their job is. Retail clerks have a single task: to help you buy something. That's their function. How they do it depends on what they are selling and what level of help the customer needs.

Retail salespeople are paid to know more about the products offered than do the customers. Of course, finding a knowledgeable clerk can sometimes be a chore in itself. Megastores often don't pay well enough to draw knowledgeable—or motivated—salespeople. That means your professional attitude, product knowledge, and desire to help will set you above many retail salespeople and give you opportunities they don't earn.

How much product knowledge do you need? Again, more than the customer. Imagine buying a car from a seller who didn't know the product or its features. Even a shoe salesperson should know more about shoes and fitting them than any customer who walks in the door. Customers who know more than you do will probably serve themselves anyway. Concentrate on those who need your help in making a selection.

In addition, retail salespeople assist in the transaction. Some also take payment and prepare merchandise for transfer to the customer. Retail workers should know how to use transaction tools: cash register, point-of-sale (POS) systems, merchant card (debit, credit) equipment, and so forth.

Want to know more about retail sales jobs? Read the Sunday classified ads in metropolitan newspapers. Under headings of Retail, Retailing, and Retail Sales, you may find dozens of job descriptions from a variety of local retailers. Some also are inserted by employment services. You also can apply for these positions and be interviewed. During the interview, the employer will attempt to sell you on the benefits of working for them. A few interviews will help you decide if retail sales is for you and, if so, for what employer.

Working Conditions

In most retail stores, salespeople work in the same environment as customers shop: clean, comfortable, and well lit. However, they often have to stand on their feet for long hours and may need to stretch and stoop to remove merchandise from shelves.

Your work hours in retail may be similar to that of office workers, Monday through Friday, 9 A.M. to 5 P.M. However, most retailers also are open evenings and weekends, so your hours may be those instead, especially if you are a part-time worker. New employees often are given evening and weekend hours, saving the weekday schedules for employees with seniority.

Because retail's busiest season is from Thanksgiving to Christmas, most retail clerks work longer hours during this period. In fact, some retailers extend their hours during the holidays and need clerks and cashiers to work them. Vacation days typically aren't allowed during this period.

Training and Advancement

Major retail stores have initial and ongoing training sessions. Because the employee is paid for training time, many employers only cover the skills needed to be functional. Retail clerks who want to sell more or move on to better sales jobs should invest in their career by getting additional training. Though many employers offer minimal training, most have additional training tools (DVD courses and books) that employees can use on their own time. Others have advancement training packages that help employees work toward better jobs within the store: department manager, assistant manager, store manager, and so on.

Pay and Benefits

Retail stores that offer merchandise based on price—discount stores—typically pay employees less than those that promote knowledgeable service. Retail cashiers are usually paid at or slightly above minimum wage, depending on the employer. Retail clerks who are more involved in the customer's buying decision often start at about one-and-a-half times minimum wage. Some clerks earn commissions and bonuses that supplement their wages.

Most retailers offer minimal benefit packages. The cost of health care has driven insurance premiums high and few retail employers offer comprehensive packages, even to their managers. Many retail employees must rely on a spouse's health insurance plan or on plans for low-income or retired workers to provide medical coverage.

Your first or next job in retail sales probably won't earn a living wage, but it can offer you an opportunity to learn more about selling and to eventually find a more rewarding career in retail management or in another sales profession. Many high-paid salespeople began in retailing.

Retail Sales 101

That's a quick look at what a retail salesperson does. To better understand the job, here are some more specifics.

Retail is the sale of small quantities of goods directly to the user. Somewhere in the world, a factory manufactures a million widgets. A regional wholesaler buys 50,000 of them for resale to its customers: retail stores. One customer, Bob's Widgets, buys 100 widgets from the wholesaler and sells one to a customer. That's retailing.

Retail Employment

Retailing employers include all types and sizes of businesses from the largest Sam's Club and Costco to the mom-and-pop neighborhood store. Each follows the same process: buy at wholesale and sell at retail. Buy a lot of 100 or so and sell them one at a time. Of course, it's not quite that simple—otherwise *everyone* would own a retail store. There also are distributors, consolidators, and importers in the process. Shippers physically distribute the products from manufacturer to wholesaler and on to the retailer. Suggested retail pricing (SRP) must be established. Discounts are determined. Store shelves are stocked. Lights are installed and electric bills paid. Management is hired. Taxes are collected. The point of all these actions is to present products (and services) to potential buyers, your retail customers.

As a *retail clerk*, selling is *your* job. And it's a very important job. Retail sales in the United States is now approximately $4 trillion ($4,000,000,000,000) annually and increasing by an average of about 5 percent a year, reports Plunkett Research. Retailing is the second largest U.S. industry (manufacturing is first). Your job as a retail salesperson is vital. Without retail clerks to help customers in the buying process, less merchandise would be sold and factories would have to cut employment, as would transportation companies.

As a *retail cashier*, your function is to help customers with the transaction. The customer has made the decision to purchase the product and brings it to your station to complete the sale. Though you may not be involved in the merchandise buying decision, you can influence it with helpful service, and you can impress customers with friendliness and encourage them to return. You are selling the store and the shopping experience.

In many stores, the retail clerk and cashier are the same person. In others, employees often begin as cashiers, then are promoted to clerks who work more directly in the selling process with customers. Many retail store managers come from the ranks of cashiers and clerks.

Your Pay

Depending on what is being sold, your employer typically calculates that about 15 to 35 percent of the transaction total (less sales tax) goes to pay employee wages and benefits. In fact, other than the wholesale price of the merchandise, the cost of employees is the largest expense that retail stores typically have.

Retail employers often encourage their employees to use fundamental selling skills. They provide basic training in customer service and related skills that can potentially increase sales. Most retailers have a training program for new hires that helps employees understand what is expected of them and how to assist customers in the buying process.

In addition, some retail employers develop commission and bonus systems to encourage helpful sales efforts. Commissions are a percentage of the sale value, while bonuses are payment for sales or service over a longer period, such as a yearly bonus.

The purpose of retailing, again, is to profitably offer products and services to individual buyers. To achieve that purpose, stores require retail clerks and cashiers who not only provide benefit to customers and employers, but also derive benefit from the transaction. By understanding the retail process and your significant place within it, you can both give more to and get more from your job.

ALERT!

The function of any business is to make a profit for the owner(s). Have fun, share your knowledge with your customers, help them fulfill their lives with your merchandise—but never lose track of the fact that if your employer's business isn't profitable you won't be employed for very long. If a ship sinks, it isn't just the ship and captain that are lost.

The Retail Process

Wouldn't it be easier if all a retailer had to do was place the products on a table and let the customers pick up what they wanted and pay for it? Maybe the first retailers got away with that, but competition among retailers has made simple retailing a thing of the past. That's because customers wouldn't long put up with sloppy retailing. "Bob's Widgets has a much better selection in all sizes, and the clerks are so helpful." Bob's business grows and the sloppy retailer is soon looking for another trade. Obviously, there's more to the merchandising process than just placing products out on a table. There's selection, presentation, and transaction. That's where retail clerks can be useful.

Product Selection

Customers want choices. They don't want shoes, they want a wide variety of shoes for men, women, and children in a variety of sizes. A single customer wants just one pair of shoes in his or her size. Your shoe store sells to more than just one customer so you must stock a wide selection. And the selection must meet the current and anticipated needs of the diverse group of people who make up your store's customers.

QUESTION?

Who exactly are my store's customers?
The store's owners probably spent thousands of dollars attempting to answer this question as precisely as possible. Business owners typically know typical customers' gross income, discretionary income, family size, primary needs for the store's products, and what makes them buy. Your store manager or department supervisor can give you a broad description of the store's customers and market. The specifics are proprietary—and valuable. All you need is a better understanding of who your store's customers are and a willingness to help them buy.

Product Presentation

Products that you have put away in a forgotten location won't sell because the customer doesn't know about them. A product that is placed in a logical location within a well-designed store has a better chance of being purchased. And if the product's packaging illustrates its use or explains the value or application of the product, the product—if value priced—may soon be part of a sales transaction. Many retail clerks participate in presentation by restocking shelves and setting up displays to make products more attractive to buyers.

Sales Transaction

A *sales transaction* occurs when a seller and a buyer agree to trade ownership of a product or service for money. That's the goal of your employer's retail store: sales transactions. Lots of *profitable* sales transactions. These transactions occur because the products offered sufficiently meet the needs of your customers and they are willing to purchase them for your price.

That's the retail process. Your job within it is to sell products and services and/or sell the shopping experience to customers. To do that effectively, you must understand the selling process.

Working for a big-box retailer may not give you many opportunities to help customers buy. Most large stores focus, instead, on price and selection, meaning lower wages and more work at stocking shelves. If you prefer to spend more time helping people buy, consider a job in an independent or specialty retail store. Most encourage customer service. In addition, many independent retailers, wanting more experienced and helpful clerks, pay more than minimum wage. Some even offer commission and bonus programs that can offer a living wage.

The Selling Process

The reason your employer invested the time and money to start a store and hire you is to sell something at a profit to people who need or want it. The process of selling at the retail level is really about helping customers buy. In fact, few independent retail stores use hard-sell techniques to move product. Most use Golden Rule Selling and other sales methods (see Chapter 4). They help customers to identify their needs and make the best purchase decision. No pressure.

Customer Needs

What does your customer need? Because you will have many types of customers, each with a variety of needs, this question may seem difficult to answer. It is. In fact, it's not within your power to know what your customer needs until the customer expresses it by a purchase or a question. With experience you will be able to make a good guess at your customer's current needs, but not until they act or ask will you know.

Of course, when a customer comes into your widget store, you know that they probably want a widget. That's obvious. But which widget? For whom? What is their budget? Would they like suggestions? The overall question is: Why did they come into your store today? Your job, as a retail clerk, is to discover—and gratify—your customers' needs.

The Decision Process

For some retail products, the decision process is simple: a red widget or a blue one. For others, making a purchasing decision can get more complicated: red, blue, yellow with orange stripes, large, small, portable, under $10, less than $50, and so on. Within your employer's retail store, you probably will have merchandise that requires simple and complex decisions. In addition, you will have customers who are more comfortable with making these decisions on their own while others prefer some help. So let's break the decision process down into three easy steps: need, choice, and commitment.

As an example, a new customer comes into your store and walks to your widget section indicating a perceived need for a widget. There are four types on the shelf and the customer picks each up to examine it and the price tag. Based on the need for a medium-size widget costing about $5, the customer picks one up, walks over to the cashier and makes a commitment by purchasing it. Simple enough. The customer didn't even need your help.

Another customer soon walks in and looks around the store for ten minutes, then stops in front of the widget section and stares at them for a couple of minutes, obviously thinking. You walk by and smile to make yourself available for questions. The customer asks you which widget would be best for a specific task and you offer your knowledge (without explaining the history and various uses of widgets). The customer then makes a decision and hands you the product to ring up the sale.

These are different customers with different needs and methods of making a decision, but the process they followed is the same: need, choice, and commitment. Your job is to help customers define their need, consider the best choices, and make a commitment.

Selling Against Your Competition

Every retail store has competition. Even if the merchandise sold is unique to the area, buyers still have choices. They can buy online. They can buy similar things. They can buy just about anything else. Your employer's store is competing for not only the customer's widget dollars (money they plan to spend on widgets), but also the customer's discretionary dollars (money they will spend on things besides food, rent, and other necessary bills).

How can you, a retail clerk or cashier, sell against your competition? First, by knowing who your competition is and what they offer. Then use the basic techniques of selling against price, selection, and service. Your customers have choices. Help them make appropriate decisions. You may lose a sale, but you will keep a customer.

Selling Against Price

Superduper Stores Inc. has a staff of hundreds of buyers at their corporate headquarters, each with the mandate of getting the lowest price on the products they buy for their department. And each department buys millions of dollars in wholesale goods each year, often cutting out the wholesaler and working directly with the manufacturer. In some cases, the super retailers *own* the manufacturer. How can your employer's retail store compete on price with deep-discount stores?

It can't. Instead, clerks can help customers understand value. *Value* is worth. As noted in Chapter 4, your merchandise may cost customers more because it is worth more. Even if it is the exact same product available at the discount store, your job is to point out why buying it from your store is a greater value. For example, your store may offer a 100 percent satisfaction money-back guarantee, it may offer a wider selection from which to choose, or it may donate to local charities. Help your customers understand the value of buying from your store.

Selling Against Selection

Some retail stores can beat the competition on price, hands down. However, the competitor has extensive selection. They offer 143 models to your store's twelve. How can you, as a retail salesperson, compete with that?

By developing product knowledge. Customers probably don't want to consider 143 models of anything. Actually, they'd like to select among two or three of the most appropriate models that fit their needs. That's your job: to help them consider their best choices. By developing knowledge about the retail products you sell, you are better prepared to help customers make appropriate decisions. Customers don't want 143 widgets—they want one. Help them figure out which one and you'll be a retail hero.

Who are your store's competitors? As a consumer, you should be able to answer that question. If you were shopping for what you sell, where would you go? Would you buy online? Would you visit a nearby town? In what stores would you shop? These are the retail stores that your customers probably shop as well. Know who your employer's competitors are, and know why customers should shop at your store instead.

Selling Better Service

"Where's a clerk when you need one?" "Can you tell me the difference between these two models?" Good luck. Finding knowledgeable and friendly help can be frustrating. Your job, as a professional retail salesperson, is to ensure that your customers get better service than they can find from any other clerk at any other store. How can you do that? By selling as you want to be sold!

What do you, as a customer, want? You probably want to be left alone until you have a question. Once a question occurs, you want a courteous representative of the store to answer it knowledgeably without trying to "sell" you something—bias your decision. You'd like that representative to be nearby, where you can see her or him, but not within your physical comfort zone. And you'd like that person to be friendly without trying to be a pal. Once the question is answered, you may allow related questions from the representative—questions that can help in your selection. Finally, if you do make an appropriate selection, you'd like the representative to help you make the purchase quickly and easily. That's your job description as a professional retail seller. Be knowledgeable, available, friendly, and assistive. Don't presume that you automatically know the customer or his or her needs. Treat your customers as individuals. Sell as you want to be sold.

Encouraging Impulse Buying

Another sign of a good retail salesperson is anticipating the customer's related needs. It is suggesting associated products and services that may be of interest to the buyer. In retailing, it's called an impulse buy. An impulse is a force that produces an action. An impulse buy is an unplanned purchase triggered by an outside source that touches a need or desire. Impulse buys typically are more profitable for your retail employer. The customer is already there and doesn't have to make a return trip. Your suggestions may save the customer a trip back—or a trip to a competitor. As appropriate, helping your customers make impulse purchases of needed items will be appreciated by customers—and your employer. For example, once a product selection is made, clerks at Bob's Widgets often suggest related products:

- Widget cases
- Widget replacement parts
- Widget tools
- Mini-widgets

In addition, the retail cashier at the checkout stand offers:

- Widget gift certificates
- Widget batteries

You get the idea. Impulse items are related to the need that the customer already has confirmed. A no-pressure suggestion from a retail clerk or cashier sometimes can help the customer fulfill related needs. Without high-pressure tactics, the decision is totally up to the customer.

CHAPTER 6

Selling by Phone

"Watson, come here! I want to see you!" With those historic words in 1875, Alexander Graham Bell solicited Thomas Watson over a telephone and the world of phone sales began. Most would call the medium a mixed blessing, bringing humanity both 9-1-1 and telemarketers. For nearly a million salespeople, it is the way they conduct business without travel. It is a powerful tool that is loved and hated, but few people would consider doing without their phone. This chapter shows how responsible telephone sales can help buyers, sellers, and the environment.

Telephone Sales 101

Selling by phone isn't a bad thing; in fact, for many selling situations it is a more responsible method of selling. Rather than wasting the time and fuel to visit a current or prospective customer, the salesperson simply calls him or her on the telephone. It is more efficient for both parties.

It also is less expensive and uses fewer natural resources. A telephone call can save fuel, waiting in offices, and related travel expenses. Billions of dollars in products and services are sold every year without the buyer and seller physically in the same location.

Don't Call Me! I'll Call You!

The negative side of telephone sales comes from *unsolicited* telephone calls from persistent and sometimes obnoxious salespeople. Most modern buyers simply hang up on them. Telemarketers then automate calls with recorded messages in hopes of getting a small fraction of 1 percent of those called to buy what is being sold. The problem has become so burdensome that the Federal Trade Commission established a Do-Not-Call Registry. There are now 145 million numbers in this registry. People don't like to be bothered with unsolicited telephone calls.

QUESTION?

Are the do-not-call laws enforceable?
Definitely. The FTC has announced numerous settlements from major telephone sales businesses since the registry was established in 2003. Most have been for $1 million or more. Complaints can be filed at the Do-Not-Call Registry website *(www.donotcall.gov)* or by calling 877-FTC-HELP. Be aware that there are some types of calls that are not covered by the DNC rules, including those from political organizations, charities, and telephone surveyors.

So are telephone sales dead? Hardly. It still is a primary method of selling goods and services to businesses and industry. In addition, buyers continue to use the telephone to initiate purchases from sellers. The Do-Not-Call Registry is an attempt by reputable sellers and consumer groups to police the industry and to return a level of confidence and trust to buying and selling by phone.

Inside Sales

In business-to-business (B2B) selling, many firms employ two types of salespeople: outside and inside. An outside salesperson travels to the customer. An inside salesperson doesn't and instead helps the customer by telephone and sends needed information by fax machine and by the mail or parcel delivery systems. In some businesses, the salesperson may travel one or two days a week and work inside an office the rest of the time. Other salespeople will travel a week of the month or a month of the year, spending the rest of her or his time in the office contacting customers by phone.

For example, a computer software company that developed a system for scheduling and tracking commercials on radio stations, called a traffic system, hired outside and inside salespeople. The outside salesperson works regionally, visiting current and prospective customers for face-to-face meetings and demonstrations at radio stations. Once sold, the inside salesperson helps the customer with product upgrades, supplies, and assistance with technical questions. Also called customer relations, the inside salesperson is responsible for keeping the customer happy with the system as well as knowledgeable about new and extended features.

Once a relationship is developed with the customer, inside sales can be more efficient in terms of time and cost. Customers will appreciate the call because it helps them make or save money with little effort on their part. In addition, inside sales jobs often lead to more lucrative outside sales positions.

Golden Rule Phone Sales

The Golden Rule of Selling—sell as you want to be sold—can easily be applied to inside or telephone sales. For example, you can establish your own rules similar to these:

- Don't call unless you have a compelling reason to do so.
- Be friendly, but get to the point quickly so you don't waste the customer's time.

- Ask the buyer, "Is this a good time to talk to you about (what you sell)?"
- If not, ask for a better time to call.
- Confirm any agreements at the end of the conversation and via a follow-up note or e-mail.
- As needed, verify contact information: phone numbers, fax numbers, e-mail addresses, time zone, mailing address, hours in the office, best time to call.
- Use your best selling voice.
- Always speak sincerely, confidently, and with appropriate politeness.

As you sell by phone, you will develop an extended list of how to sell by the Golden Rule based on what you sell, to whom, why, when, and how. Inside salespeople are professionals.

Developing Voice Power

As a telephone salesperson, you may never meet your customer in person, so it is vital that you develop your vocal skills to accurately represent you. You must help the listener develop confidence and trust in you by what you say as well as how you say it. You must speak in a relaxed voice that sets the tone for your customer's responses.

There are numerous books available on how to develop a professional speaking voice. It is an asset to any seller, but especially to one selling by telephone. The basic components of voice are: pitch, volume, quality, rate, and speech habits. Following is a summary.

Pitch

In voice, *pitch* is the tone range that the voice produces. In singing, choral voices range from soprano (highest frequency) to bass (lowest frequency). Normal speaking voices are in between. On a piano, a woman's voice typically is near middle C and a man's voice is about one octave (twelve black and white keys) lower. Most people have a speaking range of less than two octaves. The voice you use to impress someone has a different pitch from one that yells at the cat.

To find your optimum or most relaxed vocal pitch, do the following:

- Hum the highest tone you can comfortably reach and find that tone on a piano.
- Hum the lowest tone you can comfortably reach and find that tone on a piano.
- Identify the note exactly in the middle between your highest and lowest notes.
- Play the note three or four keys below (to the left of) the middle-note key.
- Read something using a voice of approximately this pitch to see if it is comfortable.

There is no best vocal pitch for selling. Instead, find the one that allows you to speak comfortably and confidently.

Your vocal cords typically are more relaxed in the morning when you awaken than at any time during the day. In addition, hot or warm liquids, such as coffee or tea, can help relax vocal cords. If you notice that your voice is increasing in pitch during the sales day, sip on coffee, tea, or warm water to relax them. Some speakers put a spot of honey or sugar and lemon in the liquid to soothe the throat. A relaxed voice portrays confidence.

Volume

Volume is the loudness of your voice. In normal conversation, people typically talk as loudly as the other speakers, depending on extraneous sounds. In amplified conversation, such as on the telephone, a loud voice isn't necessary. In fact, it can easily distort the pickup microphone in the phone and muffle the vocal signal, making words unclear.

Because telephone selling requires many hours on the phone each day, professionals develop a vocal volume that is easy to understand without tiring the speaker. Professional speakers develop their diaphragm, a muscle below the lungs, to control air in the lungs and reduce the effort needed to talk. In addition, they make sure that their throat, mouth, and lips are relaxed.

Quality

What people call the quality of a voice is its *timbre*, its characteristics. You probably have heard people with voices that can be described as harsh, smooth, breathy, nasal, or muffled. Professional salespeople, especially those that depend on the phone as a tool, develop a smooth vocal quality. What does that mean?

FACT

Further vocal training is available from voice teachers, speech pathologists, public speaking schools, and broadcasting schools. Some public speakers take singing lessons to improve the quality and resonance of their voices. Online, the Barbershop Harmony Society *(www .barbershop.org)* offers lessons on how to improve vocal resonance and other singing and speaking tips. Community colleges also offer speaking and singing courses to the public.

Vocal sounds are made in three parts of the head and neck: nose, mouth, and throat. A smooth voice is one that uses all three resonators in balance. That is, the voice sounds neither nasal nor throaty. Instead, all three components work together, just as a singing trio would, to offer a balanced sound.

You can develop vocal balance by practicing. The sound of "N" comes more from the nasal area, "O" and "W" are formed primarily in the mouth, and "UH" is formed more in the throat. Slowly repeating made-up words like "now-uh" can help you identify their source and help you practice balancing them so they resonate in all three areas. There are numerous other vocal exercises you can do to balance your voice's resonance and quality.

Rate

"Slow down! I can't understand you!" That's the last thing you want to be told when excitedly selling your product or service. Unfortunately, most listeners won't tell you. Instead, they will tune you out. Speech *rate* is the speed at which words are spoken. In normal conversation, most people speak at a rate of about 120 words per minute or two words a second. A radio announcer may speak at 150 or more words a minute. Commercial announcers have been clocked in excess of 240 words a minute. Time is money, they say.

FACT

A number of books, courses, and services are available for those who wish to reduce or eliminate their native accent or dialect and speak a more standard American English. One recommended is the accent-reduction services of leading vocal coach Paul Meier *(www .paulmeier.com).* He is a professor of voice, an actor, and cofounder of the International Dialects of English Archive. Professor Meier also is a dialect coach for movies and the theatre.

Depending on what you are selling and to whom, your speech rate should not be higher than a normal conversation rate. If your listener is a nonnative speaker, you should reduce that rate to make sure your words are understood. In addition, your rate will depend on stress and phrasing. *Stress* is the amount of intonation or inflection you use to convey the meaning of your message. By slowing down your delivery rate, you can emphasize specific words and phrases. *Phrasing* is the length of what you say without stopping, such as at the end of a sentence. To identify the difference, listen to a television news story, then read the same story in the newspaper. Television news is written for the ear, so sentences and phrases are shorter than they are in the paper. As you sell, your delivery style and rate should be for the ear, with a moderate rate, appropriate inflection, and bite-size phrases.

Speech Habits

In addition to vocal quality, your sales message will be clearer if you articulate your words and pronounce them as commonly used. In addition, many professional speakers and telephone salespeople strive to minimize regional accents and dialects.

Articulation is the forming of words by the voice. Clearly forming words and phrases helps you in presenting your sales message and your thoughts. Articulation requires that you use your tongue, jaw, lips, and the mouth's soft palate to form words so others easily understand them. The best way to learn articulation on your own is to read aloud to a tape recorder, enunciating every word, and then review the tape for clarity. In addition, speech coaches can help.

Pronunciation is forming words as they typically are heard. In the United States, standard pronunciation for the word *nuclear,* is *NU-cle-ar* rather than *NU-que-ler.* Make sure that you know the generally accepted pronunciation of words in your sales vocabulary before you use them.

Television has nearly standardized the pronunciation and delivery of English words in the United States and Canada, dramatically reducing the ability of listeners to identify the region from which speakers hail. News announcers in the South, for example, sound the same as those from the Northeast or the West. They are said to have a neutral American accent. In sales, the only reason to attempt to modify your accent toward one more widely used is to be better understood by your customers and prospects.

Building Belief and Trust

Understanding basic telephone sales techniques and developing a professional speaking voice are good attributes, but if your customer doesn't believe what you say, your sales message is lost. You first need the prospect's trust.

Trust is reliance on the honesty and character of another. Trust is vital to a transaction. As a buyer, you wouldn't buy from someone you didn't trust. How can you build trust in your prospect's mind? By acting professionally and not emulating the stereotypical seller: loud and obnoxious.

Be courteous and friendly from your first contact onward and most prospects will offer you *the opportunity* to develop trust. Build on that opportunity by:

- Being accurate in all statements you make.
- Offering respect and trust to your prospect.
- Using a smooth and confident telephone voice.
- Being prepared with your message so you don't waste the prospect's time.
- Being courteous.

In other words, once you have the opportunity to build trust, do things that will increase rather than reduce trust. Because you are selling by telephone and the prospect cannot see your facial expressions and body language, make sure that your voice and delivery are professional and encourage trust.

Belief is developed in a similar manner. When you make a factual statement regarding your product or service, you want the prospect or customer to believe you and not ask for supporting documentation every time. How can you gain believability? By offering supporting information, such as studies or reports that confirm what you have stated. If the buyer accepts that you can back up what you say, the thought of "Is this true?" will not occur. The buyer will believe you. You are closer to a sale.

Using Phone Sales Tools

Selling by phone is big business. Fortunately, technology has given telephone salespeople dozens of invaluable tools that make their job easier and more efficient. The future will bring even more. Currently, there are phone systems with a variety of features, teleconferencing tools, voice mail, and powerful e-mail systems. Your sales office or call center will have many of them at your disposal.

Phone Systems

Phone systems range from one or two phones to hundreds interconnected in a call center. Smaller systems are connected to individual outgoing lines. Phone systems with more than ten telephones typically are connected together in a Private Branch Exchange (PBX). The largest systems have a large dedicated line, called a trunk, to the telephone company's service office.

All telephones used to be physically wired to terminals, branches, and trunks, called landlines. Now, many are sent over network cable and the Internet in a system called Voice over Internet Protocol (VoIP). In addition, businesses and consumers have come to rely on cellular, or cell, phones. Using these handy gadgets, you can make voice calls transferred through cell sites or towers connected to the main phone system using the Public Switched Telephone Network (PSTN). In addition, cell phones can be used to send text messages (SMS), and photos and videos (MMS). Satellite telephone systems are also available, but they are costly and typically only used in remote locations that aren't covered by cellular phone service.

Most inside salespeople use landlines or VoIP systems in the office and cell phones if they travel. Most PBX and other business phone systems can be set up for automatic call forwarding to other phones as needed.

A boon to people who talk on the phone all day are the numerous hands-free microphones available for various phone systems. Some are wired to the phone, but many are wireless and allow the person to move around without being tethered to a desk phone. In addition, many cellular phones are compatible with wireless personal area networks (PANs) that can interconnect cell phones, laptop computers, and other electronic communication devices. The standard for these devices is developed by the Bluetooth Special Interest Group, so the devices are referred to as Bluetooth-compatible. The most popular use is to wirelessly connect a cell phone to a separate headset that the user wears on one ear. These phones are especially popular with salespeople, engineers, and other businesspeople who must stay in contact with others as part of their job but need mobility.

Voice Mail

One of the greatest inventions to be added to phone systems is voice mail. Voice mail systems (VMS) function as a directable answering system. The main difference between voice mail and answering systems is that voice mail systems are centralized while answering systems are installed on individual phones. Callers can directly access or be referred to a person's voice mail system and leave a message, a fax, a page, or other communication, depending on the system. The person receiving the message can access it from any telephone using a security code. Receipt of a message can be forwarded to another phone. Messages can be replayed, saved, deleted, or forwarded.

Salespeople appreciate the benefits of getting callback messages when they are on another phone or at lunch. However, salespeople usually don't like to leave messages on people's voice mail system. They want to talk with a live person. Of course, many prospects don't want to directly talk with salespeople, which is why they love voice mail.

Salespeople can turn voice mail systems into selling tools. Professionals have short scripts they use for voice mail systems, depending on the function of the call. The scripts help them remember to include pertinent information without wasting time. Script topics include:

- Returning your call. Sorry I missed you. Here's how to contact me again.
- Following up on your question. Please call me back for the answer you need.
- We have a new product or feature that may be profitable to you. Please call me.
- Calling to make sure that your product arrived safely and to answer any installation questions.

Of course, your script will be more conversational and will include needed contact information, such as a reminder of your phone number, alternate numbers, and your availability. However, having scripts like these near your telephone can help you take advantage of voice mail without having to strain your brain. It also reminds you to leave a call-back number.

As a professional seller, make sure that you have a legitimate reason to call first. Chances are that the person you call is busy, too, and may not appreciate a how-ya-doin' call in the middle of a deadline project. In fact, you may lose some trust points for the call. Instead, determine the call's objective—announce a new feature, offer installation help, offer a discount, etc.—before you pick up the telephone. And have a short and relevant script nearby in case you get switched to voice mail.

E-mail

Electronic mail (e-mail) is another technical advance that has benefited selling. Unfortunately, it also has been gravely abused. Most people with e-mail accounts get dozens and even hundreds of unsolicited e-mails each day. Software programs called spam filters can remove many of them from e-mail inboxes, but enough get through to make people fearful of the words "You've got mail!"

Make sure that any spam filters or security systems that you use offer you a second chance to see e-mails identified as spam before they are deleted. Some will put them in a separate inbox that you can quickly review by subject line or sender and keep or delete. No one likes spam messages, but you don't want to throw out those from prospects and customers along with the spam. Just in case, ask your computer system administrator if backups are kept of e-mails and, if so, for how long.

Like voice mails, e-mails can be valuable sales tools that can succinctly present your information to others with the least effort and expense. Depending on what you are selling and to whom, you can develop standard selling and response messages in your e-mail software's draft box, then customize and send them as needed.

When sending e-mail to others, make sure that the subject line clearly states something of interest to the receiver, such as "Widget upgrade reduces downtime" or "20% Discount Thru 12/31." Also make sure that each of the e-mails you send out includes a *signature*, an automatic appendage to all outgoing e-mails that include your contact information.

Teleconferencing

In many forms of sales and in larger businesses, meetings need to be held among multiple people. In years past, all members would have to travel to a specific location for the meeting. Technology, again, has dramatically enhanced opportunities for meetings without requiring travel. *Teleconferencing* is a real-time exchange of information and ideas among many people over telephone lines. Telephone sets are readily available that can help connect buyers in Houston and Seattle with wholesalers in Toronto and the manufacturer in Poland. The call can be set up in minutes and phone lines can be encrypted for security.

One step farther, videoconferencing systems offer two-way real-time audio and video signals so all participants can both hear and see each other, making presentations possible. With a fax machine nearby, product orders can be sent and signed, reducing the necessity for travel. Videoconferencing is also used by schools to conduct classes and by governments to gain agreement on accords.

The earliest videoconferencing systems used landline phone systems. Many now use satellite services, and a growing number are Internet-based videoconferencing systems. They are used for product demonstrations and sales, customer service calls, and even personal calls. Teleconferencing and videoconferencing are dynamic tools for professional salespeople.

Web Presentations

Through the magic of telephones and electronics, salespeople can offer full visual presentations to prospects and customers via the Internet. Businesses have used Microsoft PowerPoint, Adobe Persuasion, and other presentation software programs for many years. Other products are now available that can easily be delivered over the Internet as either real-time or on-demand presentations. They even can be interactive, allowing multiple users to move pointers anywhere on the screen.

Web presentations are powerful tools for selling prospects and servicing customers without physically traveling. They are used by *Fortune* 500 companies as well as one-person sales offices that contract with web presentation services as needed. There are dozens of options, including WebEx (*www.webex.com*), an online meeting center. For a current list of web presentation and web conferencing packages and services, search for these terms using your favorite online search engine.

CHAPTER 7

Improving Your People Skills

One of the greatest assets a salesperson can have is "people skills": abilities to relate to customers and prospects. To help people solve their buying problems, you must first understand what they are saying, be able to express your own thoughts and influence how others think, and be willing to collaborate with them toward a solution. These are primary skills for Golden Rule Sellers. This chapter will help you improve these skills for yourself so you can help others.

Understand People

The first job of a professional seller is to sell themselves to other people. They must help customers, prospects, suppliers, managers, and service providers trust them. Without trust, there will be no transaction.

But people come in all sizes, shapes, temperaments, inclinations, moods, and positions of authority. How can you really understand them? How can you quickly determine what type of person you are dealing with and how that person prefers to be helped in the buying process? Behavioral scientists suggest that you can listen to what people say, read how they say it, relate to their communications, and then respond appropriately. Applying these four easy steps can help you to better understand the people you come in contact with in your job and your life.

FACT

The Meyers-Briggs Type Indicator (MBTI) is a method of identifying and communicating the personalities of individuals. They code the types based on attitudes (extroversion, introversion); functions (sensing, intuition, thinking, feeling); and lifestyles (judging, perceiving). Career counselors, leadership trainers, marriage counselors, and people interested in personal development use MBTI. It can help salespeople understand themselves, their prospective buyers, and how best to interrelate with them. More information is available online at *www.myersbriggs.org*.

Listen

It is difficult to simultaneously speak and listen. Yet many salespeople attempt to make the sale only by talking. They are actually blocking out what the buyer wants to say. Remember that the job of a seller is to help others buy, not to talk about every feature and benefit of the product.

You can become a better listener by asking the buyer essential questions, then listening to and utilizing their answers. As suggested in Chapter 2, asking open- and closed-ended questions can help you—and the buyer—discover what information is needed to make the sale. Examples of open-ended questions include:

- How will you be using this product?
- What experiences have you had with buying this product?
- What experiences have you had with using this product?
- Please tell me about the person that you're buying this for.

Following are a few examples of closed-ended questions for buyers:

- Do you have a budget for buying this product?
- When do you need this product?
- Which of these do you think will do the job for you?
- Do you prefer the red one or the blue one?

Depending on what is sold, most salespeople start with open-ended questions to learn as much as they can about the buyer, his or her needs, and the problem that the product is intended to solve. Then the seller moves to closed-ended questions to narrow the search and help guide the buyer toward an appropriate selection.

FACT

The study of body language is valuable to salespeople, especially to those who offer products to reluctant buyers. One popular book on the topic is *The Definitive Book on Body Language* by Barbara and Allan Pease. It is an introduction to nonverbal communication among business and professional people, but it also can be used in other situations. It also includes tips on how to adjust your body language to assist the buyer in making appropriate decisions.

Read

Not all communications are heard. In fact, reluctant talkers may tell you more by their body language. There are numerous books on how to ready body language, but observation and common sense also are good teachers. By watching customers respond to other salespeople you can learn to read your own customers. What do they do with their hands during the stages of the buying process? Do they look at the seller, the product, or somewhere else when talking and listening? Do they stand facing the seller or toward the product or display? Can you, by watching the customer, successfully predict what will happen next?

Relate

Listening and watching are key components of understanding others. However, you need to understand what you hear and see. The easiest way to understanding is through empathy. Don't just hear or see what they are telling you, feel it. Put yourself in their shoes. Consider how you would feel and what you would think if you were in their position. Then sell them as you want to be sold.

Relating to others is a learned skill and may take time for some to develop. However, it's worth the effort, as it can empower you in many ways by helping you better understand your buyers, your employer, and others in your life.

Respond

As you learn more about your buyer, the problem that needs to be solved, and how she or he makes buying decisions, you will be ready to help with appropriate responses. Often, the best response is another question. Carefully probing with questions can help direct the buyer toward a decision.

- Will this model meet your needs?
- What other features would help you?
- If I offered a 10 percent discount today would that help you make your decision?

Listen, read, relate, and respond to your buyer. It's probably how you would like to be sold.

Clearly Express Your Thoughts

The reason why many salespeople talk too much is because they haven't trained themselves to summarize their thoughts. It's not an easy skill to develop. It takes practice. However, the rewards of clear expression are invaluable. They can help you minimize the confusion factor that most buyers feel.

How can you summarize your thoughts? First, by knowing what you want to say in advance. It's like taking a trip; if you know where you are going and the most direct path to get there, making an efficient trip is easy. However, if you don't quite know your destination or the available paths, you'll probably wander for a while. Conversations are similar.

Too many salespeople offer a solution before they really know what problem the buyer has. So they don't really listen to the buyer's communication, nor do they respond appropriately. A salesperson may know all the answers, but it is the professional seller who first makes sure that the right solution is offered by asking the right questions. Knowing and applying this will put you ahead of the majority of salespeople.

Choose Your Destination

Your ultimate destination in the selling process is, of course, the sale. That requires you to help the buyer solve a specific problem. And that means first defining the problem to the buyer's satisfaction. Each of these steps is a stop on your trip to that destination.

By keeping your destination in mind as you define and solve the buyer's problem, you will be able to more clearly communicate your knowledge, skills, and thoughts. The adage is true: If you don't know where you are going, how will you know when you get there? Know where your conversation is going.

Select the Best Path

Between two locations or two positions, there are hundreds of paths that can be taken. Your job as a professional seller is to help your buyers take the most appropriate path from where they are to where they want to be. It may not be the most direct route, but it will be one that best matches your perceptions of the buyers' needs. That's why it's important for you to listen, read, relate, and respond when helping the buyer define those needs.

In some sales situations, the path is relatively direct and requires few steps. When selling large-ticket products or services, such as industrial equipment, the process is more complex. However, as you develop sales experience, you also will develop your skills at selecting the best paths for the buying decision. With this knowledge, you can better help buyers reach goals.

Getting Feedback

During a trip, you probably look for landmarks that can help you verify that you are traveling the chosen path. Traveling north on Highway 101, the sign for the Highway 20 intersection says that you are nearly home. In the sales process, you will occasionally test buyers to make sure that they are with you on the path toward the sale. You will ask for feedback.

Feedback is information transmitted and received regarding the current status of a process. Feedback is used extensively to control industrial processes, such as the making of food and fuels. At an important point, the process is tested and appropriate adjustments are made. In working with buyers, asking questions about their thinking can give you feedback and help you in making adjustments to your sales presentation. "How does that solution sound to you?" The answer can help you determine if the buyer is ready to move to the next step or not.

Communication Skills

A vital component of clearly expressing your thoughts is to develop your communication skills. You can have the greatest thoughts and ideas in the world, but if you can't communicate them to others, they only are of use to you.

Professional salespeople continually develop their communication skills. They focus on building vocabulary, especially terms relevant to the products or services they sell. They build writing skills, particularly if they are required to develop written sales proposals. They work on public speaking skills, taking any opportunities they can to become more comfortable in front of audiences large and small.

QUESTION?

How can I develop my public speaking skills?
Many sales and other business people become members of Toastmasters International *(www.toastmasters.org)*. Toastmasters is a supportive group that offers opportunities for members to make short speeches on interesting topics to members for positive critiques. There are more than 220,000 members in 11,300 local clubs in ninety countries around the world. In addition, their website offers tips on overcoming the fear of public speaking and how to make business presentations.

Analyze your own communication skills and develop a plan to improve your vocabulary, writing, and speaking skills. They are primary tools in your sales career.

Influence How Others Think

Your job as a professional seller is to influence how others think. As a Golden Rule Seller, you will strive to do that responsibly, just as you would wish to be influenced. How can you positively influence others?

You're already doing it. If you smile at someone, you are influencing that person in a positive way. The same goes if you use any of the other supporting actions or emotions. *Influence* is the act of producing an effect without exerting apparent force or giving a command. Influence is subtler. In many cases, people don't even recognize that they have been influenced.

You can use positive influence in your business and personal relationships in many ways. For example:

- Smile at someone.
- Make an affirmative comment about someone.
- Appreciate someone's ideas or actions.
- Act on someone's suggestion.

The subtlest persuaders used by salespeople are positive actions that communicate friendliness, appreciation, and trust to others. Once you've earned a buyer's trust and respect, you have significant power to influence him or her.

In some buying situations, a purchaser will ask your opinion on the relative merits of specific products or services. That's a good thing. It means the buyer respects your opinions. It also means that you have a responsibility to maintain or increase trust as you answer. Make your answer appropriate to the buyer's needs rather than to your own or those of your employer. Doing so will expand your influence as well as build a more trusting relationship.

How can you develop your skills of influence? The most important step is to develop an *attitude* of influence. That is, be aware that many buyers and others will look to you for assistance and advice. Appreciate it and strive to responsibly use it. Then use your power of influence to help your buyers along the process toward the best solution.

Resolve Conflicts

The world is full of conflict. Conflict is oppositional action. It's physical, verbal, and mental differences that impede solutions. Many people strive to avoid conflict. Golden Rule Sellers learn to resolve it.

In buying, conflict occurs when a buyer stops the process or takes other evasive action because of internal or external disparities. The conflict may be that the price for the desired product or service is outside of the buyer's budget. The conflict may be a difference of understandings or opinions between co-buyers or the buyer and the seller. Other conflicts can arise and stop the sales process.

The solution is not to ignore the conflict, but to try to resolve it. It is an impediment to moving forward in the sales process and should be addressed as soon as it is evident. And it's usually the seller's job to do so. This requires questions to help draw out and define the conflict.

- Is this price outside of your current budget? Let's review why it is of greater value.
- Am I misunderstanding the application? Please tell me more about how you would use it.
- Am I sensing that you're not as excited about this product as your partner? Can you tell me how you would use it?

Resolving a conflict requires agreeing that there is a conflict, defining what the conflict is, and then working on a resolution. Ignoring the conflict, if significant to the sale, is not an appropriate option.

Getting Agreement

Conflicts can pop up at many points in the sales process. Some of the conflicts are easy to see and identify. Two co-buyers walk in arguing about the product or service. A buyer, though in the store, avoids looking at merchandise. A buyer clearly needs your solution, but doesn't want to answer questions. How can a seller get agreement on the probable conflict? By asking questions.

- "What questions can I answer for you today?"
- "If you could take anything in the store home with you today, what would it be?"
- "Are you having some difficulty deciding?"
- "May I ask what brings you here today?"

By answering, your buyer is agreeing with you that there is a conflict. It is up to you to help the buyer then define it. Remember that you are a problem solver.

Defining the Conflict

Responses from buyers can help you define the probable cause of the conflict. For example:

- "I'm not quite sure what I'm looking for" (indecision).
- "I really don't want to buy anything, but I thought I'd come in and browse" (lack of identified need and product knowledge).
- "We can't seem to agree on which one of these is better" (clarification of benefits).

Developing a Resolution

Once you identify the conflict, you can offer a resolution. You can help the buyer(s) make appropriate decisions, offer relevant product knowledge, or review the primary benefits of your product or service.

In some situations, the conflict is greater. There may be other issues outside of your control, such as a personal conflict between co-buyers. Once identified as outside of your area of influence, your best solution is to either help disarm it or to simply allow it to work itself out. You can assist in disarming it by avoiding the conflict issue and focusing on things that all can agree upon, such as the weather or any other distraction. In doing so, you may help the buyers mentally step away from the conflict and return to the buying process. If not, give the buyer a sincere smile, offer to assist when needed, and step away without communicating judgment.

Collaborate Toward Solutions

Smart buyers don't want salespeople making decisions for them. However, most appreciate assistance in the buying process. Many seek collaboration—to work jointly, or "co-labor,"—with someone who knows more than they do about the product or service.

To collaborate, buyers and sellers need to identify a common goal, then share needs and knowledge to develop a consensus. As important, collaboration requires that one accept the role of leader through the joint process.

Leadership

The leader in a collaborative selling process should be the seller. He or she is the more experienced in using the product or service and offers solutions to specific buying problems. The seller better understands the process and the various applications and has helped other buyers to reach their goals.

Your job, then, as a collaborative seller is to help buyers by gently leading them through the process that you know so well. Yet you must do so in a way that makes them feel that they are in control. They must not sense coercion. They must see your role as advisory. A true leader is collaborative toward a common goal.

Common Goal

The buyer's goal is to make a good purchase. If your goal is to sell something, you don't have a common goal. Instead, see your goal as *helping the buyer make a good purchase*. That's Golden Rule Selling. It's also how most people prefer to buy things.

The way to establish a common goal is to help the buyer identify the goal, then agree that it is yours, too. This is done, again, by asking questions.

- So are you looking for a widget that you can use in the kitchen as well as the workshop?
- Is your goal, then, to find what you believe is the perfect gift for your granddaughter for less than $25?
- Are you looking for a service that can reduce your mailing costs by 15 percent?

Each of these statements will be answered either by a "yes" or a qualifier that helps you restate the common goal more accurately, such as:

- Yes, a dual-purpose widget would be my choice.

- Actually, I can spend up to $35 on my granddaughter's gift.
- If I can be assured of saving 15 percent on mailing costs, I'll be quite happy.

With that affirmation, you now have a specific problem to solve, a common goal. Your task of helping your buyer just got much easier.

Sharing

Collaborative selling requires that both you and the buyer share with each other. Share what? Appropriate information. You don't need the buyer's hat size—unless you are selling hats. Instead, you want to know what criteria the buyer uses in making the decision. This requires more questions and responses from you.

- How will you typically use a widget in your kitchen? In your workshop?
- Can you tell me more about your granddaughter's interests?
- What expenses take up more of your mailing budget: printing or postage?

Your responses to the answers may be informational or may be additional focusing questions. As appropriate, you will share your own knowledge, such as "Many businesses find that by using high-run printers they save as much as 25 percent on printing costs." You then follow up with a question, such as "Can you plan a year's printing in advance to take advantage of these savings?" Both the buyer and seller can share appropriate information toward a consensus and a sale.

Consensus

A consensus is an agreement—the goal of selling. As a seller, it's *your* goal. Using questions and appropriate information to get a consensus, you lead buyers toward purchasing decisions that will benefit them.

Unfortunately, some salespeople continue beyond the point of consensus and actually exit the opportunity for a sale. Once there is a consensus between the buyer and seller that a specific product or service will solve the defined problem, all that's needed to close the sale is to ask for or assume the transaction. "Will that be cash or charge?" "Please sign this order and I'll get the unit shipped to you next week."

If a consensus is reached, but the buyer seems reluctant to close the sale, the stated problem may not be solved in the buyer's mind. Often, all the seller needs to do is summarize what was discovered in the collaboration. "We agreed that your granddaughter would love this Harry Potter book and the price is under your budget. Is there anything else you need to know before making the decision?" You are simply reminding the buyer of the common goal, what was learned during sharing, and restating the consensus. You are helping your buyer think through and accept her decision.

Change Paths as Needed

Selling is an art rather than a science. Sometimes during the buying process, prospects will make statements that aren't fully thought out and accurate. "I think I need a widget that I can use while driving." Your task, as a collaborative seller, is to ask questions to verify or qualify that statement. However, you may get far into the buying process based on an erroneous assumption. You may, near the close of the sale, learn that what the buyer wanted was a widget that can be operated while the car is parked. Now what?

QUESTION?

How can I know where we are in the buying process?
Based on the type of product or service you are selling, develop a simple map of the most effective process for helping people buy. A retail sales map will be vastly different from that for selling truck parts to manufacturers. Once you know the buying destination and steps, you can more easily move through it without getting lost. Remember to update your map as you learn more about the buying process that's best for your customers.

No problem. The buying process isn't totally linear. You can make changes to the progression and even back up as needed to help the buyer solve the stated problem—even if the problem wasn't accurately stated.

Once you determine what went awry, you can return to the point where facts need to be modified and move forward from there. For example:

- So you'll only use it when the car is parked, and not when it is in motion? Is that correct?
- Is the only difference then that you don't need the remote control feature?
- So our goal is to find a widget that can be used when the car is stationary, correct?
- The unit we selected can be operated in both manners, so our choice is still the best one, right? Or: This unit doesn't include the remote control feature and is identical except for a lower price. Would you prefer this one?

As a professional seller, don't be afraid to use your good judgment when guiding a prospect through the buying process. You may not need to make all of the stops along the way—as long as you have your destination clearly in mind and you are collaborating with your buyer. Your people skills will be invaluable.

CHAPTER 8

Presentation Skills

All sales jobs require some type of presentation of products or services. The bigger the sale, the more information and specifics the buyer needs to make an informed decision. Your job as a Golden Rule Seller is to present the features and benefits in a relevant, concise, and interesting way. This chapter offers dozens of proven ideas and tips on how to make winning sales presentations, no matter what you are selling.

8

Sales Presentations 101

Big-ticket items—computer systems, business services, industrial equipment—typically aren't sold without a sales presentation. The buyer wants to know more than the color, size, and price. Thousands and some-times millions of dollars are being spent, and the buyer needs to ensure that the product or service will do the job. So the seller offers a "presentation."

What is a *sales presentation*? It's a descriptive and/or persuasive account that introduces or explains the facts, features, and benefits of a product or service. Retail presentations are quite simple: the package shows the prod-uct in use and lists its features. Presentation over. A presentation for selling an aircraft to a corporation is actually numerous presentations to various management and financial groups who participate in the final decision. Each presentation has a unique purpose but a similar function.

Before making a sales presentation, you need to determine the presen-tation's objectives and requirements as well as decide what tools you will use. No matter what you sell, presentation skills can help you be a more effective seller.

Presentation Objectives

The first task in developing a sales presentation is deciding what you want it to accomplish. The more detailed and costly the product, the more things you may want to cover in the presentation. However, the presentation should have no more than three primary goals. More than that can become confusing to some of the people who see it. A few viewers will ask clarify-ing questions, but many will not, and you will wonder why the presentation didn't succeed. It may be because it was trying to do too much.

What goals should a sales presentation have? Much depends on the complexity of what is being offered and the level of understanding among the people who view your presentation. If they are all technicians, an expla-nation of the underlying science may bore them. If the audience is financial advisors, technical descriptions may be lost on them. Know your audience.

For example, three primary goals for a sales presentation to school administrators on a new health plan may be:

1. Summarize their current health plan, noting its limits.

2. Explain the features and benefits of the proposed health plan, including costs.
3. Get an agreement that the new plan is more cost-effective than the old one.

One way of determining the presentation's goals is to identify what the audience knows now and then determine what they need to know to make an informed decision. It may require that you interview a few of the participants before developing the presentation. Identify the primary decision makers in your audience and ask for their suggestions before you make a presentation to the larger group.

Presentation Requirements

Once you have a goal, a destination, for your presentation, developing a list of requirements is much easier. For example, before you can summarize the current situation for members, you must determine what they already know. If they are well aware of the current health plan's features and limits, you will bore them by spending much time rehashing it. Summarize and move on.

What does your presentation need to help the audience understand your points? At the least, a clear map of what is being presented, such as a simple agenda or handout. In addition, many people benefit from visual summaries of what is being said, charts and graphs that review or reinforce the spoken points. They can be printed handouts, product literature, projected slides, or other graphics. The choice depends on what similar audiences prefer as well as what tools are available to you.

One of the requirements that many presenters forget is time. Few people have the time or inclination to listen for hours to a sales presentation. The ones that do probably aren't the decision makers. Establish a time limit for the presentation and, no matter what happens, don't exceed it. In fact, your audience will appreciate your telling them how much time the presentation will take in advance. If you take less time, you will be a hero. Structuring a presentation will be covered in the next section of this chapter.

Presentation Tools

The level of tools needed to make a presentation can range from copies of your outline to animated graphics projected on a large screen. Simpler sales presentations with a small group can be in flip books—notebooks with one-page graphics that can be flipped through as the presentation is made. Artistic presentations can be made with a simple white board and various colored markers.

However, most business presentations today are developed using one of the many presentation software programs available. The programs can be installed on a laptop computer for viewing or plugged into a separate projector that will display the graphics on a larger surface. Most take the form of a prepared slide show. The advantage of these programs is that they are easy to modify during the meeting if the presentation takes a different direction. In addition, the presentations can be viewed online by other prospects.

FACT

The most commonly used presentation programs include Microsoft PowerPoint *(office.microsoft.com)*, OpenOffice Impress *(www.openoffice .org)*, and Apple Keynote *(www.apple.com)*. Each has its advantages and disadvantages. All offer slide show presentations with drawings, outlines, and notes. Some have animation and 3D effects to enhance sales presentations. A primary advantage of OO Impress is that it is free.

Structuring a Presentation

To ensure that you say what you want to say in the allotted time, you must structure your presentation. The typical structure includes an introduction, the body or sales pitch, and the close. The length and organization of each depends on the purpose, audience, and goals of the presentation. However, following are some guidelines used by professional presenters.

Introduction

The purpose of the introduction is to help the audience relax and become focused on the topic. Some presenters use humor, while others are simply friendly and relaxed. The introduction should take up less than 10 percent of the allotted time: about five minutes for a one-hour presentation. In that time, the introduction should:

- Outline your goals for the presentation.
- Tell how the audience will benefit from the presentation.
- Explain the structure of your presentation.
- Note whether there will be a question-and-answer session at the end or whether they should interrupt your presentation with any questions.

By the end of the introduction, your audience should be attentive, interested, and sold on investing additional time in learning the benefits to *them* of what you have to offer.

QUESTION?

How many slides should my presentation have?
The answer depends on what you are selling and whether photos of the product and its applications should be included. In general, plan on using one slide for every three to five minutes of the presentation. That's twelve to twenty slides for a one-hour presentation. Each slide should have five to eight bulleted phrases. Additional graphics and animation can help in some sales messages, but make sure that they don't detract from your message.

Body

Most of your presentation will be offered in the body and it will take up about 80 percent of the prearranged time. That's about fifty minutes for a one-hour presentation, depending on how many questions you expect during the close. The body will be up to twenty-five minutes of a thirty-minute presentation.

The body of your presentation expands on the outline you previously offered. You will cover each logic point in your presentation with features and benefits. Most presenters use the problem-solution structure. Describe a problem that members of the audience face together, then offer your product or service as the solution. Finally, clarify why your product or service is the best solution, going through each primary feature and benefit.

As you prepare your presentation, remember its goals and keep referring to the benefits the audience will derive from it. That's really what they want to know: WIIFM—what's in it for me. As you present a feature, also explain the benefit. Personalize the benefit as much as possible, giving examples. Strive to keep your audience's attention.

Close

The final thing you want to offer is a summary of what you've said—and why it is important to the audience. A summarizing close should take no more than 10 percent of available time, about five minutes for a one-hour presentation.

Before you start your presentation, write out a sentence that you want indelibly in your audience's mind when you finish. "Acme Widgets offer greater value than those from competitors." "Our health insurance plan needs to be updated to fit current economic conditions and Acme Health is the best vendor to do so." Use that summary to guide you as the presentation is outlined and developed.

Make sure that your summary clearly includes the benefits of your solution to the audience. Remember: WIIFM—what's in it for me? Finally, thank your audience for their time and help. Don't start picking up your tools and materials. Instead, stay where you are and purposely look at each person and smile as they exit. Any with additional questions will approach you.

They want additional help in the buying process. In many presentations, the sale is made after the presentation is done.

ALERT!

Don't hand out supporting literature too early in your presentation or you will find members of the audience reading it instead of listening to you. Rather, hold up each supporting document as you mention it, then place them nearby where they can be retrieved by the audience after the presentation. You want the full attention of each member of your audience.

Supplementing Your Presentation

Sales presentations are just a moment in time for many busy people in your audience. In fact, they may see numerous presentations every week, each designed to sell something. How can you make your presentation memorable? By giving them something of value.

Instead of just giving participants a sales brochure, give them something that will reinforce your presentation *and* help them in their decision process. This can take the form of articles, white papers (authoritative reports), presentation outlines, and supporting documents. Put yourself in the buyer's shoes: What other information would *you* like to take with you from the meeting?

Another point: When developing printed handouts, make sure that you leave sufficient white space on the sheets for audience members to make notes. This is especially important if you pass out a basic outline early in your presentation.

Some presentation software programs allow you to easily print out slides in various formats. Optionally, your presentation may fit well on a CD for audience members to review in their leisure. Before preparing supporting documents, ask your presentation host what audience members may prefer.

Delivering Your Presentation

How you deliver your presentation can be as important as what you say. Otherwise, you could write out your presentation and mail it to them. Some people are uncomfortable making sales presentations to groups, especially early in their career. Chapter 7 offered suggestions on developing communication skills, including joining Toastmasters International. In addition, experience will reduce the anxiety that most people face when they are the center of attention.

Professional salespeople know that making effective presentations is a craft; it can be learned. They suggest that you make eye contact with your audience, look around rather than at one point, vary your voice delivery, and keep your body calm and relaxed.

Make Eye Contact

Though you are making your presentation to a group, it is made up of *individual* decision makers. To be most effective, recognize each participant as an individual. If you know their names (recommended), use their names when answering questions. If you don't know names, ask for them; it can help you personalize your response.

Throughout your presentation, make eye contact with each participant at least a few times, but not in a recognizable pattern. That is, don't look at the first person on your left, then the next, followed by the next. Instead, look at them in seeming random order and engage them with a smile. Remember that some participants will not be naturally friendly toward you, your ideas, or your presentation. You must win them over with friendliness and trust. Making sincere eye contact can help.

Look Around

Many presenters identify the primary decision maker in the room and focus all attention on that person. Instead, be democratic. You may know who the decision maker is, but you may not yet recognize those who influence the decision maker.

Instead, look around the group, large or small. Also, use your body movements to direct participants' attention to a slide, a product sample, or other selling tool. If buyers seem uncomfortable with your continual gaze, look off to the walls or ceiling periodically.

Some participants in your presentation may feel obligated to look directly at you as you speak while looking in their direction. This can be good. However, if you would rather they look up to your current slide or presentation sheet, release their gaze by looking away or to the object you want them to see. You are then giving them permission to look elsewhere.

Vary Delivery

Presentations should be alive and vibrant, not on life support. They should flow logically and smoothly, but they shouldn't be mundane. Within your presentation, you can vary delivery and even style to keep your audience's attention and interest. For example:

- Use hesitation to suggest that you are thinking through your next point before delivery.
- If you are standing, consider sitting when you want participants to take time to read a specific slide or document.
- Vary your voice level from softer to louder as appropriate to make your points.
- Build your energy level during the presentation from moderate to high by the end.
- If participants look tense, help them relax with some humor or a humorous observation.

As you build your presentation skills, you will develop your own delivery style. However, also watch the styles of others and apply some of their techniques to your repertoire. Each of your audiences will be different; vary your delivery to match the needs of your latest audience.

Calm Your Body

Public speaking can be stressful, especially at first. The professionals say that the trick is to teach those butterflies in your stomach to fly in formation. Tension is natural, especially when lots of people and dollars seemingly depend on a successful presentation. However, you will discover that the presentation is just one component of a sale and, in some sales, only a formality. The decision to buy or not buy may already be made. In addition, even a bad presentation can often be reversed. So relax!

Professional salespeople have many proven ways to help them relax before a presentation. Here are a few.

- Make sure that you have all needed sales tools before you begin so you aren't worried about finding things during the presentation.
- Practice your presentation in advance so you are comfortable with your message and delivery.
- Take a few moments before the presentation begins to relax your body and your mind with yoga, meditation, or prayer.
- Every few minutes, such as when changing a slide or flipping a page, take a deep breath and slowly let it out, then smile.

Also, if you are still nervous, use a support, such as a podium or table, to hold your script or other papers so the shaking of your hands isn't obvious. All public speakers struggle with excessive energy and adrenaline when making presentations. Most learn techniques for controlling it and appearing calm and relaxed.

Overcoming Presentation Fears

It is quite natural for buyers to see presenters as "the enemy." After all, you are using skills of persuasion to get them to buy something. The larger the group to which you present, the more varied the responses you will have. Some will sit down ready to buy while others will be ready to say "No!" One of your primary tasks will be to eliminate the sense of confrontation that is common when buyers and sellers meet. Building trust (see Chapter 2) is critical. In addition, there are other techniques that can help.

One proven way of minimizing confrontation is to remove the barrier between you and your buyers. For example, in many selling situations and presentations, the buyers are on one side of the table and the seller is on the other. From that vantage point, it is natural for a buyer to see you as an opponent. Figuratively, you want the buyer to come to your side of the table—to your way of thinking. How can you do this?

By first going to the buyer's side of the table! There are many ways of doing this. Some sales presenters actually sit in the audience so they can be seen as a participant rather than a presenter. They control the conversation and the slides from within the group.

In presenting to individuals or small groups, the seller can sit next to the buyer or within the group of buyers, pointing to the product or sales brochure and making eye contact with each participant.

QUESTION?

What can I do if I just can't sit in the audience for my presentation?
Many pros will stand to one side or another of the audience and direct attention to the product or slides. Alternately, with smaller groups, you can walk around the group so they see you up close and less as an adversary. This technique can be used for all or just a portion of your presentation to help buyers understand that you see things from their perspective.

Remember that it is your job, as a Golden Rule Seller, to figuratively get your buyers from their side of the table to yours. You want them to see your product or service from your vantage point. To do so, you must first go to their side of the table—see their problem from their vantage point. This can mean making your presentation from within the group or next to individuals. Though you already know what problem they want to solve—and the probable solution—you must be recognized as understanding their needs before you are allowed to offer a solution. Meet them on *their* side of the table.

Personalizing Presentations

In many sales positions, you will have a standard presentation for most buyers, customized to specific variations. The presentation may be written and sharpened by others well before you are hired. Some employers may require that you learn their sales presentation script by rote. You must know it inside out.

However, most people don't knowingly buy from canned presentations. Instead, they want to know that the solution offered is customized to their needs. That's the task of a Golden Rule Seller: personalize the sales presentation to the needs of the buyer. To do so, you must know your buyer, what you're selling, how best to present it, and be adaptable.

Know Your Buyer

The product or service you sell probably has been standardized to meet the needs of a large market. That market has been identified by homogenous needs and traits. However, the individual products or services are purchased by individual people. Part of your job is to help buyers understand that what they are purchasing will fit their individual needs. To do that, you must know your buyer.

Sell as you want to be sold. As a buyer, you want sellers to fully understand your needs and offer a solution of appropriate value. You understand that the product or service offered isn't totally unique and custom-made for you. But you do want to ensure that it will fit your requirements and solve your problem. To do that, the Golden Rule Seller should ask you questions about your needs and application, your budget, and other pertinent factors. You also want your salesperson to understand that you aren't a consumer, you are an individual, and want to be treated as such.

As a Golden Rule Seller, then, you should know your buyer as an individual and acknowledge their uniqueness. Personalize your presentation to them. If you are selling to a group, make the presentation as personal to the individuals and their needs as you can. That's what you would want as a buyer.

Know What You're Selling

It is too often obvious when buying most consumer products that the seller doesn't know much about the products or services represented. In their defense, many salespeople offer dozens of products with hundreds of combinations. It's difficult to know everything about everything. However, even minimum-wage retail salespeople should have a basic knowledge of what their employer offers. Many don't seem to.

If selling is a career to you, rather than just a job, strive to know as much as you can about what you sell. Be a user. Be a buyer. Take time to read the product packaging and literature. Know more than the customer does. Help your customer make better buying decisions.

Know Your Presentation

Whoever employs you as a salesperson probably will give you training on how they want their company and its products or services presented. (If not, you may have to develop your own based on this book.) Whatever your sales presentation is, learn it well. It will make your job much easier, allow you to help customers better, and lead to more sales.

In addition, put on your buyer's hat and consider what related questions you would ask the seller—then go get the answers. Know your presentation and any possible variations. If you are asked questions that you can't answer during a presentation, make a note of them and get the answer as soon as possible. Sales presentations should be dynamic rather than static.

QUESTION?

My current sales job is just temporary. Why should I put very much effort into it?

First, because, as a buyer, you don't want to ask an important question about a product and receive the answer: "I don't know. I'm just temporary." Second, whatever you learn about the skill of selling will help you in your career and your life. Your minimum-wage job can soon lead to a high-paying sales career if you apply yourself to what you are doing now.

Be Adaptable

Presentations rarely go exactly as planned. Along the way, a buyer asks a tough question or gets you sidetracked from your presentation. You may forget what should be covered next. A technical problem may force you to present without selling aids. Stuff happens.

The time to consider these problems—and develop their solutions—is *before* you make the presentation. Ask yourself what you would do in these situations:

- A buyer challenges your statement of facts.
- A buyer begins ranting about a problem he or she has had with what you're selling.
- A buyer gets up and walks out.
- Your presentation program or computer fails.
- The primary buyer is called away from the presentation.
- Power to the room goes out.
- Your demonstration model breaks.

Dozens of problems can happen during your presentation. A professional seller is ready for each of them and is prepared with a responding action. As you develop your professional selling skills, prepare yourself for the inevitability of problems. A well-thought-out response can turn a problem into a selling opportunity.

CHAPTER 9

Essential Recordkeeping

Paperwork is the bane of salespeople. Orders to take. Forms to fill out. Prospect records to update and file. It often seems like a salesperson is simply a commissioned clerk. Computers have, on one hand, made recordkeeping easier; on the other hand, they make more records necessary. What is the Golden Rule Seller to do? Decide which records are essential and focus on them, delegating others to support staff and software. This chapter offers proven methods of identifying and using essential sales records to work smarter rather than harder.

The Right Records

In developing and keeping sales records, how much is enough? Which records? What should you track? For how long? How can you efficiently use them to make more sales? These are all good questions asked by professional salespeople. Some develop a focused system of effective recordkeeping, while others simply do what they are told.

The level of recordkeeping needed also depends on what you are selling. Records for selling wholesale consumer products are less complex than for selling big business or industrial systems. However, all sales record systems have some things in common. To be effective, you must keep records of the products or services you offer, the prospects and customers to whom you sell them, and the profits you make from selling.

QUESTION?

How am I going to keep all of these records and still have time to sell?
Don't worry about the how just yet. First, consider the what. Later in this chapter, you'll learn about manual and automated tools that professional salespeople use to minimize the drudgery of recordkeeping yet get the benefits of accurate records.

Product Records

Whatever you sell, you need to know data about it. For example, in selling real estate, you need:

- Legal and street address
- Type and size of the land and structures
- Information about zoning and neighborhoods
- Price and terms
- Owners' names and contact information
- Contact information for listing agent (if not you)
- Special features, inclusions, exclusions, amenities

There's much more. In most cases, this is offered in the listing report submitted by the listing office to the local multiple listing service (MLS). Even so, you will want to make additional notes and keep your own product records. What properties have you shown? To whom? What were their reactions? What is your opinion of the property?

Other products and services have their own data that the seller needs to represent. A salesperson for a carpet cleaning service, for example, must know how to calculate prices for various services, how to identify carpet material, what additional or upgrade services are offered, and so on. Product or service data sheets, sometimes called sales sheets, often include most of these facts. However, productive salespeople will want additional information to help prospects buy. Salespeople need adequate product records.

Prospect Records

In retail selling, customers walk in and all the seller may require to know about them is that they have a need and some money. However, as the value of a sale increases, professional salespeople must begin compiling records about prospects and customers. Again, in real estate sales, pro sellers will develop and update detailed records on prospective buyers and sellers. For example:

- Names of all decision makers in the family or company
- Living requirements and preferences
- Current housing and, if owned, equity
- Approximate income or ability to purchase including down payment available
- Time frame in which they need to sell, buy, or both
- Date and results of all contacts with prospects, including list of properties shown and feedback

Wholesale salespeople will develop and keep records of prospects, customers, referrals, and other potential buyers. Industrial salespeople also will develop records on the companies to which they sell, their industry, primary products, and financial status. Each sales job has different specifics, but all have prospects to be tracked.

Historically, many salespeople used business cards as their contact database. Business card wallets were a collection point for the numerous business cards that salespeople received daily. Unfortunately, the cards are too small for making many notes, so electronic customer databases became preferable. In the past these had to be updated manually. Today, lightweight and portable business card scanners are available that can scan, read, and export data into most contact-management software programs. They plug in to a port on your computer. Most business card scanners are priced between $100 and $200.

Profit Records

The bottom line to salespeople is often how much they sold and, if appropriate, what commission was earned. Some of this is automatically calculated by employers and reported to the sales staff. Even so, professional salespeople should keep their own records to ensure that errors don't cost them income. In addition, knowing which of your customers are the most profitable can help you prioritize your efforts.

What profit records should you keep? The most common include:

- Customer, buyer(s) or decision maker(s)
- Details of specific orders including date, components, prices, and delivery instructions
- Details of returns or damaged goods
- Special-order, delivery, or follow-up instructions
- Applicable commissions and when it will be paid

Keeping track of sales and commissions will not only help you measure your selling, but also will help you prioritize what and how you sell in the future.

Perils of Sloppy Sales Records

Let's consider what happens when you *don't* keep adequate sales records. A number of situations can occur, none of them good for your career:

- Customer orders don't get processed quickly or at all.
- Customers receive the wrong or insufficient merchandise.

- You lose valuable customer contact information.
- You call buyers by the wrong name.
- You forget to call back a customer when promised.
- You don't receive commissions or bonuses on products or services you've sold.
- You miss opportunities for referral business.
- Your employer doesn't recognize and reward your efforts.

Many otherwise good salespeople have moved to lower paying jobs simply because they kept sloppy sales records. Professional salespeople, whether required by the employer or not, strive to set up and maintain a recordkeeping system that ensures their success.

Prioritizing Sales Efforts

There are 1,440 minutes in a day, but not all of them can be spent selling. Take time out for sleeping, eating, commuting, relaxing, and other nonselling efforts and you'll probably wind up with about one-third of that time. That's why prioritizing your sales time is critical. Time is money.

Setting Priorities

If you're new to professional sales—or feel like you are wasting time—learning how to prioritize your time and efforts can dramatically increase your efficiency and your income. Many pro salespeople will tell you that it is one of your most essential skills. A *priority* is something that gets prior attention over other things. More commonly, it is establishing a sequence of important things based on a desired outcome. If your sales career is a top priority in your life, you will spend extra time learning as much as you can about how to do it well. If Customer A buys more from you than Customer B, serving A will probably be the higher priority.

How can you determine what priorities you should have in selling? Should you be spending your time in training, learning about your product, visiting with customers, resolving delivery problems, or keeping records? Yes, all of the above, but which ones are your highest priorities? In what order should you work on them? To answer, you need to review your job description and your sales goals. For most sellers, they are similar:

1. Make sure that current customers are satisfied with your services.
2. Close current sales.
3. Help buyers who are nearing a decision.
4. Start new buyers in the purchasing process.
5. Find prospective buyers.
6. Learn more about what you sell so you can better answer buying questions.
7. Keep adequate records.

All of these are priorities for you as a professional seller. However, some are more important than others. Notice that the suggested priorities begin with making sure that your current customers are satisfied. They are tomorrow's sales. The next-highest priorities include moving buyers to the purchasing decision, beginning with those who are now closest. Then make sure you find new customers to replace those who drop away as well as to increase future sales. Only then should you work on training and administrative tasks. Too often, new salespeople gravitate toward the tasks that are most enjoyable to them and avoid others. They may soon be changing careers. Professional selling requires setting your priorities based on your customers' and your employer's needs over yours.

Applying Priorities

Once you've determined the order of your sales priorities—based on your goals and your job description—it becomes easier to apply or "work" your priorities. There are many ways of doing this. One is by time allocation. For example, you can allocate one hour a day toward making sure that current customers are satisfied with your service, priority one above. Then you can set aside an hour or more to priority two, closing current sales.

Of course, selling, as life, isn't quite that neat. Instead, you may spend an entire day helping a primary customer resolve an issue with the manufacturer or shipper. Then, you may decide that none of your current customers are sufficiently near closing to work with that day. Instead, you decide to focus on starting a new buyer in the purchasing process (priority four) or even finding prospective buyers (priority five). Maybe at the end of your day or during the evening at home, you can take care of some of the record-keeping that is piling up. Prioritizing your sales efforts won't tell you exactly what to do at any point in time; it only tells you what order you should consider them. Schedule management (see Chapter 18) can help you control your time and priorities.

Negotiating Priorities

In some sales jobs, your priorities are either dictated or guided by management. They have an overall sales process and plan that requires you to work by established priorities. In these jobs, there often is a salary as well as a sales commission. For the salary, they may expect you to report on your daily activities based on *their* developed priorities. If you feel that you can be more efficient with a different priority structure, you either can negotiate with your employer or find a new one. Most prefer to negotiate.

Have some great ideas on how to change your employer's selling system? Keep them to yourself—at least until you've developed experience operating under the current system and have proven yourself as a productive seller. First, work within the existing system so that you give it a full opportunity to work for you. Adapt as needed. You may discover that the current sales system isn't really broken; maybe it's just misunderstood or misapplied.

What employers understand is results: sales. If you can show that you are a productive and efficient seller, you may be given latitude in how you use priorities to organize your efforts. You may even someday be offered the job of sales manager. However, don't expect your boss to easily change the established priorities and selling system. In fact, the sales manager may have earned her or his job by coming up with a profitable system and only increased sales will make the manager change the established priorities.

More often, the negotiation of sales priorities will be within you. Should you make that sales call today or, instead, work on developing a prospect? The answer lies in knowing what your sales priorities are and in what order they should be worked. Establish these priorities during your first days on the new job and re-establish them if you find yourself lost in your profession.

Contact-Management Tools

Making—and keeping—contact with your customers and prospects is one of the most critical tasks in your job description. Without current and replacement customers, your employer won't need your services any longer.

Fortunately, there are numerous tools that can help you do your job. They include personal information management, customer management, and contact-management software.

Personal Information Managers

Computers have revolutionized recordkeeping and made it portable. A seller in Biloxi can instantaneously update a sales file in Boulder about a customer in Bangor. The tools used can be a desktop, laptop, or hand-held computer (sometimes called a personal digital assistant or PDA). In each case, the application software may be a *personal information manager.* A PIM is a program that functions as a personal organizer. It arranges data or information about specific people and companies.

FACT

Popular PIMs include ACE *(www.goace.com)*, EssentialPIM *(www .essentialpim.com)*, Heiler *(www.heiler.com)*, KDE PIM *(pim.kde.org)*, RiverSand *(www.riversand.com),* and many others. In addition, contact-management programs like ACT! *(www.act.com)* offer versions for PDAs. Your employer will suggest or supply a system that is compatible with their system and recordkeeping requirements.

Salespeople use PIMs and similar portable systems to replace index cards and even business cards when recording information about customers, prospects, suppliers, and even competitors. If their PIM is on a secure network, they can share the information with employers and other salespeople as needed. PIMs typically offer a security system for ensuring that valuable data is not stolen.

In addition to basic PIM features, those for professional salespeople also can record contact information and results, such as:

06/07/09—10:20 a.m.: Met with Cliff regarding special order for 2,500 widgets at $17.55 each. He will confirm order with me by 06/15/09.

Most professional PIMs also have daily calendars for appointments and reminders. In addition, some offer Internet access, e-mail, text messaging, and other communication services. PIMs can be your desk away from the office; many can be synchronized to ensure that the data is the same on your PDA and your office computer.

Customer Management

A *customer management* system is one that records vital information about customers and prospects. It can be as simple as index cards with customer information on them. They are portable, easy to update, and easy to back up (copy). However, they aren't as easy to search and share. Professional salespeople, instead, use software that records this information. Some are simply database programs, such as Microsoft Access or OpenOffice Base. They can be customized to include a variety of data fields, each with specific types of information: first name, last name, company, location(s), and so on.

The primary advantage of database programs is that they are searchable. Need to remember Mr. Luedemann's first name? What's the phone number of the Acme Widget Co.? A quick search gives you the answer. The fact that these programs also are customizable can be a solution as well as a problem. Because they can be easily customized, they can fit a wide variety of sales applications and be modified, as needed to make them better. However, once they are modified the data may not be easily coordinated with other versions of the database. If, for example, one version has an address field of twenty-four characters and another is of eighteen characters, a long address may be truncated during the transfer. Of course, the field can be locked to disallow changes, but that defeats the purpose of customization.

There are software programs available that have been built specifically for salespeople and include proven data formats for customer management and related tasks. In addition, they can be customized for specific salespeople within the overall design the employer requires.

Customer management software can be used on desktop, laptop, and hand-held computers and synchronized with programs at your office or sales headquarters. For most professional sales jobs, your employer will suggest or provide preferred or required customer management systems to make your job more efficient.

Contact Management

Customer records are important. You need to know your buyers and prospects. You also need to know the history of your contacts with them. When did you last visit Acme Widget Co.? What were the results? Did you give them a quote? When will you hear back from them? *Contact-management* systems can help you answer these questions.

Just a few decades ago, salespeople recorded contact information on index cards and in contact log books. However, finding information on contacts with a specific customer required lengthy searches through written records.

FACT

There are numerous customer and contact-management software programs available in the marketplace—everything from database programs to integrated network systems. Which one should you use? In many cases, your employer will make that decision. To ensure that customer record systems are consistent among all salespeople, they typically purchase a license to use one of the more popular contact-management programs throughout their company.

Today's technology offers computerized contact-management records that are easier to search. In addition, most are synchronized to or integrated with customer management systems. Search for "Acme" and you find the phone number, buyer's name and hobbies, and information about the last time you spoke. If your system is integrated with other departments in your company, you may be able to read about all other contacts with the company: service reports, customer service inquiries, invoices billed, and other valuable data.

Integrated Sales Management

Technology has developed additional tools that integrate numerous functions and instantaneously update information for management. In addition to customer and contact data, these systems electronically deliver sales orders to your employer, help you manage your sales e-mail promotions, and provide sales tracking features.

In addition, these systems often integrate product/service information so you have an up-to-date electronic catalog wherever you go. As appropriate, a separate price book may be included as well as electronic order forms so you can take or check on orders from any location. Because these systems are resident on a central computer, all information is automatically synchronized in real time. If your buyer calls customer service with a question, you can be automatically notified. In addition, these systems can be accessed with laptop computers, wireless e-mail devices (such as the BlackBerry), and wireless PDAs.

A leading integrated sales management tool is Salesforce *(www.sales-force.com)*. It combines software tools to manage sales leads, sales orders, territories, and workflow; update product catalogs and documents; and make local, regional, and global sales forecasts. It also integrates with e-mail systems and spreadsheets to offer an integrated reporting tool for entire sales organizations. Other integrated sales tools are also available.

Of course, such integrated sales systems are expensive to purchase, learn, and maintain. However, professional salespeople who represent expensive business and industrial products and services can work more efficiently—and more profitably—with these systems than with customer and contact software.

Tracking Sales Performance

The primary function of sales records is to ensure that your customers are being served as well as possible. Every relevant piece of data is available to you on who they are; what, when, and how they buy; and how transactions are most efficiently developed and completed.

A secondary function of sales records—also very important—is tracking sales performance. Full customer, contact, and sales records can help your employer in many ways:

- Show which types of customers most need your efforts
- Confirm which customers are most profitable to your company
- Identify the bestselling products or services within the company and within your customer group
- Indicate what time periods are most productive in selling
- Analyze the similarities among unprofitable customers
- Find and fix sales process problems

Tracking sales performance is primarily the job of your sales manager. With data about the productivity of numerous salespeople and territories, she or he can analyze conditions that lead to more productive sales efforts. The analysis will be used to modify sales policies and techniques for specific or all salespeople.

In addition, individual salespeople can make their own analysis of sales performance and adjust how they sell and to whom. They can learn what sales techniques are more productive for them as well as what doesn't work as well. They can match their own sales goals up to sales results and analyze whether expected results are met. Factors you will want to track include sales by:

- Customer
- Industry

- Time period (daily, weekly, monthly, quarterly, annually)
- Product
- Territory or location

Other factors should be tracked depending on what you are selling and to whom. *Analysis* is taking something apart and comparing it with similar things. In sales, analysis means comparing data about one customer to others, one industry to others, one time period to others, and so on. What can you learn from sales analysis? Plenty! You can learn what works—and what doesn't. You can discover that hours with one type of customer are more productive than days with others. You can correlate specific products with industries or territories where they sell better. You can figure out how to best serve your customers, your employer, and your sales career.

Making Good Sales Records a Habit

Selling is a process. It involves specific inputs to gain defined outputs. Getting from input to output requires a process. It's the process of selling. Within it, you will develop processes for identifying prospects, interviewing them about needs, finding solutions, selling your product or service, and making sure that the customer is happy after the sale. Each of these is a process as well.

You can make accurate sales records a part of your selling process without making it a difficult chore. How? By first defining the required inputs. That is, to know relevant facts about your prospects and customers, you must identify what they are and then determine the best way to get and record them. For example, maybe you've determined that to help a prospect you need the following information:

- Name, location, and phone number
- Title and responsibilities
- Work hours and best times to contact
- Preferred methods of contact (in person, phone, e-mail, fax, etc.)
- Preferred products or services

- Alternate products or services
- Relationship opportunities (personal interests, sports, hobbies, etc.)

Your customer data process then should include a checklist to ensure that you gather each key data component on specific customers and prospects early in the selling process. You can use a printed reminder, a printed form, a CM program screen, or whatever else will make all of the data easy to gather and record.

You also can develop processes for other recordkeeping tasks. They will be your guides through the process, with reminders of what you need to know. You can have processes for the initial sales contact, completing the order form, customer order follow-up, and other components of your job as a professional seller.

CHAPTER 10

Your Sales Tool Kit

Salespeople don't sell by spoken words alone. They also use a wide variety of tools that help customers better understand features and benefits. These include a marketing kit and other sales tools that help buyers recognize how a purchase will enhance their lives or jobs. Your sales kit can be as straightforward as a sample of the product or as complex as a costly presentation with custom graphs. More important, your sales tool kit includes your knowledge, information, and trust. This chapter shows you how to recognize and build a winning tool kit for whatever you sell.

What's in Your KIT?

A drummer is a traveling salesperson who solicits orders for products using a sample and other marketing tools. Early drummers carried their samples by camel, donkey, horse, or automobile to buyers in their territory or sales area. Depending on what the drummer offers, buyers may be housewives (household brushes, vacuums, cosmetics), store owners (wholesale merchandise), or manufacturers (tools, equipment). The drummers' job is to solicit or "drum up" interest in their products using a portable sales tool kit, then take orders that will be delivered by others.

What drummers have in common is they all have knowledge of the product or service that they represent, information from customers about their needs, and the ability to develop sufficient trust to earn an order and payment. That's their sales kit.

Your sales KIT is the same: Knowledge, Information, and Trust. Whatever you sell, you must know your products and customers very well. Most important, you must earn your customers' trust so they will purchase from you. If any of these three ingredients is missing, the transaction won't happen.

Product Knowledge

Whatever you sell—razor blades, radio advertising, or industrial regulators—you must know more about it than your customer does. To be successful, you should know how it works, why it works, and—most important—what problems it can solve for others. Your employer can provide basic product knowledge, but you should be sufficiently curious to find out more. Depending on what you are selling, talk to the designers and engineers, speak with the marketing people, and ask existing customers what they know about what you're selling.

In addition, know your competitors' products. Learn more about them than your customers know. Also perform online searches to find out everything you can about your competitors and what they are telling your customers.

The products you represent were developed with guidance from a marketing department somewhere, probably employed by the manufacturer. A key to product marketing is developing a unique selling proposition or point (USP) for each product. Each selling point is a feature and its benefit(s) to the customer. Some of these points are unique to the product that you represent; your competitor cannot or does not offer the same USP. Knowing your product requires that you identify and understand each *unique* selling point that your product offers the customer. It's why *your* product is better than the competitive product in some (or maybe all) applications. Of course, you also should know what the USPs are for your competitors' products. That's product knowledge, the first component of your sales KIT.

FACT

Not all USPs are unique. Wonder Bread, for example, "helps build strong bones twelve ways" say the ads. Actually, the bread is enriched with calcium and other minerals and vitamins—the same ones used by other major bakers. What's unique is that the bakers of Wonder Bread used this feature as a primary marketing point to sell their bread.

Customer Information

Not all products are appropriate for all buyers. Some products that you represent will be the best solution for numerous specific applications, but may not be for others. For example, an automotive diagnostic tester may be the best on the market and be an excellent solution for auto repair shops. However, due to the price, it isn't appropriate for the home mechanic. In selling this tester, you must know the needs of your prospect. What is the problem that it must solve? How will it be used? What is the budget for its purchase? How much time, money, or frustration can it save the user?

How can you learn more about your customer? Chapters 2 and 4 explained how professional salespeople use questions to discover the buyer's needs. In most selling situations, begin with open-ended questions that allow the buyer to talk about those needs, then use closed-ended yes/no questions to focus the buyer on specific products and benefits. The point of your questioning is to help the customer come up with an answer to: What problem do I need to solve? Depending on the product and customer, the answer can be:

- I need a reliable automated widget that can reduce manufacturing costs.
- I need a computerized payroll program that will reduce costly errors and better track employee time.
- I need a human resources service that can ensure our company is complying with new federal and state hiring laws.
- I need an advertising program that reaches our core customers with a message that we are expanding our hours to better serve their needs.
- I need a truck that can deliver and off-load building materials at remote sites.

Until you've discovered the problem that your customer needs to solve—and helped the customer verbalize the problem—your solution is not welcomed. And you can't identify the problem if you don't gather information about the customer, the second component of your sales KIT.

Building Trust

Chapter 2 defined *trust* as "assured reliance on the character, ability, strength, or truth of someone or something." To trust someone is to not question what that person says or does. Because you are a seller by trade, you often will fall within the typical customer's definition of the job. Trustworthy is not in that definition. So, it is an important part of your job to develop trust in the minds of your prospects and customers.

There are numerous techniques for developing customer trust outlined in this book. In essence, building trust first means acting trustworthy. Customers should be able to depend on what you say; they should respect your knowledge and your opinion. If you are knowledgeable, confident, and respectful, your customers will more easily trust you to assist them in their buying decision. Most important, don't say or do anything that makes a customer mistrust you. Too many salespeople reduce customer trust by using unrealistic superlatives (fantastic, perfect, unbelievable, best ever, etc.) that most customers know cannot be true. Instead, they appreciate accurate and verifiable descriptions (most popular, proven, award-winning, good quality, etc.).

One proven technique for developing trust is to make a statement, then immediately back it up with succinct and understandable facts. "This article in *Consumer Digest* notes that the Acme Widget model 245 has more power than any of its competitors." If accepted by the customer, the seller can make additional statements about other features and probably have them accepted by the customer as fact. Of course, the seller should be ready to offer evidence of *every* statement made about products represented. That's how Golden Rule Sellers build trust, the third and most important component of your sales KIT.

Your Marketing Tools

Most products and many services sold require tangible sales tools such as samples, brochures, videos, and other devices. Your job as a Golden Rule Seller includes gathering and using these tools as part of your sales efforts.

Many of these components are available from the manufacturers or service providers and are given to you by your employer. However, don't assume that you have everything. In too many cases, wholesalers don't have the latest marketing literature from manufacturers. However, your competitors may. As possible, make sure that you have the most recent samples, printed materials, and other marketing collateral (media) available.

Samples

Imagine selling the latest computer when you don't have that model. "The new one's even better!" The customer logically asks, "Then why don't you have one?" For many products sold, one of the best sales tools you can have is one of the products. Even if you're selling industrial widgets by the thousands, a single widget can help a buyer make the connection and help you make the sale.

In some cases, a sample product isn't practical. However, you can use something that tactilely represents what you are selling. It can be a prominent component, a cutaway that shows internal components, or other visual aid. If the primary product feature is its sturdiness, the sample can be a piece of the sturdy material that it's made from. Your sample should be tangible.

Customers can become even more involved in the sales process if they receive a *free* sample. This isn't always practical, but it can be effective. For example, many computer programs today are sold by offering a crippled (limited-use) version, called a demonstration or demo version. It may be limited in features, the number of times it can be used, the number of days it can operate, or by another method. As appropriate, many wholesalers will give sample products to retailers to test themselves and even to resell. Samples help buyers become more involved in the purchase.

Printed Collateral

Marketing *collateral* is anything that supports or serves the selling of products or services. Most things sold today have some type of collateral, ranging from packaging to brochures and videos. Following is a partial list of printed collateral available for many things sold:

- Sales brochures
- Signs
- Posters
- White papers (research reports)
- Pamphlets
- Product data sheets
- Sales scripts
- Business cards

Manufacturers and service providers typically have a marketing department or a division called marketing communications, or mar-com, that is responsible for developing these sales tools. In some cases, outside vendors of marketing services develop and publish these collateral tools based on meetings with their client, the manufacturer. Big companies spend thousands and even millions of dollars producing printed collateral for one express purpose: to help salespeople market their products.

Audio/Video Collateral

In the past two decades, more emphasis has been put on developing audio and video collateral for salespeople. A/V collateral is everything from

PowerPoint presentations to video guides that customers can use to install or maintain purchased products. Audio/video collateral includes:

- Presentation slides and programs
- Audio sales tapes
- Videotape and DVD presentations
- Web content

Yes, web content is considered A/V marketing collateral. In fact, it is a powerful application of the Internet, helping salespeople know their products, inform customers, and build trust: KIT. Internet-based sales tools will be covered in greater detail later in this chapter.

Image Collateral

Another component in your sales tool kit should be image collateral—things that help you establish your company's image. These tools include anything with your brand name on it: coffee mugs, T-shirts, hats, emblem jackets, key chain fobs, and football stadiums.

QUESTION?

What does a football stadium have to do with image collateral?
Plenty. For example, San Francisco's Candlestick Park became 3Com Park in 1996 in a naming rights deal with 3Com, a computer network manufacturer. The license expired in 2002 and it became San Francisco Stadium—until Monster Cable (not Monster.com) purchased naming rights. Those rights expired in 2008 and the home of the San Francisco 49ers is again referred to as Candlestick Park. Many other sport stadiums have sold naming rights to corporations who wish to promote their name and image. Selling is big business.

Using Your Sales Tools KIT

Once you've collected your sales KIT and your marketing tools, you're probably anxious to put them to work. Hold on! There's more that you need to know: how to use these powerful tools. Imagine buying a large chest of tools at the hardware store before you really know how to use them. Without some initial guidance, you might use a large wrench to pound in a nail.

Of course, there are many variables, including what, how, to whom, and when you are selling, as well as what sales tools are available to you. Following are some general guidelines for ways to put your sales tool kit to work efficiently.

Opening the Sales KIT

Your product knowledge, customer information, and trustworthiness can be used within any part of the sales process. However, you and your customer will benefit most if you measure it out as needed rather than dump everything you know on the new buyer. That means you should first take some measurements of what your buyer knows. How can you do that?

- Ask questions about the buyer's job.
- Ask about the most critical problems the buyer must solve.
- As possible, determine what training level and expertise the buyer has.
- If the buyer uses a technical term, ask for a clarification. How it is answered can help you determine what level of technical understanding the buyer has.

It's critical that you don't get ahead of your buyer when offering your product knowledge. You must match the buyer's pace rather than force the buyer to keep up with you. For example, explaining how your new hydraulic widget works won't be helpful to the buyer if you haven't determined that first there is a basic understanding of hydraulics. "Have you had much experience with hydraulic components?" Don't assume this knowledge unless you're talking with a mechanical engineer.

Earning trust, too, must be carefully gained. If you already know exactly how to solve your buyer's problem with the model 928 widget, don't blurt it out and expect an order. Instead, walk the buyer through the purchasing process so that he or she first recognizes that the best solution is the 928.

Your job is not to just offer solutions, but to *sell* solutions. Doing so will help you build valuable trust.

In your sales career, you must dedicate time and effort to learning new things: details of new products, new applications for current products, what your competitors are offering, and how best to help buyers solve their relevant problems. Make sure that you dedicate at least 10 percent of your time to learning new things for your job. This percentage should never become zero. If you stop learning you will stop selling.

Using Marketing Tools

As noted earlier, there are numerous types of marketing tools—samples, printed and A/V collateral, and image collateral. How and when you use them can be as important as what.

Your first task is to identify your primary marketing tools and how best to use them. For example, a business card is often an initial collateral that tells who you are and how to contact you. A pamphlet will tell more about your products and/or services, but no one buys products from a pamphlet. Printed brochures may be appropriate for introducing a new buyer to your merchandise line. White papers offer more detail and can answer comparative questions for the buyer. A catalog can offer more specifics on a group of products and can encourage ordering. Each component has a function. It is your job to use the appropriate collateral to help your buyer learn and trust.

Audio and video collateral can help build customer knowledge and trust, though it typically doesn't have the detail that printed material offers. A/V collateral is more useful earlier in the selling process to help the buyer understand the product and the seller. Once trust is developed, most buyers want more detail that is better offered in printed collateral.

Using the Internet to Sell

The Internet is a bunch of computers talking to each other in their native language, data. Their "words" are ones and zeros. Fortunately, computer programs have been developed so that Internet users don't have to use digits to communicate. Instead, they use a special language (hypertext markup language or HTML) that is interpreted as words and images that humans can read. These computers talk across telephones, data lines, satellite links, and other transmission systems. Over them, retirees in Belgrade can plan trips to the Grand Canyon, books can be selected and even read online, and table saws can be compared and purchased via the Internet. What was once the toy of college students is now a necessity of business.

In your job as a professional seller, you may be required to use the Internet to find and communicate with buyers, order products and supplies, send reports to your managers, and perform other functions. Knowing how to use the Internet as a sales tool can enhance your career. Following is an introduction to using the Internet to sell.

E-mail Sales

Electronic mail or e-mail has dramatically changed how people communicate. Friends are found, friendships developed, and even marriage proposals are made without any face-to-face contact. In business, prospects are identified and courted, products are offered and discussed, and sales are made, again, without in-person contact.

QUESTION?

How rampant is e-mail spam?
E-mail is about thirty years old, but the number sent each day didn't reach 1 billion until about ten years ago. By 2005, the number of unsolicited bulk e-mails sent daily passed 50 billion and in early 2008 passed 100 billion daily. That's nearly 15 UBEs for every person on the earth—every day. Fortunately, the tools available to businesses are robust and very powerful at minimizing UBE for its employees. But they aren't perfect.

Unfortunately, the ease of e-mailing and its negligible cost has encouraged people selling just about everything to offer it for sale via e-mail messages. Sometimes called e-mail spam, the industry calls it unsolicited bulk e-mail (UBE). It makes receivers cautious about all e-mail they receive, but modern businesses thrive on fast communications so e-mail is here to stay.

How can you use e-mail to sell more?

- Respond to inquiries by sending product information in or attached to e-mails.
- Ask current customers if you can contact them via e-mail (opt-in) and at what address.
- Ask website visitors to sign up (opt-in) for a newsletter or other sales information.
- Develop an informational product that helps buyers and ask if you can send it to them (opt-in).

Depending on what you sell, to whom, and how, you may discover that e-mail is a significant tool in helping buyers solve problems. In addition, e-mails can bridge the time differences between seller and buyer. For example, a West Coast salesperson can review e-mails at noon daily and send responses to East Coast buyers before they go home for the day. Or you can send e-mails to buyers even though they are half-way around the world and fast asleep. They will receive your message when they next log on to their e-mail account.

Make sure you get a signature file for your e-mail system. It is an automatic addition to outgoing e-mails that note your position, how to contact you, and anything else you want to routinely include. Virtually all e-mail systems allow signatures. The signature can be a text or graphic file and can be a default for all your e-mail addresses or unique signatures for individual accounts.

Your Employer's Website

Your employer—retailer, wholesaler, manufacturer, service provider—probably will have a website used to assist sales. It may simply support your efforts with online collateral, or it may be an electronic commerce (e-commerce) site that sells products, parts, or supporting services. Chances are that you won't have much control over it. Management probably has decided its purpose and components. It will be your job to use it efficiently in your own sales efforts.

The first step in using your employer's Internet website is to study it. You can be a customer, looking at how it interfaces with you. You can speak with the site developer to discover its functions and features. You can ask the webmaster, the person or service that actually manages the site, about how it works. You will learn about server-side publishing, Java scripts, and maybe about shopping cards and auto responders, depending on the function and structure of the site. Each of these components is a tool that you may be able to put to work for you as a seller.

If your sales job involves inside sales or customer relations, you may be assigned a territory or customer group that you will serve. In this case, your primary tools may be your employer's website and e-mail system. In this case, be certain that you get full training on how they can work for you—even if you have to train yourself by reviewing software manuals and reading books.

ALERT!

Once hired by a firm with an Internet website, find out if your name and contact information should be on the website. If so, strive to get it done expeditiously. You will have one or more e-mail addresses assigned to you and should make sure they work. Then verify that they get on your business cards and other appropriate collateral.

Resource Websites

If you work for an independent sales office, your employer may have a minimal or no website. It may link to the manufacturer(s) it represents. In addition, the manufacturer's website may include contact information for your territorial sales office. Verify that it is accurate and up-to-date.

If your employer has no website and you feel you would benefit from at least a small one, consider setting up your own. The cost of a simple website can be just a few hundred dollars or less. However, first make sure that it has the approval of your employer.

You also can promote your sales efforts using association and network websites. For example, if your employer is a member of a trade association, visit the site and analyze whether you can submit your e-mail or website address for inclusion as a link. Networks are groups of similar businesses that allow reciprocal links on their websites. Be cautious, as it can direct your prospects to your competitors. Chapter 17 offers additional guidance in leveraging Golden Rule Selling on the Internet.

CHAPTER 11

Finding Sales Prospects

You made a sale! Congratulations! Now what? The process starts over again, either with an existing customer or with a new prospect. But where can you find prospects? Where are they hiding and how can you turn them into customers? Tomorrow's sales depend on your answer. This chapter focuses on where and how to find qualified buyers for what you sell. The rules of engagement are similar, whether you are selling consumer commodities, business products, or industrial services. Learn how to find sales prospects in any situation and your sales career will grow.

Identifying Prospects

Prospective buyers are all around you. In fact, every one you know or meet is a prospective buyer of something, as are you. The question is: Who is a prospective buyer for what you sell?

The question may seem straightforward, but the answer can be multifaceted, depending on exactly what you sell. It can entail geographic, economic, title, and other factors. It can depend on the time of year or the status of your employer's inventory. It also is dictated by your job description. If you are an inside salesperson, your prospects may be your employer's customers who have purchased initial products or systems from outside salespeople.

A *prospect* is a potential buyer of what you sell. It is a person or entity (corporation, government office, etc.) who needs the solutions your products offer, who has purchased them in the past from your employer or your competitors, or who may need these solutions in the future.

FACT

An excellent and free source of market data is the U.S. Census Bureau (*www.census.gov*). It includes current and historic data on people and households, business, industry, and geography. It should be the first place you look for population numbers. In addition, you can analyze the makeup of that population by a variety of criteria including age, race, economics, and other factors that impact business.

Prospect Needs

Earlier chapters explained that products and services are designed and marketed to solve specific problems that an identified group of buyers has. Reviewing a list of product features and benefits can help you analyze who your potential prospects are. For example, if what you are selling is displays designed to increase traffic into a retail clothing store, then your prospects, obviously, are clothing retailers.

The benefits list may continue with specifics that can help you focus your prospect definition even more.

Product Feature	Buyer Trait
Displays are easily moved to entryways.	The prospective store is either in a mall or on a street that allows and has security for large outside displays.
Display components can be changed to fit a variety of clothing merchandise.	The prospective store offers a variety of clothing and prefers to rotate what the rack holds.
Displays include signage racks.	The prospective store wants to draw attention to the displays.

By understanding what your products do, you can better understand who needs them. Then it becomes much easier to use sales lead resources (below) to identify and contact prospective buyers.

Previous Customers

You may have prospective buyers waiting to order from you. Who are they? Previous customers. So why aren't they buying from your company right now? The reasons include:

- Your firm's customer service department lost the customer.
- Your competitors made them a better offer.
- A prior seller for your employer lost them.
- Their business changed.
- They found other suppliers.
- They simply forgot about your employer.

How can you get them back? First, by identifying who they are. Your employer can help you identify previous customers who have not ordered within a specified period, such as a year. It will be your job, then, to prioritize your efforts, then update the contact information before making a call to identify the reason(s) why they aren't buying from you.

Fortunately, you are in a good position to help these previous customers become current. You are not the problem. By being friendly and helpful, you may be able to discover what the problem is and help solve it.

"I've just joined Acme Widgets and wondered if you can help me. I see that you used to purchase from us, but now you don't. Can you tell me why so that I can do a better job in the future?"

One of the most powerful techniques you can use to disarm a prospect, customer, supplier, or coworker is to ask for their help. If asked sincerely, most people will take a moment to help another. Then make sure that you listen to what is being said. Once you learn how to use this technique, you can diffuse a variety of business and personal situations. Don't over-use it, but do learn how to use the power of "help me."

In many cases, you'll find that prospects only need a reminder, a short sales message, to get thinking about your company again. If a prior order or contact has made the problem, your sincerely listening to it can help re-establish a relationship. If you can somehow resolve the problem to the person's satisfaction, you may have a new prospective customer. If not, your efforts to help can at least neutralize the effect of prior problems and open the buyer's mind to considering your company again.

Competitor's Customers

You also can find prospects among your competitor's customers. As you contact your prospects and customers, you will soon identify who your competitor's customers are. They also are your prospects. Never give them fully up to your competitors. Instead, identify why your competitors have won their business and, if you can, determine how you can win them away.

Why do you want them as customers? First, because if they are buying from your competitors, they are potential buyers for what you are selling. Second, because if your products or services can better satisfy the buyer's needs, they should be *your* customers. Of course, that's not up to you to decide; it's up to the buyer. But if you don't at least treat your competitor's customers as your prospects, they may never have the choice.

Future Buyers

Once you've identified who should consider buying from you, it's easier to recognize future prospects. For example, if you are selling display units to retail clothing stores, as above, future prospects will include those who are contemplating opening, remodeling, or buying an existing clothing store. Using various sales lead services, discussed below, as well as your own knowledge of the business, you begin courting future buyers.

In addition, you should be courting those who can help you find future buyers. That is, if you want to be aware of what retail stores are coming to your area, make contacts with shopping mall management, business permit offices, chambers of commerce, and other gatekeepers. Developing a relationship of mutual assistance and trust can pay off in identifying potential customers.

Locating Prospects

Finding prospective buyers is not only about identifying who prospects are, but also where they are. In some sales jobs, it's relatively easy; all your prospects and customers are located in a single zip code, county, state, or region. Other sales jobs ignore physical locations and focus on prospects in specific businesses or industries. Or prospects are identified by title: CFO, book buyer, parts buyer, marketing manager, or whatever.

Geographic Prospects

Many employers offer exclusive geographic territories to their salespeople. The salesperson is their representative within an area, such as lower Manhattan (with specific street borders), Utah, or Canadian Maritime Provinces. The purpose of geographic territories is to keep salespeople from wasting time and confusing customers. Without geographic boundaries, customers would get too many or too few salespeople representing your employer.

If you are given a geographic sales territory, ask what supporting information the employer has about it. It may be minimal, in which case you'll have to do your own research. However, they may have access to databases that can help you more easily identify prospective buyers within the area. Some business databases have financial information that can help you in prioritizing prospects so you work with the best opportunities first.

Business/Industry Prospects

Depending on what you sell, your prospective buyers may not have geography in common. They may be spread across the country or the globe. You may be selling to widget buyers in Queens, New York, and Queensland, Australia, on the same day. Using the phone, e-mail, and delivery services, you can serve them from Quinter, Kansas ("the half-mile-high city").

QUESTION?

What is NAICS?
The North American Industry Classification System (pronounced nakes) was introduced in 1997 as a method of classifying industries in the United States, Canada, and Mexico. The six-digit number identifies the sector, subsector, industry group, industry, and country. For example, 339941 identifies a pen and mechanical pencil manufacturer in the United States. NAICS replaces the older four-digit Standard Industrial Classification (SIC) in use since the 1930s, though some federal government entities haven't made the change over to the newer system.

As with other prospecting, your employer will help you identify the businesses or industries that you will sell to. They may be identified by name or by North American Industry Classification System (NAICS).

Title Prospects

In some cases, your prospects and customers will be identified best by their title, such as widget buyer. Alternatively, your sales territory may also include geographic areas and possibly even industry codes. For example, you may be selling to widget buyers at nuclear power construction sites (NAICS 237130) in New England. That's specific.

Titles can be vague. A "documentation engineer" is better known as a technical writer. Even this title often doesn't help identify a person's responsibilities. The documentation engineer you contact may be a data clerk or she may be responsible for buying large computer systems for document publication worldwide.

If your sales responsibilities are focused on a specific job title, make sure that it also has a function component. What level of buying authority should the title have? Do they decide or do they just recommend to others? Fortunately, you can get guidance in developing a functional title by reviewing your employer's current customers. What are their titles and functions? Are there patterns, such as job grade levels? Locating good prospects for future sales requires knowing as much as you can about them, what they buy, why, and how.

Contacting Prospects

Developing new sales prospects is an important priority, no matter what you are selling. However, it is not your first priority. Remember from Chapter 9 that finding prospective buyers is fifth on your priority list. Even so, your future sales depend on finding and developing prospective buyers. You must allocate some of your sales time to prospecting. Your time must include prospecting.

What's the best time from the prospect's view to reach them? Within their need cycle. A *need* is a condition that requires supply or relief. The prospects need replacement inventory or the solution to a business problem. That is their point of need. Many purchases aren't made until there is a perceived need and a requirement for action. It may even be a future need, recognized as requiring an action now. You may not need toothpaste right now, but you will soon, so you buy it now.

As a professional seller, you can contact prospective buyers before they identify the need, when it is recognized, or after it is acknowledged. Depending on what and how you sell, one point in the need cycle may be a better time to contact prospects than another.

You can lead a horse to water, but you can't make it drink—unless you first make it thirsty! This sales truism suggests that you must first help prospects and customers identify and see the value for fulfilling a specific need. If you don't, you will continue struggling and any effort to offer a solution will probably be fruitless. In fact, the more you help intensify the need, the less work you will have to do in selling the solution.

Before the Need

All people and businesses have needs. A restaurant that doesn't want to run out of tomatoes will plan ahead and buy before they open the last crate. If you're selling tomatoes and other produce to restaurants, you can help them in estimating usage and supplying fresh produce before it becomes a need. Of course, you can't supply them too early or they won't be fresh when used.

Many products and services sold require that they be delivered before the need arises, when a future need is identified. If you primarily sell before the need, make sure that you can identify when the need occurs for various buyers. In addition, learn how to sell based on anticipated needs.

During the Need

A plumbing contractor often sells during the need. A pipe is busted and needs to be fixed right now. The plumbing contractor also offers other services, water heater installation, the plumbing system in a new home, and so on. In many cases, the selling is done either before or during the need. Selling products and services at the point of need actually can be easier. If it is an emergency, it is easier to convince the buyer of the needed products or services. In many cases, prospective buyers will approach you once they identify an immediate need—if you have previously identified yourself as a fulfiller of specific needs. Maybe you've contacted the buyer in the past and left your business card, or you advertise in the telephone book or other directory. Anticipating buyer needs, you can be prepared to be known by the buyer when a need point arises.

After the Need

An insurance agent often sells before the need arises, pointing out a predictable need. However, insurance agents also sell after the need. That is, an auto accident will either solidify a relationship with an insurance agent or damage it, depending on how the claim was handled. After an accident is reported, some insurance agents will call those involved to determine if the claim to a competitor was handled satisfactorily. If not, this gives the agent an opportunity to sell after the need is recognized and before the next need occurs.

Selling the Need

What you sell may be best offered before, during, or after the need is acknowledged. However, when prospecting, the best time to approach is before the need, then help the buyer understand that the consequences of the unfulfilled need are greater than the cost of fulfilling it now.

- Ordering two cases now will ensure that you don't run out of fresh tomatoes over the busy weekend.
- We can perform a plumbing system check tomorrow afternoon to make sure you don't have a plumbing emergency over the winter.
- Signing up with Acme Insurance now can guarantee that you don't have frustrating claim problems again.

The best time to contact prospects is before they identify the need; in this way you can help them to recognize it. It's called proactive selling and it gives you a viable reason to help prospective buyers.

Sales Lead Resources

Your employer probably will define for you how to identify and locate prospective buyers. You may be assigned a territory or even be furnished with some sales leads. These leads may be "prequalified" or "nonqualified." Prequalified leads are those that meet defined criteria, usually involving their interest in buying as well as their ability and authority to buy what you sell. Nonqualified leads are simply names and basic contact information for people and companies who might buy from you. Obviously, salespeople prefer prequalified leads.

Where do these sales leads come from? The sources depend on what you are selling and to whom. They can be derived from referrals, advertising campaigns, or from a list of possible prospects, called suspects. Each type is identified and approached in a different way.

Referrals

The best prospects are those that have been referred to you by current customers. Your initial call to them has credibility because you are being recommended by someone that they know and probably trust. Remember that trust is a key to selling and a major component in your sales KIT (see Chapter 10). It is invaluable to be able to use your customer's trust as an opening tool when contacting a prospect.

Referrals should be followed up while they are still fresh. If possible, ask referrers to let the prospects know that you will be contacting them. For example:

> "Mr. Jones, I was just speaking with your friend, Mr. Smith, who suggested that I call you. My company, Acme Widgets, has been providing wholesale widgets to Mr. Smith for three years, and he is very pleased with them. Is there a time when I can meet with you to discuss your future widget needs?"

Proactive salespeople often ask for referrals any time that a customer expresses satisfaction with the products or services that you provide. "I like how you got that order to me fast, Ralph." "Thanks, Bob. Can you think of any of your associates who might appreciate fast service?" Always be ready to ask for and develop referral business.

Ad Leads

Most businesses advertise. Some develop branding advertising that builds customer recognition for their brand name. Others use ads to elicit a response from readers. They often will offer something, such as a free report or a token gift, if the reader will inquire with their contact information. Depending on the value of the potential sale, some businesses will then use follow-ups to identify the inquirer's needs and ability to purchase, called inquiry qualification. This data then is passed on to appropriate salespeople as prospects.

The value of these prospects depends on how deep the prequalifying goes. The inquirer may simply want something for free. Others may have legitimate needs and respond truthfully to qualifying questions—or not. In any case, some form of prequalification can assist the seller in determining the value of the prospect.

For many years, most inquiry leads came from magazine advertising, especially in industry publications where the readers already have an identified need: process controls, bottling equipment, remodeling materials, computer networks, or whatever else the magazine is focused on. Ads would include reader service numbers that could be checked off on a postpaid card at the back of the magazine. Readers give their contact information and indicate what products or reports they want to receive. The magazine or a service processes the inquiries and reports them to the appropriate advertisers or their inquiry management service.

In recent years, more inquiries are being developed through Internet websites. The process is automated so that requested information is immediately delivered to the inquirer using autoresponders and other software. Questionnaires are sometimes used to help identify and qualify inquirers and, as appropriate, pass them on to salespeople as prospects.

The key to utilizing inquiries from ads and the Internet is to somehow prequalify them. To do that, you need to know what the primary qualification questions are for what you sell. For example, maybe the qualifying question is: Do you have a computer network that is more than three years old? Or: Are you considering buying a new car in the next month? Identifying the best qualifying questions for your prospects can help you identify which are the most likely to purchase from you.

Suspects

In selling, a *suspect* is a prospective prospect. It is someone who is probably qualified and interested in buying from you in the future. For example, a school district is *not* a suspect for a wholesale liquor salesperson, but a nightclub is.

ALERT!

Sometimes suspects will become prospects without any help from you. As a low priority, they don't seem like significant buyers, but a perceived need on their part will require that they quickly find a solution. You are a solution. So they contact you and present their problem, making them a qualified prospect. If they subsequently buy, they become a customer. Initiation of the process, however, was out of your hands, though you are the beneficiary.

Finding suspects for what you sell is relatively easy; qualifying them for need and interest is more challenging. If you are selling pneumatic nailers at wholesale, your suspects include all building material retailers and contractors in your sales territory. That's probably a long list. Your job, then, is to narrow down the list of suspects into prospects. That requires some qualifying. You can broadly qualify your suspects by determining not only if they buy pneumatic nailers, but also if they buy the type of nailers that you offer. If yours are designed for factory use, they may not be appropriate for retailers who sell to consumers. You can then qualify them even further by researching your suspects to determine who has purchased your type of product or service in the past. Business databases and sales lead services, covered next, can help you in separating prospects from suspects. Once you have more information about your prospects, you are more ready to contact them and offer your knowledge and assistance.

Buying Sales Leads

In addition to using prequalified ad and Internet inquiries, there are other ways you can purchase sales leads. You can buy contact lists or sales lead services or hire prequalifiers. Each has its advantages and disadvantages. The key to using them is determining which are investments and which are simply expenses. This requires trial and error, testing sales lead sources and comparing the outcome (sales) with the costs. If they are profitable, repeat the process until they are not. In most sales organizations, your manager will purchase and test sales leads, though your efforts and reporting can help in ensuring that results are accurately tracked.

Contact Lists

Contact lists are the simplest and least expensive of purchased sales leads. Actually, they really aren't sales leads. Depending on how much prequalifying is done, they either are lists of prospects or suspects. In most cases, the more you pay for the list, the greater the prequalifying level. However, you probably still will have do some qualifying to discover whether they are hot, warm, or cold prospects.

Contact lists typically include information such as: name, title, company, address, industry code, annual sales, and other data. For example, ZapData (*www.zapdata.com*) is a Dun & Bradstreet division that sells data about companies. Others include InfoUSA (*www.infousa.com*) and Hoovers (*www.hoovers.com*).

FACT

Direct marketing is a business function that can help salespeople qualify sales leads. Persons on contact lists can be mailed product collateral (see Chapter 9) and asked to indicate their needs and their authority in purchasing. Those who respond, often encouraged by a premium, are, to some extent, prequalified. As appropriate, they can be passed on to a sales rep for further contact and qualifying.

Depending on the list and from whom purchased, there can be some fact verification, but most are built from existing—and not always up-to-date—

databases. Error levels can be just a few percent or up to 20 percent if the list is old. People change jobs or responsibilities and lists that are more than six months old can already be out of date in some industries. When purchasing contact lists, ask how recently *all* data has been verified and updated. Some may be very recent additions while others are years old and unverified.

Sales Lead Services

Sales lead services take contact lists one step further. They contact the suspect and ask qualifying questions, either generic or industry specific. It will save you time, as a seller, to know which of the contact list names is planning to purchase what you sell in the next six months rather than never. Sales lead services perform this function.

In some cases, the prequalifying is done via direct mail, telephone or fax, or the Internet. In each case, standardized qualifying questions are asked and the responses noted. Those questions typically answer:

- What is their area of purchasing responsibility?
- What are their current and future purchasing needs?
- How and why do they buy?

Accurate answers to these questions can help salespeople more efficiently identify prospects within a pool of suspects. Of course, the cost of this value-added service is higher than that of contact lists. However, for high-ticket products and services, sales lead services can help salespeople work more efficiently and actually save money over doing their own qualifying.

Prequalifiers

Some products and services are focused on a narrow market, and finding qualified prospects is difficult, but rewarding. In those situations, many sales organizations will use contact lists and have their own staff or a service contractor make the calls and pass the leads to their salespeople.

The advantage to inside prequalifiers is that the qualifying questions can be tailored to the exact needs of the sales staff. The questions can be focused on the elements identified by sales managers as buying points. In addition, the questions can be modified as needed to better identify prospective buyers. Imagine receiving sales leads that indicate that specific individuals are planning to purchase your type of product or service within the next month and their budget is in place. That's a hot lead.

Sales leads can be profitable or a waste of time. As your sales career grows, you will learn how better to turn suspects into prospects, then into customers who provide qualified referrals. The sales process will continue, and you will enjoy the rewards of being a Golden Rule Seller.

CHAPTER 12

Getting Appointments

Finding prospects is a vital step in the sales process. Once done, the next step is to meet with those prospects to learn how you can help solve problems for them. You must meet them in person or by phone to analyze their needs. You must get appointments. How can you get productive appointments? Good question. This chapter offers proven methods for setting up meetings with prospective buyers in a variety of sales situations.

Toughest Job in Sales

Professional sellers agree that just about the toughest job in sales is getting time with a buyer. In retail sales, the problem is easier to solve. Buyers walk in. Getting time with the retail buyer typically means making yourself available to help. However, as the price of things sold goes up, so do the barriers that buyers erect. If they make decisions on major purchases for their company, they are inundated by salespeople with requests for their time and attention.

Obviously, they can't see everyone. So many buyers take the stance of: We're not buying right now! This can be frustrating, especially for salespeople who sincerely believe that the solutions they offer could really help the buyer—if the seller could just get some time with the buyer.

The solution for professional sellers is to focus your message, develop buyer trust, and be patient yet persistent. Following are some guidelines for making the toughest job in sales easier.

Your Message

Buyers are busy. They don't have time to listen to salespeople stutter over their sales pitch in hopes of gaining the buyer's interest. Their initial message must be focused, clear, and attention grabbing.

The products or services that you represent probably are designed to solve a number of generic problems for buyers. But buyers really don't care about other people's problems; they want to know how to solve their own problems. Your sales message must focus on how it can benefit the buyer. For example:

- Acme Widgets are the most popular brand among consumers and are the most profitable for retailers.
- Our umbrella business insurance plans can increase covered events at lower premiums.
- Wholesalers can reduce inventory with our just-in-time delivery system.
- Conventions at our resort have a 97 percent satisfaction rate.

You will have many unique selling points like these in your sales arsenal. It is vital that you use the appropriate one to focus your message on the specific buyer's needs.

In addition, your message must be clear and specific. Saying "conventions at our resort are satisfied with our service" has less meaning than specifying that the verifiable satisfaction rate is 97 percent. Being clear and accurate can help buyers understand that you recognize their problem and that you have a solution.

As much as possible, make your message attention getting. Stating a primary benefit can gain a buyer's notice: most popular, most profitable, lower premiums, reduce inventory, high satisfaction. Before you ask a prospect for an appointment, make sure you have a focused, clear, and attention-getting message. Know what problem you can solve for your buyer and present it as succinctly and vividly as possible. That's the first step in getting a quality sales appointment.

Developing Trust

As noted throughout this book, trust is the key to gaining a buyer's confidence. You must encourage and develop a level of trust in your buyer so that she or he can believe what you say and do. Without trust, there is no transaction.

How can you build a level of trust in a prospect that you barely know? Most often, initial trust is transferred from another source. That is, a trusted business associate or friend recommends you. "Mike Simpson, your golfing partner, just bought a set of our new clubs from me and suggested that you might like to know about how they improved his game."

In some cases the product or service that you offer has developed brand-name recognition that you can use. "I'm Dave Jones from Acme Widgets, the bestselling brand in the United States." Use this associated trust to your advantage. Just make sure that the trust you attempt to transfer is valuable. If, for example, you are calling an expired customer who may not have had a good experience with your company in the past, start with an apology. Then you can begin to rebuild the lost trust.

Being Patient

Don't expect buyers to be awaiting your phone call for an appointment. Most are much too busy for that. Instead, your call may be an interruption to them. Always ask if they have time to discuss an appointment. Be prepared to hear answers like:

- We don't have any needs to buy right now.
- I'm too busy to discuss it right now.
- Call me back in a couple of months.

Responses like this can indicate a very busy buyer. More often, they point to a buyer who doesn't see an advantage to an appointment with you. That's why having a valuable message and developing trust can help you. Be prepared to respond to a "No!" and you may get a "Yes" or at least a "Maybe."

Once you get some experience at setting appointments, you'll probably be able to identify which of the "No" reasons a buyer uses before it's even used. Great! Then take the power out of it. "I know you're a busy person and don't want to take your time without giving you something valuable for it, so can I buy you lunch?" "You're probably not in the market for widgets right now, but I can show you how to save 20 percent when you are."

Being Persistent

Professional sellers don't easily take "No!" for an answer. They are persistent. But they aren't pests. They are careful not to ask questions that will end the discussion, such as "Would you ever buy from us?" Instead, they ask questions that typically bring a positive answer, such as "Do you buy widgets?" or "Do you have a few minutes to discuss how to save $500 on your next widget purchase?"

In some calls to request an appointment, the buyer will put you off until another time. Don't be dissuaded. Instead, thank the prospect for the opportunity, then get a date and time when you can call back. Most important, when you do call back, remind the buyer that you were asked to call back now and why.

The Live Appointment

What type of sales appointment are you asking for? Must you meet the person face-to-face or will a telephone appointment suffice? The answer often depends on what you are selling and to whom. For example, if you are selling business systems that require technical assistance, your sales call probably will be a live presentation (see Chapter 8) to one or more people.

Live appointments are preferable for many sales situations. One primary reason is that it is more difficult for most buyers to say "No" to someone who is right there. This is especially true if it is obvious that the salesperson has spent time and effort to prepare for and make the presentation. Live appointments are more commonly made for business and industry products where there are multiple buyers (see Chapter 16). In addition, larger-ticket consumer items also may require live appointments, such as selling financial services to a couple.

Don't get lost. Many a sales meeting has started off on the wrong foot because directions to the site or the meeting room weren't sufficiently clear. Get full directions or GPS mapping coordinates so you can find your way. In addition, ask for a cell number that you can call if you expect to be late. If at all possible, plan to arrive at least fifteen minutes early to check out the room, prepare your presentation, and get comfortable.

Once you've determined that a live sales appointment is better—for the customer and for you—than a phone appointment, define its goals and specifics. For example, the goal of your live sales appointment may simply be to introduce your line of widgets to a new buyer. Or it may be to help solve a specific problem the buyer has with widget inventory. That's the goal of your live appointment.

Next, where is the best place to meet with your buyer? In most cases, the buyer's office is the preferred choice. This is especially true if there are multiple decision makers who would otherwise have to travel to your location. However, if the buyer will have technical questions, you may prefer to meet at the manufacturer's office or at another site where the products can be shown and questions answered.

Finally, the question becomes: When? Obviously, you want to accommodate the buyer's schedule. Some buyers prefer to meet with sellers on a specific day of the week or during a period of the month. Others meet with sellers in the mornings or the afternoons; a few meet sellers only during lunches—which the sellers pay for. "When is most convenient for you, Mr. Buyer?" It's helpful if you can indicate how long the meeting is expected to realistically take. "I'll need about an hour of your time to show you why Acme Widgets are a greater value."

The Phone Appointment

For many reasons, you and the buyer may opt for a telephone sales appointment rather than a live one. For example, if the meeting only requires an hour, yet is many miles away, it may be more efficient for you to meet by telephone. Fortunately, there are many technical advances that can make a phone appointment productive. Refer to Chapter 6 for details.

Telephone appointments often require as much preparation as live appointments, depending on what is being sold. For example, perhaps presentation collateral and sample products will need to be shipped to the buyer prior to the appointment. If a web presentation service, such as WebEx (*www.webex.com*) is used, the software must be downloaded, installed, and tested on all computers prior to the appointment. In addition, contingency plans should be made in case there is a technical problem during the presentation.

As with live appointments, make sure that you identify the purpose of the meeting, where it will be conducted, when, and how. It's especially important that you get alternate telephone numbers in case the buyer must move the meeting to a different location at the last minute because of increased attendance or room scheduling conflicts.

Also remember to verify the *local* time of the meeting. A 9 A.M. meeting in London is at 1 A.M. in San Francisco and 6 P.M. in Seoul! In addition, be aware that some world time zones change on the half hour and even at forty-five minutes. Others are on daylight savings time during a portion of the year. Synchronize your watches.

QUESTION?

Are there any options to phone appointments that don't require extensive planning and preparation?

Yes, there are. One popular solution is to rent a presentation room in a nearby business center. For example, Office Business Center Association International *(www.obcai.org)* has 600 metropolitan business center members around the world. In addition to executive offices with full secretarial services, most have presentation rooms that are set up for video conference calls and other sales opportunities. Salespeople who travel extensively use these centers as away-offices as well as presentation sites.

Getting Past the Gatekeepers

Every buyer with any authority will have a gatekeeper, a person whose job includes keeping salespeople from wasting the boss's time. Gatekeepers can be very effective at this task; the ones that aren't are soon looking for other work. How can you identify and get through the gatekeepers?

Gatekeepers include the general receptionist, department secretary, and possibly a private secretary or assistant. In retail stores, the gatekeeper may be a clerk or even a manager—someone who has no buying authority. Each will have numerous responsibilities, one of which is to help buyers screen salespeople as appropriate.

The Gatekeeper's Job

Understand that, just like you, the gatekeeper has a job to do. Initially, it may seem like that job is to keep you from getting an appointment. Actually, the gatekeeper has a different function: to help the boss work more efficiently. The gatekeeper is often an assistant who provides a variety of important services to the boss, depending on the job description. The gatekeeper may perform office duties or be responsible for transactions or simply serve as an appointment maker for the boss. In each case, the gatekeeper will not let you pass until you are identified as someone who is valuable to the company. If the gatekeeper judges that you meet the entry criteria, you're in.

Selling the Gatekeeper

What is the entry criteria? You probably won't know for certain, but you can make an educated guess. If the buyer you want to see is responsible for buying all office supplies for the company, then the criteria probably is that all salespeople must first prove to the gatekeeper that she or he can provide better product, better service, or lower prices than current suppliers. Your first sales job, then, is to sell the gatekeeper.

Gatekeepers typically have even less time to hear sales pitches than do their bosses. And less interest. You must tailor your appointment pitch to the needs of the gatekeeper. Your goal: get an appointment.

- I only need fifteen minutes of your boss's time to show your company how to reduce inventory while increasing profits.
- I recently sold Bluebird Widgets an automation device that cut their production costs by 15 percent and I'd like to show it to your boss.
- Can I send you a copy of our catalog and call you back in a week to see if your boss is interested in meeting?

In most cases, your initial contact with the gatekeeper will be by telephone, though it may be in person or by letter. Review the telephone techniques in Chapter 6 and make your pitch succinct. Understand that the gatekeeper's responsibility is not to keep you out, but to make sure that you have something of value to offer the boss. Understand what that is and communicate it—sell it—to the gatekeeper and you have improved chances of getting in.

Developing the Gatekeeper

Once you've had an appointment with the boss—whether you sold anything or not—make sure that you show the gatekeeper appreciation for the attempt. However, never present it as a bribe. It's not. It's an appreciation; if it is seen as a bribe, chances are that your next efforts to get by will be stopped.

Appreciation can come in a variety of forms. By arriving early for an appointment, you may get the opportunity to personally thank the gatekeeper. In addition, you can find out more about the individual. Look for photos and mementos on the wall or desk. In most cases, simply taking an interest in the individual and appreciating the work done is sufficient to begin building a positive relationship. Keep it sincere.

FACT

The gift for gatekeepers that keeps on giving is any useful item with your company name on it. For example, coffee cups, key chains, coasters, and other token gifts. If your gatekeeper works in the factory, warehouse, or other area where the temperature may be lower, an emblem hat, jacket, or sweater may be appropriate. Just make sure that it doesn't look like a walking billboard. And make sure that you get the appropriate size, if applicable.

If you feel that a gift is appropriate, make sure that it is something that acknowledges the individuality of the gatekeeper or helps her on the job. Appreciations can include relevant samples of your product, tickets to sporting or music events that you've identified as of interest to the gatekeeper, or something decorative for the desk. Again, make sure that it is seen as appreciation for extra efforts, not as a bribe. Give the gift *after* the service rather than before.

Getting Through to the Prospect

In some cases, your efforts to get through the gatekeeper and speak directly with a buyer about setting up a sales presentation will be rewarded. Your call is put through to the buyer and you must sell him or her on a meeting. Now what?

It's a good thing that you're prepared for this eventuality. You're ready to impress the buyer sufficiently to earn a sales appointment. Your plan is to introduce yourself, appreciate the call, state its purpose, ask for the appointment, and thank the buyer. Following are proven suggestions for speaking directly with the buyer about a sales appointment.

Introduce Yourself

The first step—introducing yourself—sounds easy. However, to do it efficiently, consider what the buyer wants to know. Who are you, who do you represent, and why should I care?

The who is easy. The why isn't as obvious. However, it's a vital question to ask yourself before you begin talking: why should the prospect care? You should know the answer. In many cases, the answer is because you can help solve a problem that the prospect probably has. But *specifically* why should the prospect want to meet with you? You probably won't get a chance to state it during your brief phone conversation, but knowing what the reason is can help you focus your request.

Buyers aren't sitting by the phone awaiting your call. They are immersed in whatever they do all day. Your call may be an interruption. Assume that it is and be clear as you speak. Begin with the buyer's name to gain attention before moving on to your specifics. For example, "Ms. Jones? My name is Art . . . Art Smith . . . and I represent Acme Widgets." By giving your first name twice, you are making it more prominent and suggesting that the prospect use it.

If you have any referrals to the prospect, state them now. For example, "Your engineer, Syed Hussaini, suggested that I give you a call today." Of course, make sure that you can respond to the question "How do you know Syed?" if asked.

Appreciate the Call

You just interrupted your prospect's day. It doesn't matter whether the prospect was planning the next great project or simply eating a donut; you've interrupted. Sincerely thank the prospect for taking your call and you will begin developing positive momentum that could end in a sales appointment.

- I'm certain that you're busy, Mr. Prospect, so I'll get to the point of my call.
- Thank you for taking my call, Ms. Prospect. I appreciate getting a couple minutes of your time.
- Pardon my interruption, Mr. Prospect. I'll be brief.

State the Call's Purpose

Here's where the prospect learns WIIFM: what's in it for me. Until now, you've been talking about yourself. Make your statement of the call's purpose as succinct and as individual as possible. In fact, write it out in advance so you don't miss it. In addition, reading it aloud will slow your delivery down and help the listener understand it easier than a rote statement.

Make sure that the purpose is as individual as you can make it at this point. For example, "I'm calling because I learned that your company is expanding into China and I want to make sure that you know of our international business services."

Ask for the Appointment

The point of your call is not to sell a product or service, but to get an appointment. In fact, if the prospect encourages you to offer your sales presentation on the telephone, you should consider whether it is in the prospect's best interest. Can you present the facts sufficiently for the prospect to make an informed decision. If not, keep pushing for the appointment.

- The purpose of my call today is to set a meeting with you that can help you reduce HR costs.
- May I meet with you to show how we have improved investment returns by 20 percent?
- Can we set up a meeting next week that explains how Acme Widgets reduces plant maintenance costs?

Again, the primary purpose of your call is to *get a sales appointment*. Of course, you should be ready for a sales opportunity, but if your presentation cannot be adequately delivered over the phone, don't try to do so. Save your full message for the appointment.

FACT

Give prospects a choice. Is this week better or is next week? Do you prefer meeting on Tuesday or Wednesday? Is morning or afternoon better for you? Does 1 P.M. sound okay, or would you like to meet later in the afternoon? Your office or mine? Notice that the choices don't lead to a Yes or No answer; they assume a Yes and work toward specifics.

Thank the Buyer

Thanking the buyer for setting an appointment does many things. First, it offers your appreciative attitude while recognizing the prospect's power. Second, it allows you to confirm and remind the prospect what you've agreed upon. "Thanks for agreeing to meet with me next Tuesday at 2 P.M. in your office, Ms. Prospect." Third, it is a natural close for your conversation. All that's needed is "goodbye."

Handling Turndowns

Not all buyers that you contact for an appointment will make one. In fact, you may find that your conversion rate of prospects to presentations is low. What can you do?

First, don't think of it as a personal message. It is not you who is being turned down; it is your offer to present. Be aware that all salespeople are turned down for sales appointments; no one gets them all.

Second, consider what you can do to improve your chances of getting a sales appointment in the future. Review the process above: polish your message, develop trust, and be patient yet persistent. Analyze what you are doing and how it can be improved. If your product or service really is valuable to buyers, you must strive to overcome their natural objection to being sold and sincerely help them buy.

Third, be prepared to counteract initial turndowns to improve your conversion rate. How? By asking yourself a few post-turndown questions:

- Did I clearly present my message?
- Did the gatekeeper seem rushed or unprofessional?
- Was I rushed or unprofessional?
- Should I have asked to call back another time?
- What reason did the gatekeeper give for not offering an appointment?
- What can I do in the future to counter the turndown?

By analyzing and learning from appointment turndowns, you can improve your conversion rate and help more buyers. You can become a better Golden Rule Seller.

CHAPTER 13

Precall Planning

You've found prospective buyers and earned an appointment to present your message to them. Good job! Now what? Your next task is to get ready for your meeting. Get your facts together. Dig into your sales KIT. Thoroughly understand your prospect's problems and needs. Be ready to represent your product or service as a viable solution. This chapter guides you through this vital sales step.

What Is Precall Planning?

Going to the store for bread doesn't take much planning. You know where the store is. You know what brand of bread you'll probably buy. You have some cash. Thinking is optional.

But planning for something as important as a big-ticket sales call is much more important. The sale of thousands of dollars in products or services is hanging on your success in helping a buyer solve a problem. Those who make, distribute, or use what you sell also depend on your success. Feel the pressure now?

Preparing for an important sales call can be demanding, especially the first few times that you present. What do you need to be ready? How can you best represent your employer while offering your buyer appropriate solutions? All good questions. The answer is to focus on your prospect, the problem your prospect faces, the product or service you have to sell, and how you can best present your product or service as a solution.

Prospect

You've contacted prospective buyers (see Chapter 12) for what you sell, but what do you really know about these buyers? Maybe their names and locations, industries, and the business problems that they face. Now that you have scheduled a sales presentation, you should learn even more about the individual buyers and the companies that they represent. As a buyer, you would want a salesperson to understand something about who you are, what you do, and the group that you represent. That's Golden Rule Selling.

What do you need to know about the prospect? As much as you can! Realistically, you may only be able to gather basic information about the person's title, job description, and position in the company hierarchy. But the more information you get, the greater your potential to help the buyer reach her or his goals.

Depending on what you sell, to whom, and your employer's resources, you may be able to gather an extensive amount of data about the prospect's company. Or not. Your employer may already have a file on the company. Or you may be able to do some online research and find out more: who they are, what they make or sell, how much they sell, to whom, who owns them, and so on.

Problem

What's the problem? Whatever you are selling, its primary function is to solve one or more problems for buyers. It can be a point-of-sale (POS) system that helps retailers better track sales, inventory, and employees. It may be an advertising program that helps manufacturers build their brand identity. It could be a new line of heavy equipment that more efficiently constructs roads. Whatever you're selling is intended to solve one or more specific problems.

What problem does your prospect want to solve? You should know what that is before you make your presentation. In fact, you should have a pretty good idea of the problem before you even contact the prospect.

QUESTION?

Where can I find reliable financial information on businesses and corporations?
There are many sources. For example, Dun & Bradstreet *(www.dnb. com)* provides credit information and reports on U.S. and international businesses. Moody's Investors Service *(www.moodys.com)* reports on business *and industrial credit and risk analysis. OneSource (www. onesource.com)* offers a variety of profiles and overviews on specific businesses. ESRI *(www.esri.com)* offers geographic and demographic information for businesses.

Before you make your presentation, be sure you can clearly define the primary problem the buyer has that your product or service can solve. If you're not sure, keep digging. You can start your presentation with a couple of clarifying questions, for example, "Is your Chicago operation more profitable than your Miami office?" But you'd better have the problem well defined before you attempt to present your solution. If you don't, your credibility as a problem solver will diminish, and the prospect may not listen to what you have to say. Understand the buyer's problems.

Product

Chances are that you represent more than one product. In fact, you may represent hundreds or even thousands of related products. You don't have to memorize every detail of every product, but you must know how to get those details if needed. If your company has a catalog, you should know it almost by heart. You should know the features and benefits of most, if not all, products that you represent—especially those that you intend to offer as a solution at your sales call.

Part of the trust you need to build with your buyer is a trust that you know more about your products than the buyer does. Unfortunately, some salespeople forget this. A buyer asks about the model 497 widget, and the seller scrambles to find product literature and read it for the first time. Know your products!

QUESTION?

As a Golden Rule Seller, do I have to know everything about all my products or services?
No, you don't. However, you do need to know at least the basics about them. You can ask your prospect for a moment while you look up the specifics on a product, but don't offer "I'm not sure if that's in our line or not." You'd better know. You must know at least the basic facts about everything you sell. That's your job.

Presentation

As covered in Chapter 8, your presentation must have a specific goal. It's not a fact-finding meeting. It's an opportunity for you to show that you understand the buyer's problem and that you have a viable solution. Your presentation must have a goal or objective. What do you want the buyer to think when your presentation is over? Knowing this is an important part of precall planning.

Precall planning also requires that you prepare the tools you will need. Make sure that you have the hardware and software necessary to make an effective presentation. Also make sure that you have product samples, promotional collateral, and other components of your presentation.

Be sure that your mechanicals—slides, screens, handouts—are ready to use. Take backups if needed to give you sufficient confidence. Final preparation for your presentation will be covered in greater detail later in this chapter.

Prequalifying Your Buyer

Before calling prospects, you determined that they buy what you sell and probably have a need for it. However, there is more to prequalifying a buyer than probable need. Can they actually afford what you are selling? And how can you know that?

Prequalifying a prospect's ability to purchase requires some facts and a few assumptions. You can gain financial facts from a variety of business database sources (as mentioned previously). You can analyze the company's financial position and relate it to the cost of what you are selling. For example, if you're selling wholesale widgets to a retail store, financial records can tell you that the store is solvent, profitable, and buys a specific amount of widgets annually. You can also visit the store and approximate how many widgets they sell each year.

FACT

What should you do if a prospect balks at furnishing credit references? Beware! Credit apps are an accepted part of doing business, especially when large sums are involved. Buyers who don't recognize and cooperate with this requirement often aren't good credit risks. Most will complete your credit application without any questions. Remember that if the buyer becomes a bad debt, you probably lose your commission on those sales and you won't be popular with your boss.

Business credit information can prequalify your buyer as well. But newer business prospects may be more difficult to prequalify in this way. Depending on your employer's credit requirements, a prospect may need to complete an application before being allowed to purchase from your company on credit. Many wholesalers offer cash-only or short-term credit terms (net: thirty days) until a business has been an established and proven customer. If your employer requires a credit application, determine when in the selling process it is needed and how long it takes to get an approval. In most cases, an order can be placed but cannot be shipped without a line of credit established. Alternatively, the first order or two can be paid COD (collect on delivery) when the products arrive. Know your employer's requirements and policies in advance of your prospect meeting.

Anticipating Objections

"Sounds wonderful. I'll take two million of whatever you're selling!"

Don't expect to hear these words during any sales presentation in the real world. In fact, what you will hear are objections like:

- They're too expensive.
- I never heard of your company.
- I don't have time right now.

Ad infinitum. Chapter 14 offers ideas on how to respond to objections during a sales call. However, before the presentation you should start to anticipate and respond to common sales objections.

People will buy something when they want it more than they want the money that it costs. All buyers are looking for value, the equal or greater worth in an exchange. Businesses buy because they trust that their purchase is of greater value to them than the price. They believe that they can turn a profit. The seller, too, sees the profit value of selling their products or services for money.

The key to answering sales objections is understanding what they truly are: questions. In most cases, objections are presented to ask you why the prospect should buy. It's often a delay tactic that prospects use because their questions and concerns haven't yet been answered. By anticipating common objections, you can answer them in your presentation even before they are asked.

- Acme widgets are less expensive than any other brand of similar quality.
- Acme Widgets is a *Fortune 500* company employing more than 10,000 people worldwide.
- I can help you save more than $1,000,000 in the next hour by acting on my suggestions.

Planting responses to common objections within your sales presentation can diffuse the buyer's natural reluctance to make a decision.

An important aspect of preparing for your sales call is anticipating common objections of buyers and developing viable answers. If possible, make the case against the objection before it even develops in the buyer's mind. However, if the buyer does voice an objection, you should be ready with a well-thought-out answer. In fact, if a common objection isn't voiced by a buyer, smart sellers will bring it up.

- As you consider your purchase, you may think that our products are too expensive. Let me respond to that . . .
- I sometimes hear buyers ask to know more about our company. It's a good question. Acme Widgets is . . .

Golden Rule Sellers anticipate buyer objections and either answer them in advance or offer considered responses when they are presented. Understanding how a buyer thinks can help you build trust, a prime component of every transaction.

Final Preparation

You soon will be standing in front of a prequalified buyer whose business problems you understand. Better yet, you know the approximate solution that will bring the prospect to purchase from you. What can you do to be ready?

First, make sure that you have all the tools you need to make an effective presentation: check your list. Second, visualize your successful presentation. Third, ask more questions that confirm the meeting and illustrate your understanding of the problems to be solved.

Check Your List

As you develop your presentation skills, with experience you will discover specifically what you need and don't need to make a successful sales call. You may be bringing too much or too little of what you need in terms of samples, equipment, or literature. You may be intimidating buyers by the mass of boxes and cases that you bring to a meeting. You'll learn.

As you do learn from experience, develop and revise a list of basic presentation components that you need: audiovisual equipment, outlines, collateral, samples, pens, paper, and so on. This will become your checklist for ensuring that future presentations are easier.

Visualization

Professional golfers often visualize their swing before they make it. Other sports players perform similar visualizations as a mental practice before the physical event. It helps them prepare for action. As a Golden Rule Seller, you can do the same before making important presentations.

Pro sellers suggest that you visualize a successful sales call just prior to making it. Spend a few extra minutes in your car, step into a coffee shop, or find some other way to take a moment to reflect on how you can help your buyer before you actually do so. It can give you the confidence needed to offer your best efforts.

Visualization requires that you relax your mind and imagine the location where you will be presenting. If you're not sure, visualize yourself in a generic office or conference room. You're early for the meeting and have ample time to set up your presentation equipment. If you are working from a sales flip notebook, you have decided where to sit in relation to the prospect. You are comfortable and confident, and certain that your prospect is, too. You mentally go through your presentation and answer any questions or objections raised. You are successful, and the prospect places an order for what you are selling. Win-win.

Ask More Questions

As you plan for your sales call, additional questions may occur to you. Some of them can wait until the meeting. However, the answers to other questions may be helpful in making a better presentation. In addition, asking a question or two before the presentation can do three things for you:

1. Remind the prospect of the meeting.
2. Illustrate that you are putting effort into solving the prospect's problem.
3. Give you additional information that you can use to help the prospect.

What kind of questions are appropriate for your precall conversation? Following are some examples:

- You told me that your division buys $100,000 in widgets annually. Is all of that purchased by your North American office?
- The last time we talked, we estimated that there will be twelve people at our presentation. To make sure I have enough information packets, is that number still the same now?
- Bob Smith mentioned that he may be away on business and not able to attend our meeting. Have you heard anything new about that?

Your final call to the prospect before the meeting gives you another chance to sell. It also offers the prospect an opportunity to bring up any problems or objections that can be better handled prior to the meeting.

The Exit Survey

Chapter 14 will walk you step-by-step through common sales call structures. You will see how professional salespeople successfully handle each stage toward solving the buyer's problem. Hopefully, you will get a purchase order from the meeting—or at least be one step closer to buyer approval. However, there will be an additional step after the meeting that you should consider now: the exit survey.

Just as in an election, pollsters take an exit survey to help politicians understand the reasons why voters made their decisions. Politicians want to know what worked, what didn't, and what to do next. Sales professionals can perform their own exit survey using their personal perceptions as well as asking prospects these questions. Feedback is a vital component of all processes, including sales.

What Worked?

Once the presentation is over and the "vote" is in, you'll have a relatively good idea of what worked. You may be able to identify what points of your presentation were best received or seemed to garner the greatest interest. Future sales presentations will tell you even more about what elements of your efforts were best understood and acted upon by participants. Whether you present to one or one hundred, you will have a sense of what worked.

However, that is only your perception. To make your analysis more complete, you must go beyond your own observations and ask participants what worked. Of course, some will say "great presentation," but still not buy. They may not want to hurt your feelings, or they may not have analyzed their own. Instead, you must ask open-ended questions that require more detail than a "yes" or "no" answer: "What was the main point that encouraged you to purchase?" The discussion following can help you analyze how prospects buy. You will see your presentation from their perspective—the only one that ultimately matters.

What Didn't Work?

Whether your sales presentation met your goal or didn't, chances are that some elements weren't as effective as others. What were they? You probably know what at least some of them were. Maybe a sample that broke when handled or a handout that had spelling errors. You know what went wrong maybe even better than your prospects.

However, you still need their perceptions. Buyers may have laughed off the broken sample but were bothered by the spelling errors. Or vice versa. In any case, the prospect's opinions are more valid than your own. Make sure that you ask for them.

Your buyer's answers, especially if you encourage candidness, can help you not only in the current sales process, but also in future ones.

What's Next?

Everyone makes mistakes. Not everyone learns from them. A professional salesperson cannot afford *not* to learn from what worked and what didn't in a sales call or presentation. That's why an exit survey is critical to your success. The mistakes may be avoidable in the future. Make sure that every sales presentation you make, large or small, includes an exit survey of some type. Avoid closed-ended yes/no questions, and encourage participants to be frank with you. Your future as a salesperson and the satisfaction of your buyers may depend on it.

CHAPTER 14

Anatomy of a Sales Call

The day you've been working for has arrived. Today you're making a sales call to Ms. Big, the widget buyer for Amalgamated Industries. You've done your homework and developed an outstanding presentation. You know your buyer well and are anxious to help. This chapter offers proven methods for making sales calls to major prospects. You can use it for smaller clients, too. The process is the same; the scale is different. Check the mirror once more and grab your briefcase.

The Opening

You're face to face with the prospect. What do you say first? How do you get the prospect to totally focus on your message? How can you offer your message without boring the prospect? All are good questions that you must answer before you step into the buyer's comfort zone.

No matter what you are selling, to whom, or where, the opening of your sales call should follow the common process: the greeting, breaking the ice, making the transition, and stating the goal. That's your four-step opener. You'll follow it, with few exceptions, whether you are meeting a major prospect for the first time or a secondary customer for the twenty-first time. Once you develop a relationship with the buyer, the steps will be shortened and may even be combined, but they are there. They give you a proven structure for opening the minds of prospects to what you have to offer.

QUESTION?

Who sets the pace for the opening of a sales call?
Fast or slow, let your prospect set the pace. If you know from phone conversations and prior meetings what speaking pace the prospect uses, emulate it. If not, start at a moderate speaking pace and adjust as needed. Be aware that speaking paces also depend on other factors: the time of day, the amount of coffee consumed, the proximity to lunch, nervousness, and outside factors. To be heard, listen to your prospect and emulate the speaking pace that she or he prefers.

The Greeting

The first step in the opening is greeting the prospect. How you greet depends on your relationship. "Good morning, Mr. Johnson." "Hey, Bill!" Initial greetings require that you clearly recognize the prospect as well as clearly identify who you are. Pro sellers typically use the prospect's name first in order to gain attention.

Hello, Ms. Buyer" (smile, offer hand to shake, pause). *I'm Frank Seller with Acme Machine.*

Your sales call begins the moment you greet the prospect. You are selling yourself as a person who will help solve buyer problems without making more. You are beginning to sell your knowledge, information, and trust—your KIT. The greeting doesn't need to be long, but it does need to be informative and sincere. First impressions can make your selling job easier or more difficult.

Breaking the Ice

When meeting new prospects, don't be nervous about the meeting. You've prepared for it and know your products or services well. You don't know as much about the prospect, but you have done some work to find a common point of interest. If you need clues about the prospect, make some quick observations about the person or work area to identify signs of interests that you may have in common.

- Bill Turner suggested that I give you a call to meet you in person.
- I see you're a golfer. Where do you play?
- I read your recent article on robotic widgets. Very impressive!
- This restaurant has a great sushi bar. Have you been here before?

The purpose of breaking the ice is simply to begin developing a relationship of mutual trust. Whether that relationship will include any personal elements—golf, sushi—depends on the prospect and what you are selling. The pros say that it is better to start with a nonpersonal icebreaker until you know your prospect better. However, if you already know that the prospect has a passion for golf or sushi, it's probably okay to begin there.

Some sellers use humor to break the ice. It can be effective—and it can be deadly. Depending on the topic and the prospect's sense of humor, telling a joke can backfire and become a detriment to building a relationship of trust. Or it can be a great icebreaker. If you do choose humor to help a prospect relax and be comfortable with you, make sure it is not offensive.

Making the Transition

Both you and the prospect know that the purpose of your visit is to sell something. Some prospects prefer to avoid the inevitable sales presentation and instead continue the transition, discussing common interests or sharing jokes. Others prefer to get to the point. To know when to make the transition to selling your product (rather than yourself), watch and listen.

The signals that prospects use to indicate their interest to move to the topic include:

- Pausing and looking at you expectantly.
- Asking something like: What can I do for you today? or What do you have for me?
- Showing any signs of boredom or impatience.

As you develop sales call experience, you will better recognize when the prospect is sufficiently comfortable with you to want to begin the presentation. In some cases, there will be no obvious signs and you will need to take the initiative and transition the conversation to the selling process.

Stating the Goal

It's time to move ahead. You're already selling with your greeting, ice-breaker, and transition. Now you must officially kick off the sales call by stating the goal of your meeting.

The three steps of presenting are: tell them what you're going to tell them, tell them, then tell them what you told them. In other words: introduction, development, and summary. Stating the goal of your sales call is the introduction. It defines what you will be discussing and solicits a confirmation. Once the goal is confirmed by the prospect, you can begin your sales presentation.

You already have determined the goal of your presentation. Depending on what you offer and the needs of your prospect, the goal may be:

- Increase the sale of widgets in your prospect's retail store.
- Show how the new improved widget can save the prospect time and money.
- Get agreement from the prospect that Acme Machine should be their company's primary provider.
- Resolve a problem with quality control that can improve customer relations.

There are hundreds of other potential goals for sales presentations. Whatever it is, you must clearly state it before beginning the presentation. It defines the meeting's goal.

By stating the goal, you may discover that the prospect sees the goal differently. It's important to identify that difference before continuing. Maybe the prospect says, "I thought we were going to discuss increasing widget sales only at our Denver store." Your response can be to focus on the Denver store or to discuss all stores, as the result will impact the Denver store. Whatever adjustments are needed to modify the goal, make sure that you get an agreement on the goal of the meeting before continuing.

Identifying the Problem

The purpose of selling is to solve a problem for the buyer. The problem may be low profits, high costs, labor problems, tax problems, or some other difficulty of business that stands in the way of growth. Your job as a professional salesperson is to help the prospect identify the problem and then offer a viable solution.

How can you identify the prospect's relevant problem? You probably already know what it is, at least in general terms. However, before you attempt to solve it, make sure you know it explicitly. And make sure that the prospect clearly recognizes it. That requires your asking questions, listening to responses, analyzing the information, and selecting an appropriate solution. Only then can you present a solution to the prospect.

Asking Questions

Questions can do two things: get answers and illustrate understanding. A question to a prospect such as "What level of returns have you had on model 485 widgets?" seeks information while also confirming that you understand where the problem lies. As you help the prospect solve the agreed-upon problem, you will need to develop relevant and knowledgeable questions to guide the transaction.

FACT

What's the problem? The majority of your prospects, buyers, and customers have a job that is similar to yours. Their function is to solve problems for their employers. The problem to be solved may be to increase profits, reduce costs, improve relationships with customers, or to accurately track business information. Your function is to solve problems not only for your employer, but also for your customers. Learning how to identify and solve problems is a valuable asset in selling.

Listening to Responses

If you've done your homework, you may already know the answers to questions posed to the prospect. The purpose of these questions may be to help the prospect recognize the problem. Even so, you *must* listen to the responses. In addition to confirmation, the responses may offer new information that you need to help the prospect define and solve the stated problem.

Some responses will need clarification that can be developed by asking additional questions. "You said that model 485 widget returns are now at 28 percent. Can you tell me how that compares with return rates for other model widgets?" As needed, make notes both to record useful information and to show that you are interested in what the prospect says.

Analyzing the Information

Once you've gathered relevant facts to help solve the problem, you need to analyze them before selecting and offering a solution. Again, you may already know what the probable solution is, based on your experience. However, don't move forward faster than your prospect does. In order to seemingly reach the same destination at approximately the same time, you must move at the same pace.

Once your prospect has answered all relevant questions, summarize the responses to make sure you both agree on them. Then take time to consider the facts presented.

- Model 485 widget returns are at 28 percent.
- Other model widgets are returned at a rate of about 6 percent.
- Many of the returners complain of the same issue: defective flanges.
- The flanges are made using a cold-weld process.
- All other widget flanges use a hot-weld process.
- Cold welding has been proven to be stronger than hot-welding in most applications.

Summarizing the information gathered can help both you and the prospect find a solution. A problem defined is half solved.

Selecting a Solution

There still may be more than one solution to the defined problem. The solution may be better training on cold welding. If so, you should ask the prospect about training and determine whether it is the full solution. If not, your job is to select an appropriate solution to the prospect's stated problem.

For example, based on your product knowledge and prior experience, you may recommend the Acme Cold Welder Deluxe to the buyer. You do so because it has a higher power level and operates faster. In your experience, the Deluxe makes cold welds that are superior to hot welds in this application. You know the problem, understand your products, and have a genuine desire to solve the prospect's problem with the most appropriate solution. You, in your mind, select the Acme Cold Welder Deluxe. Now what?

Next, you must *sell* your selection to the buyer. If you've followed the sales process above, you are nearly done. You've already agreed on the problem. It's now your job to help the buyer understand *why* the Deluxe is the best choice.

Offering the Solution

You could blurt out the solution and ask for the order. However, the chances of the buyer agreeing with you are greater if you help him or her come to the same conclusion that you did. As noted previously, to reach the same destination at approximately the same time, you must move at the same pace. You now must bring the buyer along the path to the best solution.

How can you do that? By summarizing and developing the need before offering the solution. Following are the suggested steps.

Summarizing the Need

To begin selling the solution, first summarize the need. Restate the problem. In the example, the problem is that the return rate on one type of widget is high due to poor flanges caused by inadequate cold welding. That's the problem. By summarizing it you not only move toward offering a solution, you also get the prospect to move with you. You get agreement on the problem before you continue.

Developing the Need

The problem has many implications and causes related problems. Developing the example to illustrate, poorly cold-welded flanges can cause many other problems:

- Returned widgets reduce customer confidence in your products.
- Returning widgets can be expensive to the company.
- Broken widgets can lead to product recalls and lawsuits.
- Widget problems give your competitors a sales opportunity.

Developing the problem and the need for a solution helps you sell your solution. You are helping your prospect understand what you already know. They can see that the value of a solution is greater than the cost. They are anxious to hear what your solution is.

FACT

Professional salespeople don't create needs for prospects, they identify them. In some situations, the prospect fully understands the need. In others, the need must be defined and the related problems recognized. In all cases, the prospect will not act on a need until it is identified and acknowledged. In addition, the prospect must realize that the value of the solution is greater than its cost. That's your job.

Offering the Solution

"Based on what we've learned today, Ms. Buyer, I recommend the Acme Cold Welder Deluxe."

As you offer your solution for their problem, remember what and why: features and benefits. Continuing our example, the Acme Cold Welder Deluxe can solve the identified problem because:

- It has 2,000 watts of power (feature) to ensure the strongest weld (benefit).
- It has automatic controls (feature) to make operation easier (benefit).
- The Acme is cost-effective (feature) and can pay for itself in energy savings within six months (benefit).
- I can offer you a thirty-day trial (feature) to verify that the Deluxe solves your model 485 widget returns problem (benefit).

The solution you've selected for your buyer has features and benefits that can solve the stated problem. You know that because you've researched and analyzed the problem, then compared it to the features and benefits that your line of products or services offers. Most important, you have guided your prospect through this process, helping her clearly see that the *value* of your solution is greater than its cost.

Summarizing the Solution

All the facts, figures, questions, and answers may be confusing to your prospect. Or your prospect may have followed you willingly at every step of the selling process thus far. In either case, it is important that you summarize the solution. For example, "The Acme Cold Welder Deluxe can reduce widget returns and quickly pay for itself." That's your bottom line. That's the statement you've been working to make since you first greeted the prospect. You are offering a collaborative solution to the stated problem.

Handling Objections

In some sales situations, your prospect's questions will all be answered and you can proceed to closing the sale. More often, however, the prospect will have what are often called objections, in most cases they simply are questions or concerns. An objection is an opposing viewpoint or disagreement. A question is simply a request for additional information. By developing a relationship of trust and clarity, the questions prospects have can actually help you in the sales process. Some professional salespeople say that the sale doesn't begin until the prospect begins asking relevant questions.

How should you handle post-presentation questions? Professionally. Even if you've already answered the question, don't patronize the prospect. Instead, summarize what you previously stated without saying, "What I said before was . . ." or "As I already mentioned . . ." If the prospect does recognize the statement as previously made, she will appreciate that you don't point it out. In any case, never argue or minimize the prospect's question. In fact, you should be thankful that the prospect asks clarifying questions, as it indicates that the sales process is continuing.

How should you respond to additional questions? By listening, recognizing the concern, restating it, answering it, and confirming the answer. Each question should be responded to in the same manner, removing any objection that the prospect has to closing the sale.

Listen to the Question

Many salespeople talk too much when they should be listening. Listening not only helps you gather more sales information, it also shows respect for your prospect. Both are requirements of a sale. You can listen with ears, your mind, and your body. Hear the words that the prospect is saying, but also attempt to understand what it means. If you need clarification, ask for it.

Also listen with your body. In other words, show the prospect that you are listening. Don't rummage through your sales literature or stare out the window. Instead, engage the prospect's eyes and show that you are sincerely concerned and listening.

Recognize the Question

Exactly what is the prospect asking? Is there a technical question that needs to be answered, or is the prospect attempting to delay the inevitable decision whether to buy or not? Your response will depend on what type of concern the prospect shares. For example, "Does the Deluxe model come with a rolling platform?" is a technical question that you can answer, then use to move toward the close. "Why do we need the Deluxe model?" is probably a delaying question if you've already answered it in your presentation. Knowing the *purpose* of the question can help you in answering it better.

Restate the Question

Whatever the question, the prospect needs your answer. To ensure that your answer is accurate, first restate the question or concern.

- You're asking if the Deluxe model has a heavy-duty rolling platform as an option?
- Are you asking about the differences between the Deluxe and Standard models?

Restating the concern tells the prospect that you are listening and that you understand the question. It also gives the prospect an opportunity to hear the question. As appropriate, the prospect may then revise or clarify the question, or even withdraw it.

Answer the Question

By answering the agreed-upon question, you are recognizing the prospect's interest in buying. It also gives you an opportunity to validate the buyer. "That's a good question, Mary. Yes, the Deluxe model does have an optional rolling platform that can hold up to 500 pounds yet is easily moved with one hand so it can be quickly moved to various assembly stations." The answer offers both a feature and a benefit.

Many professional salespeople use prospect questions to do more than answer concerns. They answer them with a question that will help move the sales process toward a close. "If the Deluxe model had an optional rolling platform, would you like to have one here by next week?" Don't overuse this technique, but consider how the answer to each question can help the prospect make a better decision.

Confirm the Answer

The prospect's question was asked, you listened attentively, recognized and restated the question, then answered it. What's next? Make sure that your question was understood. How? By asking.

- Does that answer your question?
- Does that make sense to you?
- Do you have any other questions I can answer for you?

Prospect questions are an important part of the selling process. By listening attentively and asking your own clarifying questions, you can soon be ready to start the close of your sale.

Closing the Sale

The selling process involves a number of planned steps that help prospects become buyers. The prospect has a problem that you can help solve. If you present the facts as you develop trust, you may persuade the prospect to make the purchase. You won't coerce. You won't misrepresent. You will help the prospect buy.

The *close* is considered by some to be the most important step in the selling process. However, it really isn't more or less important than any other. Each step—from the opening to identifying the problem, offering a solution, and answering questions—is just as critical. In fact, in the ideal sales presentation, the prospect may ask to buy without any coaxing. However, in most situations, the professional salesperson will need to continue guiding the prospect toward a decision.

Recognize the Close

A sales *close* is the consummation or agreement to exchange. You offer the Acme Cold Weld Deluxe for a specified price. Your job as a salesperson is to show the prospect how the Deluxe will solve the stated problem and give the prospect a value that is greater than the price. Toward that end, you have mutually identified the problem and the solution and then answered questions so the prospect recognizes the value of your product. It's time for the close.

When to Start the Close

New salespeople often ask when they should begin closing the sale. Professionals answer: at the *beginning* of the sale. In fact, every step of the sales process is an effort toward reaching the close or transaction. The greeting, stating the goal, agreeing on the problem—these all require that you first have planned where you want the prospect to be when you're done. What do you want the prospect to know and believe? Your opening will begin the prospect on the path toward your close.

Ask for the Order

Now what? Most buyers still require a final step to help them in accepting the offered solution. They need to be asked for the order. Working with experienced buyers, you may find that they will make the order without additional prompting. However, many others will wait until you actually ask them to complete the transaction. Following are some suggested ways of doing so.

- Can I write your order for the Acme Cold Weld Deluxe?
- Would you like them in your factory by the end of next week?
- Would you like one or two of the Deluxe models?
- I can place the order today and have them on our next delivery truck, okay?
- Are you ready to reduce widget returns and buy the Acme Deluxe?

There are many other ways of asking a prospect for the order. Some are direct questions and some are assumptive, presuming that the decision has been made and that only the details are required. Depending on what you are selling, to whom, and your employer's requirements, you may use other types of closes. All have the same function: to elicit a decision and action from the prospect.

Handling the Paperwork

Some sales require only a handshake to complete, especially with known customers. However, the majority of sales transactions require that specifics be written down or entered into a computer and a confirmation copy be given to the buyer. The paperwork will include who is buying, who is authorizing the purchase, where and when delivery will be made, the specifics of the purchase, and how it will be paid for. Whether you are selling machinery, widgets, advertising, or janitorial services, the transaction probably won't be approved by your employer until the paperwork is completed.

Make sure that you know exactly how to complete the transaction papers before you visit your prospects. Not only can uncertainty challenge a prospect's trust in your skills, it also can mean you don't gather sufficient information to complete the sale. You should know by heart every element of the order forms you use and understand what your employer requires. It can be embarrassing for you to return to a buyer with a new order and have to resell the purchase because of inadequate paperwork.

Following Up

To ensure future sales, you must confirm the sale, make certain that the customer is satisfied and, if not, remedy the problem immediately. Then ask for a referral. Pro salespeople know that follow-up is an integral step to developing additional sales.

QUESTION?

When's the best time to confirm a sale?
Either once the order is written or just before you place it in your employer's system. It's easier to make changes to an order before it is entered into the system. In addition, it offers you an opportunity to up-sell by offering needed supplies or materials. "The unit comes with enough supplies for thirty days at no extra charge, Bill. Would you like to include an additional sixty-day supply and earn the same discount?"

Confirming the Sale

Confirming the sale simply requires a summary of the terms in plain English. It can be done when the order is completed or in a follow-up call after the order has been accepted by your employer.

Bill, I just wanted to confirm your order for two Acme Cold Weld Deluxe units at our discount price of $1,234 each plus shipping, for arrival at your Main Street plant by the 15th. Is that correct?

Verifying Satisfaction

No one likes surprises. If your buyer is unhappy with the purchase, the problem will fester until your next sales call—or the buyer will call customer service or you to resolve it. Don't let it go that far. Instead, as soon as the order is received and you know it is either in use or in stock, make a call to the buyer to verify that it solves the agreed-upon problem. If the sale is simply replacement inventory, you only need to call periodically to ensure that the buyer is satisfied with products and services received. If, however, the purchase is a performance product—one that is supposed to do something for the buyer, such as a cold welder—contact the buyer as soon as you believe it is in operation. In fact, for big-ticket items, you might even be on hand when the product arrives so you can verify satisfaction in person.

Verification is easy. Just review the problem that you both agreed upon and the assurances you made about your solution. Does it do what you said it would do? Does it solve the stated problem? Your long-term sales goal is not to just earn customers, but to develop *satisfied* customers.

Handling Buyer's Remorse

What if your buyer gets cold feet and calls you before the delivery to cancel it? It happens in sales, especially when selling one-time buys such as homes and new cars. The buyer gets home, thinks, "What have I done?" and evaluates all of the negative sides of making such a big decision.

What can you do about buyer's remorse? First, by making sure that the buyer moves through each of the selling stages in this chapter, you are minimizing opportunities for buyer's remorse. You are moving the prospect through the process at her own pace, summarizing as needed, and getting an agreement before moving on. Even so, some buyers will regret the purchase.

Whatever you do, don't argue about the sale. Instead, help the buyer to understand that buyer's remorse is a common malady when purchasing large-ticket items for the first time. In fact, many salespeople who work with first-time buyers will defuse the possibilities for buyer's remorse by explaining what it is once the sale is made. Others will offer to discuss the decision process with anyone the buyer requests, such as an influential relative or friend.

The best method of handling buyer's remorse is to pleasantly help the buyer review the problem and solution—to summarize the sales call. Don't take it personally and don't make it personal. Just review the points of agreement. Resell the product or service including benefits. If you've followed the sales process as outlined, chances are great that you can easily avoid or overcome buyer's remorse and reach customer satisfaction.

Getting Referrals

Once you know that your buyer is satisfied with the purchase, ask for referrals to new prospects. "Mr. Smith, I'm glad to hear that you really love your new car. Are any of your friends or relatives who have seen it interested in more information about it?"

How you ask for referrals will depend on what you are selling and how. In all cases, anytime a buyer expresses satisfaction with your product or efforts, thank him or her, then immediately ask for a referral. Be sure to ask for permission to contact the person and mention your name. And don't forget to ask for contact information. Your future sales will depend not only on your satisfied buyers, but also on your referral prospects. If you are a Golden Rule Seller, you will earn both.

CHAPTER 15

Winning Sales Proposals

Not all of your selling opportunities will be oral. In many B2B sales, written proposals frequently are developed and submitted to buyers. Some are offered by professional salespeople and others are requested by the buyers and must meet stated requirements. This chapter guides you through the sales proposal process, from concept through delivery and follow-up.

Types of Sales Proposals

Selling to consumers often depends on some level of emotion in the decision process. Selling to businesses usually does not; it depends more on facts and logic. If you are selling to a business, industry, or government—especially large-ticket products and services—you may spend at least some of your time developing written sales proposals.

So what are sales proposals, what do they do, and how can you make yours effective? Before answering that question, following is an introduction to proposals and how they are used in selling to businesses and governments.

Proposals 101

A *proposal* is an offer. It can be an offer of marriage, a peace proposal, or the presentation of an idea or service. In business, a *sales proposal* is an offer to sell a product or service. It's an offer to solve a business problem. In government, proposals are used in a bidding process required by law to ensure that the sale or project goes to the lowest or best-qualified bidder, depending on the criteria.

The more expensive the products and services you sell, and the more complex the buying decision, the more that you will need to develop sales proposals.

QUESTION?

Will I have to write my own sales proposals?
You may, but most sales positions that require proposals also have guidelines and tools or even support staff to help develop effective sales proposals. Some tools include Intravasion *(www.intravasion.com)*, ProposalSmartz *(www.proposalsmartz.com)*, and Proposal Master and RFP Master *(www.santcorp.com)*. In addition, some contact-management software products include a proposal-writing tool.

In some large businesses and governmental offices, buying is called *procurement*. It's the acquisition of goods and/or services at the best price and terms from qualified sellers. Some major retailers (such as Costco) call them buyers or buying agents, and many federal government and military entities use the term *procurement officer* or similar titles. In each case, the job is the same: to buy smart. Their purchases typically are large, such as a year's worth of office supplies or a $1 million piece of equipment. Because these buyers require more facts than consumer buyers do, proposals help them make informed comparative decisions.

Initiated Proposals

In some sales situations, you will offer written proposals to buyers that summarize and support whatever you're proposing that your prospects buy. For example, a radio or newspaper advertising salesperson may develop a written proposal for a retail store, showing the benefits and costs of an annual promotions plan. The proposal is often a component of the sales presentation and includes specifics developed in a prior interview with the buyer. The sales call (see Chapter 14) will present and review the written proposal, which may then be left for further consideration by other decision makers.

Guidelines or tools for writing sales proposals may come from your employer. If not, or as a supplement, planning and writing a sales proposal is covered later in this chapter.

Request for Information

In many cases, buyers will request purchasing information in the form of a proposal. For example, a construction company may request information on reinforced concrete products for use in a new structure it is building. The builder will summarize the need, including building plans, and then contact concrete suppliers and subcontractors for suggestions and further information.

A request for information (RFI) often is the first step in the selling process for some types of businesses. This is especially true when the business hasn't yet decided how to solve the problem. They want more information on the various solutions before selecting the best one. Often, you will follow up on an RFI with a written report, sometimes called a white sheet, and deliver it with an oral introduction that explains why your employer is the most qualified to develop a purchasing proposal.

Request for Quotation

If the prospect knows what it wants to purchase, a request for Quotation (RFQ) is issued to companies that offer the product or service. An RFQ typically has more specifics than an RFI. It may include dimensions, weights, units, and other requirements that allow the buyer to more easily compare your proposal with that of another supplier.

Request for Proposal

A request for proposal (RFP) is one step up in complexity from other types of proposal. For governments and large business entities, an RFP can be many pages or even volumes of technical data, cost and delivery limitations, and other information. An RFP is an invitation to suppliers to bid on specific requirements.

RFPs offer advantages to both buyers and sellers. Buyers are able to standardize the requirements of what they need and make purchasing comparisons based primarily on pricing. Sellers are able to bid on specific products or services that the buyer believes offer a solution to an identified problem.

RFPs are distributed in many ways. Smaller buyers may distribute an RFP document to a few preferred vendors or sellers. Larger projects and those involving city, state, federal, and other governmental bodies may be required to be published in specialized publications or online sites where vendors can see them. Some wholesale and retail chains will submit either to a small group or publish requirements depending on the size of the purchase. The deadline for delivery of the required products or services can dictate what method is used. An RFP for major road construction, for example, can have a proposal deadline of a year or more and a work deadline of three to ten years, depending on the project. Purchasing an earthmover for the project may be made with a thirty-day RFP.

What Sales Proposals Do

What do sales proposals actually do for buyers and sellers? Many things. First, they allow buyers to standardize the decision process when purchasing expensive products or services. It reduces the subjective components and increases the objective. Once the criteria is established and met, just about anyone with authority in the organization can make the decision to purchase.

Second, proposals offer sellers a unique opportunity to bid on exactly what the buyer wants. Instead of helping the buyer recognize the need, the seller can focus more on solving it with specific products and services.

What is the function of a sales proposal? As you've seen, each has a different purpose: to present information, pricing, specific requirements, or all of these. Some proposals are relatively informal, while others must be presented exactly as required or the proposal will be disallowed. Before covering the components of a typical sales proposal, following are some guidelines on what proposals do and don't do.

Bidding Process

A *bid* is an offer. A *request for bids* is, then, an appeal for offers. Buyers and other procurers request bids from suppliers for a wide variety of products and services. Government offices purchase the majority of what they need by making a request for bids. For example, if they need a computer program that will manage payroll for overseas employees, an RFP is published or submitted and assigned to a specific reviewer or committee for the final decision.

ALERT!

Thousands of private enterprises do business with the federal government. You can view a wide variety of federal business opportunities online at *www.fedbizopps.gov* and at specific department websites, such as the Environmental Protection Agency *(www.epa.gov)*. Many of them are government procurement opportunities with a minimum size of $25,000. State and local governments also have websites that explain how to make proposals and bids.

For many projects, the bidding process for the seller includes:

- Identifying requests that your employer could bid on
- Gathering the requirements for the bid or proposal

- Completing the bid following the buyer's requirements and meeting deadlines
- Submitting the bid
- Following up with additional requests for information, as needed
- Winning or losing the bid and learning how to improve future bids

Many metropolitan areas have specialized newspapers and other publications aimed primarily at the business community. Some industries, such as construction, also have publications that focus on requests for proposals or quotations. You or your employer should find appropriate publications or online sites where you can search for sales opportunities. However, be aware that some of the sites aren't the requesters or their primary publishers, but are other services that may or may not offer factual and dependable information about current opportunities.

Informational

The primary function of your sales proposal is to inform. It must respond to the bid requirements, including deadlines, informatively and accurately. That's why many proposals are reviewed at numerous levels within an organization before being submitted. A factual or mathematical error can void your proposal or cost thousands or millions of dollars if accepted.

The buyer or procurer who must make a decision based on facts will require that the specifications be accurate and comparable. That's why RFPs are specific. The buyer wants 2,807 widgets, not 2,000 or 3,000. And the widgets must have the specified dimensions, features, and applications. If some are larger or smaller than requested, the buyer probably will throw out your bid.

First rule of bidding: Meet the specifications and requirements.

Persuasion

You can use some persuasive techniques in your bid if it allows for explanations and notes. In these cases, you may have opportunities to educate the buyer on why your products or services offer a greater value than your competitors. However, because it is not quantitative, your persuasive efforts may be lost with some buyers.

But presenting a bid that is neat and organized and that follows requirements can help persuade some buyers that your business is substantial. That can impact their buying decisions.

Summarize

The primary decision makers may not read long sales proposals in their entirety. Instead, a clerk may make sure that the bid conforms to requirements, then pass it on to decision makers, possibly with a recommendation. How can you ensure that decision makers read it?

Many proposals allow for an executive summary. It may be at the beginning of the proposal or at the end, depending on proposal requirements. If it isn't an option, some sellers will develop their own executive summary and include it as a letter or a separate document.

An *executive summary* is an abstract or analysis written primarily for decision makers who don't have the time or inclination to wade through a thick proposal. It summarizes the main points of the proposal. Be cautious, however, because an executive summary that isn't substantive may be ignored. Instead, write a summary that clearly abridges the proposal and includes facts that a decision maker requires.

Components of a Successful Sales Proposal

Sales proposals come in all sizes. A brief letter can serve as a proposal. So can a 1,000-page document with detailed specifications and pricing. Depending on what you're selling, the proposal format is important. All proposals have the same task: to answer a buyer's questions regarding their request.

Some proposals are allowed to be free-form. That is, as long as you answer the buyer's questions, you can offer it in whatever form you think the buyer would prefer: a letter, a short document, or a notebook with supporting data. In other cases, buyers may require that you complete *their* proposal form *exactly* as offered. Governmental bodies and some industrial buyers require a standardized proposal. They do so because they will be receiving numerous proposals and they want to be able to compare the responses in each. If your employer sells by proposal to a number of buyers, there may already be examples and even written guidelines for completing the proposal. In addition, some buyers have guidelines and explanations for completing and submitting proposals. Others don't. Make sure that you know what is expected before you spend the effort to meet expectations.

QUESTION?

How can I take a look at a winning sales proposal?
Ask your boss. If your company does numerous sales proposals, chances are that some of them have been successful. Ask to see the winners and discuss with your sales manager why they won. Then ask to see some that didn't win and use your newfound knowledge to analyze why they weren't accepted. The more you know about winning proposals, the easier it will be to write one.

Meeting Requirements

The most important step in developing a successful sales proposal is understanding its requirements. Are you responding to an RFI, RFQ, or RFP? What does it want? When does it need it? What are the specific requirements of the document you will be submitting? You must know the answers to these and similar questions before beginning the writing process.

Fortunately, buyers and procurers typically include the list of requirements when they request information, quotations, or a full sales proposal. They identify to whom, what, when, where, and how required products and/or services are to be delivered.

Unfortunately, not all requests are as complete as they need to be for precise bidding. That is, they forget to mention a critical term, such as the delivery method or date. What can you do about that once you identify the absent elements? You can contact the buyer and ask. If the answer impacts your proposal, also ask that the term be put in writing as an addendum. There should be no "verbal understandings" in major proposals; everything should be in writing.

Requirements Summary

An important part of your sales document should be a summary of the requirements. You can lift them from the request for information/quotation/ proposal or, for initiated proposals, you can simply summarize the perceived problem. "Bob's Widgets is a retail store that is losing market share to Acme Super-Widget Store and needs to increase awareness of their unique offerings to local customers." The requirements summary for an RFP will be more exhaustive and include specifics of the problem and solution from the buyer's perspective. In either case, the summary is saying, "This is what the buyer and the seller/proposer agree on."

Details

The requirements summary is then backed up by details and supporting data. For example, a proposal to help Bob's Widgets increase market share may include marketing data that compares the sales of both businesses over the past few years. It will relate the sales of one to that of the other. It may also identify some of the perceived causes, primarily those expressed by the buyer with additions from the seller. The details explain the problem or solution from the buyer's perspective.

A more extensive document may analyze and develop more details offered by the buyer in the RFP. It may offer outside analysis as well, but primarily it will focus on details that the buyer has identified. Then it will tell how the seller will solve the problem and at what cost. For example, it can describe the metallurgical qualities of the widgets, the quantity, shipping date, and other data. If the RFP is a standardized form required by the buyer, it must be thoroughly and accurately completed before submission. Again, call the buyer or agent if there are questions or needed clarifications.

Executive Summary

The executive summary is important to all types of sales proposals. It can be as simple as an introductory or concluding paragraph in a letter of proposal, or it can be a one-page summary for busy decision makers. It may be the only component of a proposal that some buyers study. That means your executive summary must be your best writing.

However, it should not be a sales pitch. It must objectively summarize the information that is detailed in the full document. It typically shouldn't use unsupported superlatives like best, world-renowned, and excellent. Just the facts.

Credentials

Why should the buyer purchase from your company? Here is where you can do some selling and maybe even use a few superlatives, depending on the type of proposal and its requirements. In most cases, it's best to let the facts stand for themselves. If your company is the number one widget manufacturer in North America, say so. If it's not, identify its prominence in the market place and build the buyer's trust and confidence. If you, as a salesperson, have special credentials—such as a relevant degree or certification—offer them.

Planning and Writing a Proposal

Okay, those are the components of a successful sales proposal. But how do you go about planning and writing one? The answer depends on what you are selling, to whom, and in what format the proposal is required to be delivered. Proposals to governmental bodies, such as the U.S. General Services Administration *(www.gsa.gov)*, can be challenging documents. Contractors must first register with the GSA. The proposals can often be completed online through the Federal Acquisition Process *(eoffer.gsa.gov)*. Once the contracts are awarded, you can make changes to it as needed through their eMod service. Other federal, state, and local governments have their own systems for requesting quotes and proposals. The three most important elements to successful proposals are following the format, verifying information, and meeting deadlines. Proposal software, described above, can offer additional help in writing effective proposals.

Format

It may not seem so, but the design and format of most requests for proposals has been thoroughly considered before publication. There is a reason for every component, though it may not seem obvious. The reason, typically, is to make the buyer's decision process easier. In fact, most proposal formats are about "process." A *process* is a series of actions or operations toward a specific end. In the case of standardized proposals, the specific end is a decision based on comparative elements: the delivered price of 2,807 standard widgets from Vendor A versus Vendor B. The proposal can help make that decision easier for the buyer if the format is standardized.

The point is that to submit successful sales proposals, you must first consider, understand, and follow the required format. Most of them, especially when developed by governmental bodies, are intended to *discourage* creativity. They want objective and comparative facts, not opinions. It's about accountability. The decision maker at some point may be asked by a superior: "Why did you purchase these widgets from Vendor B instead of Vendor A?" Help your decision maker by staying with the format and requirements.

ALERT!

If your buyers prefer proposals made online, copy them to your computer so you can analyze them at leisure. Also, download documentation and other tips that will guide you in developing the proposal as required. Then spend the time to go over all documents to ensure that you understand requirements and can meet filing deadlines. Many government proposal sites also offer telephone numbers to ask relevant questions.

Reviews

In most sales operations, more than one person develops a sales proposal. It may be begun by support staff, continued by the salesperson, and then reviewed by a sales manager or other superior. Reviews are vital to accuracy. Make sure that your proposal is reviewed for technical accuracy or at least grammar before submission. In fact, your first few proposals may require a signoff by your superior.

Deadline

Proposal deadlines have a function: they close the door. Without a deadline for submissions, decisions cannot be made. All RFQs and RFPs include a deadline; most are unchangeable and cannot be extended by the buyer without notifying all participants. In a few cases, RFPs are rescinded or declared incomplete. However, the vast majority of RFPs have a set, unchangeable deadline that you are required to meet if you want your proposal to be considered.

It is vital, therefore, that as soon as you decide to bid, you begin to develop an action plan toward completing the proposal in advance of the established deadline. If the deadline for delivery is in ninety days, establish a deadline for defining all requirements, a research period to develop details, and another deadline for gathering components into a first draft with executive summary. Then allow sufficient time for fact-checking, internal review, and editing to make sure that the proposal is ready in advance of the deadline. Like all projects, other events occur that can delay progress for a week or two. If time for contingencies isn't figured into the schedule, the deadline may be missed and the time and efforts lost. Meet your proposal deadlines!

Presenting Your Proposal

Your proposal is a valuable document. In some cases, presentation of your proposal will be limited to giving it to a delivery service or submitting it online. In others, you may be able to offer the written proposal in a meeting with decision makers. If that's an option, take it.

FACT

Presentation is important. Make sure that your proposal package is easy to read. Avoid fancy bindings that can make disassembly and copying difficult. Also, verify how many copies of the proposal are requested and make sure that you meet that requirement. Some buyers prefer to make and distribute their own copies from a master, while others want you to make the required copies.

Proposals are often intended to take subjective feelings out of the buying process. The decision to buy should be based on facts only. However, buyers are human. Meeting the proposal's author or representative can help buyers add an otherwise unseen dimension that can help you—or hurt you—at decision time.

Prepare for the meeting as you would any sales call (see Chapter 14) just in case you are given an opportunity to influence the decision. However, be cautious, as some buyers may dock you points for any contacts that seem like a sales call. If in doubt, ask your sales manager how best to deliver a proposal and offer further assistance.

The Importance of Follow-Up

You've given it your best shot. Your proposal offers the facts and data needed by the buyer to make an informed and comparative decision. Now what?

Keep a log of all sales proposals, when they are due and when winners will be announced. Use this log to schedule and track follow-up. Your sales manager should have access to this log and verify that follow-up is being done.

Most RFPs will tell you what's next. In most cases, a date will be set for announcing the decision. Meantime, you may be contacted for clarifications to the proposal. In these contacts, you may get a sense of how your proposal is doing and maybe even how many competitive bids were received. However, most buyers won't share this information until the decision has been announced. Much depends on the process used by procurers and their personal relationship with you. Be cautious what you ask so you don't jeopardize future proposals.

RFPs usually indicate how your company will be notified of the bid award. It may be by mail or e-mail, or you might receive a call from support staff.

In any case, once the bid is awarded, you often can contact one of the decision makers and ask for feedback on the process.

"We want to ensure that our proposal was helpful to you, Ms. Buyer. Can you tell me why the winning bidder was selected?"

Whether you discover anything useful or not, you have made an effort to continue a positive relationship with the buyer. In addition, sending a thank-you letter can help develop that relationship. But make sure that you don't send any thank-you gifts that could be construed as bribes.

If you are able to ask the buyer for opinions about your proposal, do so. It can be a valuable education that can help you to better prepare—and win—future proposals. Even if yours is the winning bid, follow up with the buyer as appropriate so you can continue your winning streak.

CHAPTER 16

Selling to Multiple Buyers

In the ideal sales world, the proportion is one buyer
per seller. You get to speak directly with the person
who will make the final decision. It minimizes communication losses and makes accountability clearer.
However, in the real sales world, many people may
make or influence the decision to buy. What can you
do to ensure that everyone gets needed facts to make
an informed decision? This chapter shows you how
to identify, analyze, and help multiple buyers in a
transaction.

Meet the Individuals

Even in retail selling there sometimes are multiple buyers in a transaction. It may be a spouse or friend who goes shopping with the primary buyer. Or it might be someone who has asked the present buyer to make a purchase for him.

In fact, the majority of transactions have more than one seen or unseen buyer. If the transaction is simple and the primary buyer knows what the others want, you may not even be aware that there are other participants in the transaction. In buying a gift for someone, the recipient is an unseen influencer. In other sales situations, you may only hear from secondary buyers if the primary buyer crosses a line: "You know we can't afford that right now!"

There are other authorities in the transaction who may only have passing influence on the primary buyer, but they still participate in the sale. Who are they? How do they participate in the transaction? Do they need to be involved in your discussions with the primary buyer? These are all good questions that you must answer to ensure successful sales. You need to make your presentation(s) to the ultimate decision maker(s).

Deciders

There are two levels of authority within a decision to purchase: deciders and influencers. Deciders come to a decision. They are the ones who have authority to say "yes" or "no" regarding the purchase. A hungry shopper enters a restaurant and sits down. Purchasing a hamburger, the decider is asked about onions and makes the decision—yes—as the ultimate authority in the transaction.

FACT

Everyone—buyers, sellers, consumers—makes decisions every day. A decision is a choice among options. If you have no options, you have no choice, and therefore don't have to make a decision. Simply accept. Modern life offers multiple choices—and the responsibility of making good decisions. Golden Rule Sellers help buyers make better decisions among choices.

Across town, a couple is buying a car together. They are equally interested in the transaction but maybe not in the same aspects. One is buying the power and the other the styling. Of course, they both must agree before the purchase of a total car can be made. One purchase can have one or more deciders.

Influencers

There also are influencers. They have some authority in the decision through the buyer. A second person at the restaurant booth may ask the buyer, "Honey, do you *really* want stinky onions on your burger?" The buyer may then say "yes" or "no," depending on the degree of influence accepted. The influencer may be more or less subtle but exerts some level of authority in the buyer's decision.

In the case of a two-buyer car purchase, each buyer may also be an influencer to the other. "I agree with your decision about the styling, but I prefer red over blue." Add into this equation the dynamics of their relationship and you have a job on your hands selling to both. How can you do this? By first considering who the buyers and influencers are in your transactions.

Candidates

As you build your career and meet new people, you will begin categorizing them as to their needs and authority to purchase. Who are these buying and influencing candidates? In retailing and restaurants, candidates are easier to identify. In business, however, the group of candidates is larger and can include:

- Receptionists, secretaries, and other gatekeepers
- Administrative assistants
- Buyers
- Managers
- Buyers' managers
- Technical advisors
- Product or service users
- Unseen buyers and influencers

Yes, it can get confusing. That's why it is vital that you efficiently consider all candidates before deciding who the decision makers are and what level of responsibility or authority they have.

Identify the Decision Makers

So the next logical question is: How can I identify the decision makers in a purchase transaction? The best way is to ask!

- In making this purchase, who are the ultimate decision makers?
- How much authority does each of these people have in the final decision?
- Who and what influence but don't make the final decision?

Modify your questions based on what you sell and to whom. The point is to ask questions of individuals to determine who makes the decision and who influences it. You must know this in order to sell appropriately and effectively.

QUESTION?

What should I do if I can't identify all of the decision makers and the influencers before I need to start selling?
Assume that everyone is a buyer or decider until you have reason to demote or disqualify them. That means treating the receptionist or secretary as a buyer or at least an influencer in your transaction. It is better to temporarily assume greater authority than it is to later discover that you should have been selling to someone you were ignoring. Some influencers, when given authority, will use it to help your efforts.

Determine Buying Authority

Once you've identified who buys and who influences the buy, you can begin focusing your sales efforts by priority. However, keep in mind that most co-buyers have various levels of influence on other co-buyers. In the above example of co-buyers for a car, one will have decision powers for one aspect of the car purchase but also will influence other aspects. Fortunately, by asking questions—a salesperson's primary tool—you will soon identify the buying authority for all candidates. You can learn who makes decisions for various choices offered.

Then comes the hierarchy or chain of command. Must both co-buyers of the car decide equally (usually not), must they agree (probably), and how do they influence the other (it depends)? In some co-purchases, one buyer can ultimately overrule the purchase. In others, if there is no consensus there is no sale. Whatever you do as a salesperson, *never* take advantage of a weak relationship to make a sale. You ultimately will regret it.

Identifying Need

The primary reason to identify decision authority among multiple buyers is to assess who needs the most help in the buying process. For example, to be comfortable with making a clear decision about power aspects of a new car, one buyer may need some education on the latest engine and fuel-efficiency technology. You may have to fill in some knowledge holes. Because both buyers either decide or influence, you should include both in your discussion—unless the influencer opts out and starts looking at models and interiors. Then you must decide whether to truncate your power training to one buyer and focus on the other's style questions or attempt to bring them both along together on their journey to a decision. Golden Rule Selling isn't always easy. However, it always focuses on the needs of the individual and collective buyers.

The critical point is to determine buyer authority and then help each participant gain the knowledge needed to make an informed decision.

Who's Your Buyer?

Here's a dilemma: What if you cannot identify and measure the progress of one or more co-buyers? What if they're absent from your sales effort? Should you start without them? For example, what if you learn that your sales call is with a buyer who unexpectedly is replaced by an unknown individual—maybe a co-buyer and maybe just an influencer? What do you do?

The rule is: If in doubt, sell. That is, assume that the person you are presenting to has sufficient authority to make the decision or at least to influence the decision. Don't minimize the authority. You may later discover that the replacement is the buyer's boss. To clarify, you can begin the revised sales call by asking the new participant questions about purchasing influence. Then you can modify your presentation to fit the needs of the person you are helping.

Often, a business title can help you determine who the primary buyer is in a purchasing decision. Obviously, if the business card says "widget buyer" that's what he or she does. However, titles also can be deceptive. A "documentation engineer" usually is not an engineer at all, but a technical writer. You can clarify job responsibilities by simply asking what the job title entails. More specifically, ask how the job involves buying decisions for what you are selling.

Multiple Buying Groups

Another situation that can arise in major business and industrial sales is having separate groups or committees of buyers. For example, a major purchase for a corporation—such as the construction of a new shopping mall—may require that you make sales presentations to groups who have diverse interests in the transaction. One committee in Dallas decides about the size and final location of the mall, while another in Cincinnati hashes out the financial costs of construction. In addition, both may be required to report their decisions directly to the corporate headquarters in New York, which will make the final decision—based primarily on their recommendations. It can get confusing. Knowing who your decision makers are, what authority they have, and what they need to make an informed decision can make your selling job more productive.

If you eventually are involved in a complex sale like this, consider each as a separate sale. The site committee must decide where and, though you have influence, your information may not be as important to them as what they get from their own marketing department. However, the financial committee may listen intently to everything that you say about costs. You may even be allowed to present to the corporate decision makers. Each presentation has a different goal and agenda to different decision makers and influencers. Plan accordingly.

Understand Their Decision Processes

That's how buyers, in general, make and influence buying decisions. However, you're not just working with buyers; you're also helping individuals— unique people with distinctive needs and abilities. How can you best help them?

Again, the most productive method is to ask. "What information do you need to make an informed decision?" Depending on what you are selling, the individual answers may be different. However, they will have commonality. Most people, in making choices, follow a common path: gather data, add information, develop knowledge, and make the decision. By understanding how your individual buyers and influencers follow that path, you can better help them toward a successful decision.

When buyers ask for data (engine horsepower) they often are asking for information as well (how the horsepower relates to driving speed and safety). Professional salespeople respond to data questions with additional information to show the relevance of the data. In addition, they put it in terms that the buyer can relate to. "This engine can easily pass a semi-truck in less than three seconds."

Gathering Data

Data means factual information. The widget 295 weights six pounds and uses 1,700 watts of power. That's data. Whatever you are selling, the products and even services will have data. To help individual buyers make decisions, be sure that you have whatever data they require.

You do this by first asking them. "What data do you need about the widget 295?" One buyer may focus on the mechanical data while another needs the electrical or other data. You don't have to give them everything available, just everything they *need*.

In the example of the hamburger eater, she doesn't need to know the type of beef used or where the tomatoes were grown. The data she needs includes the size, the price, and what condiments are available. The menu will tell her most of that. The car buyers, however, will want to know the size of the engine, number of transmission gears, and other relevant data. Give them the data that they need by first asking, then providing.

Adding Information

Data won't always answer questions sufficiently. Buyers need to know the relevance of data, in other words, information, the application of data. For example, a 200-hoursepower engine (data) is relevant because it is more powerful (information) than a 150-hp engine. Data must be analyzed and compared to be informative.

Some buyers don't care about data or even much information. However, most do—especially as the price tag increases.

Data must be relevant to the buying decision. Help your buyers understand the relevance of product data and you will be helping them make better choices.

Developing Knowledge

Higher on the decision tree is knowledge. *Knowledge* is the integration of information and experience. It's more than just relevant facts. It's the application of appropriate information to real-life situations. It's remembering that the lower horsepower of your last car almost got you into an accident when trying to pass a slow-moving truck.

Knowledge comes from experience, but it also comes from association. That is, you don't have to actually get into a dangerous passing situation to know that, without adequate horsepower, you could. An *association* is a mental connection between facts and memories or ideas. Association keeps people from bungee jumping, even though they've never been in a similar situation.

What does all this have to do with selling? Buyers need knowledge—information combined with experience or association—to make better decisions. You can help your buyers develop needed knowledge. You can help them remember experiences and suggest associations that can be applied to their needs.

- You mentioned that your prior home had lots of problems. This home is brand new and is warranted against defects for two years. You can comfortably live in it without having to tackle repairs every weekend.
- Heavier widgets, such as the 295, are sturdier and will last longer. You won't have to worry about it breaking during use.
- We could grill the onions on your burger. That way they're less likely to bother your stomach—and they taste even better.

As you can see, knowledge can be turned into features and benefits. You are simply helping your buyers make better decisions by offering knowledge, facts combined with experience or association. You are selling as you want to be sold.

Making the Decision

You cannot—and should not—make the buying decision for your prospects. Instead, help them individually and collectively to analyze, understand, and satisfy their purchasing requisites. If you have worked with them through the entire buying process, you will know what data, information, and knowledge they require. And you will satisfy those requirements. That's your job.

Remember that no matter how large the group of buyers that makes the purchasing decision, they all are individuals with specific needs. Treat them as individuals and you will be helping them make better collective decisions.

Working Within the Decision Group

If you are working with multiple buyers, it's best if you can meet with them both collectively and individually. You may be making a sales presentation to the group. Before, during, or even after the presentation, you can identify the deciders and influencers. If you haven't previously identified them, assume that they all are buyers, and sell.

As you develop relationships with the individuals in decision groups, you'll be in a better position to determine their needs—data, information, knowledge—and help them acquire it. The best position to do that from is within the decision group. That is, make yourself a nonvoting member of the decision team.

In a retail selling environment, you can be a nonvoting member of the team by simply assisting and advising the decision makers. They are shopping for a new refrigerator—she for size and features and he for price. By being helpful, you can guide them in their decision, offering the data and information, the features and benefits, as they are identified by your questions to the buyers.

Becoming a team member can be difficult—especially when you are perceived as a "salesperson," someone who may not be honest and fair. That's why building trust (see Chapter 2) is so vital to Golden Rule Selling. The trust factor is especially important with multiple buyers because you might alienate one of them without even knowing it. You must identify each person's needs and decision process individually, then help them come to a collective decision.

In business and industrial sales, there typically are fewer emotional issues to the buying process, but group dynamics are still a concern. By becoming a nonvoting member of the decision group you can better analyze the individuals, the dynamics, and how they work to make buying decisions. You can be considered and treated as "one of us."

How can you become an integral component of the decision group? Through empathy. *Empathy* is seeing a person or event as if it were your own experience. In sales, there are different names and descriptions for empathy, such as assistive selling or consultive selling. One way of applying empathy is to see someone else's problem as your own. Analyze and solve the buyers' problem as if it were yours, then work within the group toward a solution. You are a nonvoting member, but your influence still can be significant. In fact, because of your knowledge and skills, you should be a primary influence in the decision. Again, that requires that you first build trust within the group.

FACT

The word empathy comes from the Greek word for passion. It involves feelings and emotions as well as understanding. It can be a changing force in daily life, but it also can be applied to the business world. Imagine employees who have empathy for customers and passion for their problems. Being empathetic toward your customers and their problems can help you to relate to and help them. They, in turn, may better help you in your efforts to sell.

Empathy first requires understanding. The buying group's need to find a long-term investment for pension funds should be *your* need. You should consider it as if you were trying to solve your own pension funding decision. The facts will be different, but the process will be similar. By empathizing, you are more invested in discovering an appropriate solution.

Empathy also requires communication—two-way communication. You must both listen and respond knowledgeably. As a member of the solution team, you must hear all sides and listen to each individual's input. You cannot simply make a statement and expect the group to accept it. Instead, empathize and help from within the group.

Keeping Decision Makers Aligned

As an integral member of the solution team, you may have an additional job on your hands. It may be up to you, the nonvoting decision influencer, to keep the quest focused on solving a specific problem or group of problems. From your knowledge and experience in solving similar problems for other clients, you may be looked to for leadership. You can nurture and increase your leadership role within the decision group as you collectively work toward the solution.

Unfortunately, stuff happens. There are disagreements and maybe even arguments within the decision group. Or the interest of the group in solving the problem wanes due to other, seemingly more pressing, problems. How can you help the decision makers focus on finding a solution? You can guide the group in identifying and resolving the disagreement, using your influence to focus on the buying process.

Identify the Problem

What's the problem? The signs of a problem can be anything from differences in information to angry disagreements among group members. One decider says that the plant reconstruction costs will be $11 million and another says it will be double that. Other members aren't sure which is accurate and the issue can't be resolved without accurate data.

Your job is to first identify the problem. Possibly one member is quoting an early estimate while another has the latest figures. Or not all cost factors are being considered in the lower number. Or for other reasons, one decision maker is attempting to slow or stop the buying process by objecting with misleading information.

FACT

A problem is a question. A solution is the answer. In selling, the question typically involves numerous related questions: How can I reduce job stress? Where can I go on a short vacation? How can I pay for that vacation? By thinking of selling as finding correct answers for buyer questions, you can better understand your role in the purchasing process.

By asking a few relevant questions, you may soon identify the true problem. Carefully asking questions can draw out the data and information needed without injuring members.

- When was the $11 million reconstruction estimate made?
- What did the estimate include?
- Are there logical reasons why the estimate would have doubled?

In the example, a few questions of fact may clarify their accuracy. You may help the decision group recognize that the $11 million estimate was for materials and didn't include labor.

Resolve the Problem

The last step is resolving the problem. It may simply require that prior statements be qualified: "The $11 million estimate for reconstruction was for materials; the labor estimate added another $10 million to the costs. Those estimates are current."

As a vital member of the decision team, you can inform, advise, and influence multibuyer groups from within and keep it progressing toward a sale.

CHAPTER 17

Leveraging the Internet

What does the Internet have to do with selling? Plenty! Within a decade, the Internet not only has become a major force in retailing, it also has expanded whole- sale and industrial sales around the world, bringing buyers and sellers together instantly. This chapter shows how you can use the Internet to find more prospects, serve your customers better, and keep up with the latest developments in your field.

Internet 101

One of the most practical technical advances of the twentieth century is the development of the Internet. It has changed the way that people communicate with each other. It began with simple messages that could be sent and displayed to distant computers. Then chats became games, followed by technical information and a few business transactions. Today, individuals share digital videos and businesses make sales presentations across the Internet. Chapter 6 on telephone sales mentioned a few sales opportunities, but there are many more. And there are more to come in the near future. Your sales career may depend on them.

Early Internet

The *Internet* is the *Inter*national *Net*work, an interconnection of computers around the world. There are virtually millions of them, all connected by digital data lines. Many are connected directly to telephone services. Others connect to the Internet via satellite, cable, and other data lines. They all share data using various methods, called *Internet protocols* (IPs). Some of these protocols have been around for more than twenty years, allowing computers to communicate with each other following a common structure.

In 1991, a new Internet structure was begun, called the world wide web or WWW, commonly called the web. This network was established within the Internet to share *hypertext* documents that send both text and the instructions for displaying that text. At that point, the Internet that you use today was born.

Browsers

The hypertext files could be shared and displayed because of the development of a special protocol that could read and interpret them, called hypertext transfer protocol (HTTP). The software programs that read them are called web browsers or simply browsers. One of the first browsers to become popular was called Mosaic. Microsoft Explorer is the most widely used Web browser program today. However, there still are many challengers including Mozilla Foxfire, Opera, and Safari (for Apple computers).

A browser reads and displays hypertext markup language (HTML) and other coding (such as JavaScript). The coding tells the browser where and how to display data, such as red text in a white box on the left side of the screen. The files also include the text to be displayed. As a salesperson, you don't need to write your own HTML code and design your own pages. However, it will help your understanding of this tool to know at least the basics of how the Internet, the web, browsers, and HTML have made communication and sales easier.

QUESTION?

What does HTML code look like?
Open your favorite browser, go to any website, and take a look. In Microsoft Explorer, select View, then Source to see the underlying code for that page. In Foxfire, it's View, then Page Source. You'll see the text code that built the page you were looking at. It includes the location of photos and drawings, text, and even the code for scripts that do things on the page. Some page coding is relatively easy to follow, while others are more challenging, even for webmasters.

E-mail

Some people never use the Internet as a commerce site; they don't buy or sell on it. However, they do use e-mail. It's the most widely used feature of the web. E-mail is suggested as a powerful sales tool in Chapter 6.

How does e-mail work? It, too, uses a protocol—a set of rules or guidelines. In this case, the protocol is called Simple Mail Transfer Protocol (SMTP). It's a text-based protocol that includes both data and directions. The message includes information on where it is being sent, from whom, the text itself, and how it should be displayed. The primary e-mail programs are Microsoft Outlook and Outlook Express, Mozilla Thunderbird, and Apple Mail. The next section of this chapter offers a variety of ways that you can use e-mail to enhance your sales efforts and work smarter rather than harder.

Other Internet Sales Tools

As covered in Chapter 6, there are many other Internet tools available to salespeople. One is Voice over Internet Protocol (VoIP), which allows you to make voice phone calls over Internet connections.

The most useful Internet sales tool is web presentation software. With it you can conduct a full sales presentation in a distant office while sitting at your desk—or in your home. WebEx *(www.webex.com)* is a program that manages meetings over the Internet. It's similar to a visual conference call. Using Internet cameras mounted on the computer monitor, it sends videos of participants to each other so it seems like a face-to-face meeting. In addition, presentations can be offered and participants can use their keyboards and mice to point or add to the presentation screens. Fast Internet connections are required; dialup connections don't have the speed or bandwidth to transfer the visuals. Many sales offices use similar products to hold staff meetings or to meet with suppliers around the world without traveling.

E-mail Selling

Anything that you can do with direct-mail sales you can do using e-mail. Your employer may use direct-marketing methods and direct-mail tools to help you do your job. Most sellers have applied what they know about direct marketing to e-mail marketing. It, too, can be an efficient and effective way to reach more prospects and customers with your sales message.

Direct Mail

Direct marketing is selling products or services directly to the end user. In most sales, that means individual consumers. However, direct marketing also is used in business and industry to develop prospects' interest in your product or service. Depending on what you are offering, part or all of your sales job will involve direct marketing.

Direct mail is using the mail service to deliver marketing and sales messages. Because much of the mail is delivered at third-class postage rates, the cost can be relatively inexpensive. A single postcard mailer can be delivered to a prospect for less than twenty-five cents. That's a lot cheaper than most other message-delivery systems. Because of the lower cost, sellers send out millions of direct-mail pieces every day, flooding mail boxes with what often is called "junk mail."

FACT

The Direct Marketing Association *(www.the-dma.org)* has expanded its reach to include companies and salespeople that sell using e-mail. In addition, they co-sponsor a conference with the Email Experience Council *(www.emailexperience.org)*, which helps sellers and marketers understand best practices and leading-edge strategies for e-mail selling. E-mail is becoming big business.

Why does some direct mail work and some not? Because of *target marketing*, focusing your efforts on people who have the greatest need for what you are selling. Offering refrigerators to Eskimos, for example, can be a waste of everyone's time. Target marketing means offering refrigerators to people in warmer climates, who would benefit from keeping food fresher longer. By targeting your direct mail, you can help more people at less cost. The same is true of e-mail marketing.

E-mail Opportunities

Electronic mail, or *e-mail*, is even less expensive to deliver than direct mail. The "postage" is free! The costs involved include designing a message and preparing it in a form that attracts the interest of the user, often using HTML or another tool. Your employer will help you in understanding and using their e-mail sales tools and campaigns. In essence, e-mail campaigns and functions are similar to direct mail efforts. They are designed to:

- Build a brand name
- Make prospects aware of the features and benefits of products or services

- Tell prospects and customers of sale and discount opportunities
- Assist prospects in making a decision regarding what you sell
- Help keep existing customers happy

Following is a list of some of the opportunities that salespeople have for using e-mail.

- Send a survey to find qualified prospects.
- Respond to prospect requests for additional product information.
- Confirm a sales appointment.
- Send a periodic newsletter to prospects or customers updating them on products or services you offer.
- Confirm an order placed.
- Confirm the shipment of an order.
- Check back with a customer to ensure that the order was satisfactory.

You and your employer will find hundreds of ways of using e-mail to find, help, and keep satisfied customers.

E-mail Rules

Because e-mail is sent at no cost, there is a proliferation of e-mails, the majority of it unsolicited. Unsolicited e-mail is often called "spam." In the business world, it's sometimes known as Unsolicited Commercial E-Mail (UCE).

It's estimated that there are nearly 100 billion e-mails sent per day. A small minority of these e-mails are actually received. The rest are caught by spam filters, which are software programs that recognize the fingerprints of unwanted e-mail and stop delivery. Fortunately, antispam software today is seemingly intelligent and widely available. Businesses have built-in spam filters that catch most of it. In addition, there are federal laws that attempt to regulate e-mail delivery.

CAN-SPAM

In 2003, an extensive set of laws was enacted to establish standards for what can and cannot legally be sent via e-mails. The long name for the law is Controlling the Assault of Non-Solicited Pornography and Marketing Act, or the CAN-SPAM Act. The law is enforced by the Federal Trade Commission. In essence, CAN-SPAM says that bulk e-mailers must:

- Include a relevant subject line
- Include a legitimate physical address of the advertiser and/or publisher
- If the content is of adult nature, include a label indicating so
- Provide a method of unsubscribing to, or opting out of receiving, future e-mailings from the sender
- Honor opt-out requests within ten days of receipt
- Use opt-out lists for compliance only and not resell them

Spam filters work well to reduce unwanted e-mails. However, some spammers attempt to get around them by sending e-mails from legitimate e-mail addresses, such as bobsmith@ibm.com. It's called spoofing. It's like receiving an envelope addressed to you from IBM, then opening it to discover a get-rich-quick scheme from Nigeria. Some spam filters can catch this trick. Your employer's Internet administrator can explain more about how to avoid being deceived by spoofers and other e-mail tricks.

In addition, individuals and companies can sue senders and even their Internet Service Providers (ISPs) for sending unsolicited e-mail, and addresses cannot be "harvested," that is, picked up unsolicited from the Internet. The intent is that receivers must opt-in to, or ask to be placed on, an e-mail list. Your customers can ask to subscribe to your newsletter; you cannot just search the Internet for the e-mail addresses of people you think might be interested in your newsletter.

E-mail Etiquette

In addition to laws that govern the sending of e-mails, there is etiquette. Your employer may be sending out thousands of automated e-mails, such as a monthly newsletter or weekly update, but much of your e-mailing will be to customers and suppliers. How can you make sure that you don't annoy recipients with your e-mail? By following e-mail etiquette. Here are some suggestions.

- E-mail as you want to be e-mailed.
- Clearly make your point.
- Reread messages before you send them.
- Quote all or part of the original message when replying so your response is considered in context.
- Be careful of irony and other humor that may not be understood when written.
- Don't forward e-mails without editing them down to their essence.
- Send the e-mail in plain text unless you know the receiver prefers HTML.
- DON'T SEND ALL-CAPS E-MAILS; IT'S CONSIDERED SHOUTING!
- Ask for permission before sending huge attachments, as some systems will truncate or not deliver them.
- Avoid smilies and other emoticons in business e-mails.

Use an appropriate commercial e-mail account to send business messages. Don't use HotMail, Yahoo!, Gmail, or other free accounts. Not only do they look unprofessional, but they also are scrutinized more closely by spam filters. Your message may get lost.

E-mail Signatures

Popular e-mail systems allow an ending message, called a signature, to be automatically appended to outgoing messages. This is a useful feature that can benefit sales. The signature isn't your graphic signature (unless you want it to be), but a short list of contact information, usually with a short sales message.

Your signature should be long enough to give vital information, but short enough to not be ignored. For example, if your customers don't typically use the fax line for communication, leave it off of the signature and only add it to the message if needed. The same goes for your company slogan or address. Only include what is useful to the receiver of your e-mail.

You can have alternate signature files in most e-mail management programs. You can have one automatically appended per e-mail account as the default, or you can choose among a few of them based on the recipient's needs. In addition, advanced e-mail programs can allow you to be more creative with your signature. Your employer can help you develop and use an appropriate signature for your outgoing e-mail.

Keeping Current

One of the greatest features of the Internet is its immediacy. With it, you can watch stock prices change in almost real time, you can watch a video announcement by a financial official, and you can view your factory on the other side of the world through a video camera. The Internet is an amazing tool that can improve your sales opportunities—if you know how to use its power.

The Internet also places a burden on users, especially commercial users. The burden is that your competitors are using the Internet as well. If you don't know at least as much as they do about your field, you could lose sales opportunities. Knowledge is power. The Internet isn't the source of all knowledge, for sure, but it is the largest source of data available. You can learn to mine that data and build your knowledge toward improved sales. You can do so by using search engines, finding communities, and watching your competitors online.

Search Engines

If you haven't discovered Internet search engines yet, you're in for a powerful surprise. The Internet is huge with *billions* of pieces of data. How can you find what you're looking for on the Internet?

Fortunately, there are information retrieval systems, called search engines, that have read and indexed just about everything on the Internet. These search engines know where to look for data by keywords. A *keyword* is a word or phrase that search engines can look for and report back to you. For example, a search for "widget" will return more than *24 million* entries on the Internet. Narrowing your search down to "green widget" reduces the number to about 3,000. As you learn to use search engines, you'll find out how to narrow your searches for optimum results.

The primary search engines on the Internet today include Google (*www.google.com*), Yahoo! Search (*search.yahoo.com*), and Live Search, formerly MSN Search (*search.live.com*).

QUESTION?

How can I get a crash course in search engine use?
The search engines themselves offer guidance. Take a look at *www.google.com/help/basics.html* or *help.yahoo.com/l/us/yahoo/search/basics.* They offer both an introduction and tips for effectively using search engines, including how to use keywords and phrases to get specific results. Spend a little time with the primary search engines and you can quickly learn how to use them to find what you're looking for.

One of the advantages of search engines is that you can sort by types of information. You can search for keywords across the web or more narrowly among images, on maps, in the news, among blogs, in groups, in books, or within numerous other categories. For example, a search of Google's Books category for "widget" returns nearly 1,600 entries. You then can look at sample pages with the term "widget" from many of the books. As you can see, search engines can help you search for just about anything under the sun—once you've learned how to use it.

Communities

The Internet also is a meeting place. Buyers and sellers meet there, as do professional groups. For example, salespeople in a variety of fields meet and discuss their professions and frustrations in web logs, called blogs, in user groups and other communities. Groups are available for people who fly electric model aircrafts, collect ancient Greek coins, sell on eBay, play professional hold 'em poker, and have a thousand other interests.

How can you find communities that have your professional and personal interests? By using search engines. For example, search Google Groups for a list of groups and postings on "sales," "selling," and related topics. Some groups are moderated, meaning that someone manages the group to ensure that it doesn't collect off-topic and spam messages.

Another option is to search Google Blogs for selling and you will discover numerous groups interested in the topic. You'll also find blogs in which selling is discussed, but not necessarily by professional sellers.

Another resource is trade associations to which you or your employer belong. Many have moderated forums in which members can post messages, ask each other questions, and carry on electronic conversations.

FACT

Want to be notified whenever your search term comes up on the Internet or in the news? Join free services like Google Alerts that scan the net for your keywords and send you an e-mail notice when discovered. You can then get real-time, daily, or weekly reports on those topics. To keep your e-mail inbox manageable, focus your keywords, such as "green widgets" or your competitors' names.

In addition, you can develop an online community yourself. As you meet people with common interests, exchange e-mail addresses, and develop Internet relationships, you may find friendly competitors or other salespeople who don't compete in your territory. They can help you keep up on the latest in your industry as well as share insights into the career of selling.

Competitors

Tired of having competitors get the jump on you? Know more about them, their strategies, and their efforts by periodically searching the Internet for them. If they have a website, you can visit it frequently. You may even be able to sign up to receive their e-mail newsletter.

Who are your competitors? Anyone who sells or wants to sell to your customers. They are competing for the dollars that go to you. Your primary competitors are those who sell the same things you do to your customers. It's your job, as a professional salesperson, to know what your primary and secondary competitors are doing toward taking your income. Don't wait until they announce the big sale; use the Internet and your other resources to learn what your competitors are up to right now.

Mobile Internet

Selling is a mobile profession. Because of telephones and the Internet, you can work from virtually anywhere and interface with prospects, customers, and suppliers just about anywhere else in the world. However, that means you need to be using the latest tools of technology and communication.

The most popular mobile Internet connection is the laptop computer. It can let you take your entire data office with you wherever you go. Depending on what type of connection you use, you can make VoIP telephone calls through it and connect by a Wi-Fi wireless system or a satellite Internet link. You can work at the office, at home, in an airport, or at your customer's location with equal ease. A major advantage of laptop computers is that you can take advantage of the power, graphics, and data of the Internet. You can plug in just about anywhere there is an Internet signal.

Even cellular telephones today offer opportunities to surf the Internet from anywhere. Using digital signals, they connect to a mobile transmitter just as your voice calls do, then log on to the Internet. The keyboards on these devices are very small and require some practice to use, but you can read and respond to e-mail from virtually anywhere that you can talk on a cell phone.

Many personal digital assistants (PDAs) also include an Internet hookup via Wi-Fi, phone line, or other connection. PDAs offer some of the features of a laptop, including software interface, in a larger package than available with a cell phone.

Your sales manager or employer can help you select the appropriate technology tools for your job. And today's tools will be tomorrow's toys. Keep up on what's happening in business technology with the Internet, e-mail, and the many devices that can bring them to you anywhere. One resource is Mobile Magazine (*www.mobilemag.com*). In addition, publications for sales professionals, such as Sales Magazine (*www.salesmagazine.com*), offer periodic roundups of technology tools.

CHAPTER 18

Self-Management for Sales Professionals

As your sales career grows, your professional and personal assets will increase. You will be more your own boss. That can be good, giving you new opportunities to expand your skills and manage your life. It also can be a challenge as you strive to work smarter and enjoy more. It requires self-management. This chapter offers proven methods for managing your habits, schedule, appearance, emotions, motivation, and travel. It can help you help yourself as you help others.

Habits of Success

Everyone wants to be successful in what they do. Success is a desired outcome. The outcome may be to get rich, find love, build an empire, pay the bills, or simply to help others find their success. Most people are driven by a variety of categories of success, for example, success on the job, in relationships, and in competitive situations. However, to some, success is only a vague goal, such as attaining wealth. It isn't sufficiently specific to drive them on a daily basis. At what point can they declare success? A million dollars in the bank? A big house? They need specific goals.

Success Goals

In your sales career, in order to attain success, you must first clearly define it. Set your goals. Your professional goals may be similar to these:

- Help more buyers purchase quality widgets than any other salesperson in the office.
- Earn at least $100,000 in sales commissions in the coming year.
- Earn my employer's Salesperson of the Year Award.
- Increase my sales in the next year by 20 percent over last year.
- Earn the opportunity to be considered for the new Sales Manager position.

Each of these are viable goals for your sales job. Similarly, you might have specific goals for your personal life and other endeavors.

QUESTION?

What should I do if I'm new on the job and not sure what my sales goals should be?
Ask your boss. She or he will know what goals are appropriate for you. In fact, many employers will have quotas, minimum goals that you must meet to continue employment. Sales managers know how much everyone on the team is selling and what to expect from new hires. Ask for guidance and follow it until you can establish your own sales and professional goals.

Chapter 19 offers more specifics on setting and achieving sales goals.

Making a Plan

Making a plan is similar to planning a trip. Your goal is a destination. Plans are the roads to those destinations. They identify the speed and direction of your travel, the stops along the way, and your estimated time of arrival. They also note what vehicle, fuel, and other resources you will need.

For example, if your sales goal is to help more buyers in the coming year, you first need to identify how many buyers you served last year. If it is 100 and your goal is to serve 20 percent more, then your new number is 120 buyers. That's the new goal. You can implement the plan by determining how you are going to reach the goal.

- Spend an extra hour in the office each day.
- Hire an assistant to help with the office paperwork so you can meet more prospects.
- Establish a monthly goal of serving a minimum of ten buyers.
- Work harder to increase referrals from existing customers.

Your plan should be flexible because life sometimes isn't. Emergencies come up. Health or economic issues take priority. Opportunities change. So you should not only make a plan, but also monitor it. Like checking maps and road signs along your trip path, you need to verify that you are where you should be at any point. As needed, you make adjustments to ensure success.

Making Success a Habit

A *habit* is a repetitive behavior. The advantage of habits is that they can make the steps within plans more efficient. Your goal is to have healthy teeth; the plan is to brush regularly. The habit is remembering to do so every night.

To make career success a habit, you must identify your goal, develop a plan, and repeat the required steps. For example, working an extra hour in the office each day requires that you adjust some current habits—such as setting your alarm clock—and make your mornings more efficient so you can get to work earlier. Or you may decide to change your afternoon habits, cutting your lunch hour or spending less time with mundane tasks so you can spend more on productive work.

How can you form positive habits? Experts say that the process includes:

- Knowing what habit you want to form
- Listing the benefits of your new habit to help motivate you
- Working more for consistency than performance
- Keeping on the move

Your professional and personal success is based upon dozens and even hundreds of small successes, many of them developed by habits—repetitive behaviors that fit your goals. Set your goals, make plans, and create valuable habits. They will help you reach your goal of success.

Managing Your Schedule

A schedule is a list of time-based details. It can be a schedule of appointments, meetings, phone calls, tasks, or other events, each with either a time or a priority level. Your daily efforts as a salesperson will require scheduling or planning tasks and events by date and time. In addition, your schedule must have sufficient room to manage unscheduled events. Learning to manage your schedule is a critical part of being a successful salesperson.

Calendars

Most schedules are recorded on calendars of some type. It can be a simple printed calendar book available at office supply stores or it can be an electronic device such as a personal digital assistant (PDA) or software on your computer. Exactly what the tool will be depends on what your employer prefers that you use as well as your own preferences. If you do most of your work on a laptop or a PDA, putting your scheduling calendar on it makes sense. If your scheduling requirements are limited, a simple pocket calendar book may be sufficient.

The next question is: Who manages your schedule? In most cases, you will. However, depending on what support staff you have, a gatekeeper—secretary, assistant, clerk—may be in charge of setting up your schedule and helping you to meet appointments. If there is more than one source for scheduling, make sure that it is coordinated. You don't want to go to an appointment only to discover that it has been cancelled or moved to another location through your secretary. Fortunately, many scheduling software programs can help you coordinate or match up schedules from various sources while minimizing conflict. However, it requires that you set up the coordination system. That could mean an automatic uploading or downloading of data overnight. If so, you must make sure every day that you are aware of the latest scheduling changes and are prepared for the day's events.

Calendar Feedback

Feedback is output used to adjust input. You see that the faucet you turned on is flowing too fast (output), so you to turn the faucet handle back (adjust input). The process is called feedback and you use it in a hundred ways every day as you drive, speak, eat, and work. You make correcting changes in the input to alter the output to a desired level.

Scheduling your day gives you specific outputs. For example, you meet with Mary at 3 P.M. and learn that she is prepared for your one-hour meeting and it only takes a half hour. So, when scheduling your next meeting with her, you plan it for a half hour. Other adjustments are made in your scheduling based on feedback. You learn that a new highway cuts twenty minutes off your commute and you can start the day earlier. Or you discover that Friday traffic delays your afternoon appointments. These adjustments are common and necessary. By making note of them, you can be a more efficient scheduler of your valuable time.

Dressing for Success

People are sold, in part, through visual perceptions. A salesperson of $50,000 cars who dresses like poverty will be ignored. How salespeople look enhances or decreases the customer's perception of their professionalism.

That doesn't mean all salespeople should wear business suits. They aren't appropriate for all selling situations. However, salespeople should dress to impress. Following are some guidelines.

- Select apparel, jewelry, and fragrances that don't detract from your professional image.
- Make sure that your hair is clean, neat, and professionally styled.
- Be sure that your apparel is clean, neatly pressed, and of the appropriate size.
- Choose apparel that is more formal than that of your typical customer.
- Keep colors and designs simple and not distracting.
- Select clothing that draws attention to your face rather than your body.

There are many other guidelines, depending on what you sell and to whom. Your employer probably will have a dress code for salespeople. Invest in an assortment of quality, easy-to-maintain professional clothing and it will help you make a lasting first impression.

Need more tips on dressing for success? About.com has a category on Career Planning (careerplanning.about.com) with suggestions and tips on dressing for interviews as well as in the workplace. In addition, Dress for Success (*www.dressforsuccess.org*) is a nonprofit organization that provides interview suits, confidence boosts, and career development for low-income women in over seventy-five cities worldwide.

Dealing with Emotions

Sales is a logical profession. However, it involves people, so it also involves emotions. Buyers feel happy or upset. Sellers feel confident or self-conscious. How can professional salespeople deal with the various emotions of their job and their customers?

The answer is: understanding. To deal with emotions appropriately, you must understand what they are as well as how to manage them in yourself and others.

Your Emotions

The emotions you will feel as you work and live are varied. However, salespeople are most susceptible to the emotion of acceptance or, more specifically, self-acceptance. As you invest your time, efforts, and energy into selling, the success and failure of events can drive you on an emotional roller coaster ride. You're elated at the big sale but disappointed and even depressed about the sale that fell through. Add to these variations those of daily life and you can see that selling can be an emotional job.

Because humans are emotional beings, controlling emotions can be a lifelong struggle. What can you do to manage your emotions? Experts offer these suggestions:

- Recognize it. When you become emotional about an action or words, identify the emotion you are feeling.
- Learn how to express it. Tell yourself what emotion you are feeling and describe it as clearly as you can.
- Try to understand it objectively. Impartially consider the emotion, its purpose, and what it is making you feel.
- Control it. If the emotion is appropriate, act on it. If not, modify your response or ignore it.

Why should you recognize and deal appropriately with your emotions? Because otherwise emotions can build out of proportion and impact other emotions. An unkind word to you can trigger inappropriate anger or deep depression. Dealing with your emotions as they arise can help you keep them in perspective.

Emotions of Others

The same guidelines can be applied to dealing with the emotions of others. A customer yells at you. Your boss derides you. In each case, you can help the person recognize, express, understand, and control the emotion.

Be cautious, as not allowing the person to express anger and recognize it can make it fester within them. If you cut them off or challenge them too harshly, you may receive an enhanced emotional response.

FACT

For further information on managing emotions in the workplace and in life, read Diane and Terry Berry's book, *A Peace of My Mind: A Therapist's Guide to Handling Anger and Other Difficult Emotions*. Also recommended is Scott Spradlin's *Don't Let Emotions Run Your Life*. There are other good titles available offering guidance to gain control of human emotions.

Fortunately, you are a professional salesperson and you understand the value of listening and asking questions. Tell me what you mean by that? How did that make you feel? What do you think caused it? By encouraging communication and not responding with equal emotion, you often can defuse a strong emotion and help the other person consider it more objectively.

Staying Motivated

As you sell yourself and your products, it may become increasingly difficult to stay motivated. You may soon become tired or frustrated and not recognize how important your efforts are. It's tough to stay motivated.

What can you do? *Motivation* is a reason for doing something. You were motivated to accept your sales job by income and service opportunities. You're motivated to go into work by wanting to spend time helping prospects and customers solve buying problems. The problem can sometimes be retaining that motivation through the months and years of your sales career.

Remembering Your Motives

The proven way to stay motivated in your sales job is to periodically remind yourself of the reasons that you became a salesperson. As Chapter 2 outlines, Golden Rule Selling is selling as you want to be sold. It is a sincere desire to earn personal rewards by helping others. Reminding yourself of these facts can help you stay motivated. Suggestions include the following.

- List your reasons for selling and keep them where you can easily refer to them.
- Periodically review your efforts that have helped others.
- Don't focus too much on long-term goals. Instead, recognize success reaching short-term goals.
- Live in the now. Enjoy what you are doing and with whom you are doing it.
- Reward yourself for success. Enjoy the benefits derived from your successful sales career.

Keep your selling and career motives in mind to help you focus on the positive efforts and results of what you do for a living. Remember why you became a professional salesperson.

Having trouble staying motivated on your sales job? Think you're facing the world alone? You're not. As your sales career grows, you will discover new relationships with people in your trade. Some will become your mentors. As your motivation diminishes, turn to these people for help and advice. Chances are they have felt it, too. They may be able to guide you. At least you may get a sympathetic listener who understands the problems that you face.

Taking a Break

Keeping a balance between your job and your life can sometimes be difficult, especially when selling requires more time than previously. It may seem that you must be a salesperson 24/7 to succeed. Unfortunately, no one can maintain such a schedule and survive. Relationships will suffer. Health will suffer. Yes, even income will suffer as you work without rest and replenishment. You need to take a break.

Breaks can be as short as power naps or as long as extended vacations. A power nap is simply a short sleep that renews energy. Most power naps are twenty to sixty minutes in length and offer the body and mind an opportunity to be refreshed. They can add productive hours to your day. A ten-minute power nap in your car waiting for an appointment can leave you refreshed and ready to do your job better.

Taking a Vacation

Vacations also can help keep you motivated at your job, giving you a goal as well as a reward for your hard efforts. There are two primary types of vacations: relaxation vacations and stimulation vacations.

A relaxation vacation is one that takes you mentally and emotionally as far away from your sales job as possible. It is lying on a beach in the sun or going to a spa. You should leave all of your business tools and cards at home. Forget what you do for a living and enjoy the moments. Even a few days of a relaxation vacation can bring you back renewed, motivated, and ready to sell.

A stimulation vacation arouses your mind and emotions. It can be travel to museums or popular hot spots, a family vacation, or any holiday that inspires you about life. You might take a volunteer vacation, helping to build homes for low-income people or teaching a class in business skills. Do whatever will stimulate you.

You also can mix and match the purposes of your vacation, spending some time in the sun and other time in art galleries. The goal is to renew yourself physically, mentally, and emotionally, replacing the energy that you've used helping others.

Working on the Road

Some sales jobs require that you travel more than others. The travel can be annual, seasonal, or all of the time. If you enjoy travel and don't have family obligations, the life of a traveling salesperson can be rewarding. However, for many, working on the road is difficult. Travel is a logistical strain with irregular accommodations, unpredictable food, and the frustrations of scheduling and delays. How can you get anything done on the road?

Good planning can help you survive and even enjoy road sales. You can go to exotic locations that you may not otherwise see—and be paid to do it. You can use your off-the-clock time to expand your horizon and see the diversities of this world and its inhabitants. Professional salespeople who travel offer the following suggestions:

- Know where you are going and why.
- Make sure you have the things you need.
- Be efficient in your work.
- Enjoy yourself.

Like planning any trip, a sales trip requires that you know where you're going. In addition, you must know why. Is it to meet a long-time client in Hong Kong to further the relationship? Are you inspecting outlying sales offices to ensure that they are operating efficiently? Are you traveling to Cincinnati to find prospects for a new sales territory? To get the most from your trip, you must first understand what results you want from it.

Selling on the road often is different from selling near to home. Your presentations may require equipment that you must ship ahead. Or you may need adapters for the different electrical systems in foreign countries. Maybe you will be required to attend or even host a formal dinner and need appropriate attire. Make sure that you have a comprehensive list of your needs before you make the trip, especially if you will be away from replenishment sources.

QUESTION?

What kind of assistance can I expect from my employer on a sales trip?
It's as much your employer's responsibility to organize a productive sales trip as it is yours. Interview your employer about business expectations as well as off-time opportunities at your destinations. Sales managers typically are experienced salespeople who can help you know what to pack, what to expect, and what to do if problems arise. Also use your sales support staff to help you make arrangements so that your sales trip is rewarding.

Plan your sales days efficiently to ensure that you get done what you need. However, many traveling salespeople recognize that their productivity is cut about in half by the vagaries of travel, especially foreign travel. Plan your days loosely and allow time to fix unexpected problems.

Make sure that you enjoy your trip. Sales trips often can be overwhelming, especially if it is your first trip to the area or country. Take a camera. Shop for souvenirs. Stay in contact with family and friends. Find opportunities to enjoy what you do and where you are. Enjoy your job and your life on the road.

Setting and Achieving Your Sales Goals

Salespeople are goal-oriented. They set goals for the number of prospects found, the number of customers served, and the number of sales made. They keep track of how they are doing against goals. As needed, they revise goals. Goals are in their job description. This chapter shows you how professional salespeople establish and meet sales goals in a variety of situations. Whether you set your sales goals or your boss does, you'll discover how to meet them and succeed.

Plan for Success

Success in selling isn't an accident. It's deliberate. You must plan for sales success. That planning requires that you establish professional goals, from how many hours a day spent prospecting to how many new customers you must find each month. Your ultimate goal may be to earn a specific amount of money, but it takes these other goals—and many more—to achieve your financial goal. One of the advantages of sales over many other professions is that you'll have more control over your own goals.

Understanding Goals

A *goal* is an objective, an intent put into action. Wanting to visit Shanghai is an intent or desire; planning the trip and working toward funding it is a goal. The problem many people have with goals is failing to understand what they are and how to use them as a guiding force in their daily life. Instead, they drift from one situation or desire to another without ever deciding and acting on their aspiration. They don't actually *set* goals.

The profession of selling teaches you the requirements and benefits of setting goals. As you discover this powerful tool, you may begin seeing applications within your personal life. This doesn't mean that your life will be filled only with activities intended to meet specific goals. It does mean that you will learn to prioritize your actions better because you can visualize how these actions result in meeting goals.

Using Goals

Your career and specific job goals are really a group of interrelated objectives that work toward your personal life goal. That is, earning $100,000 a year selling widgets is an admirable goal, but not your primary one. Your life goal will involve your values, your relationships, your needs and desires. It might be to enjoy your life in all its facets as well as you can. It might be to make sure that your family gets opportunities that you didn't have. Whatever your life's goal is, your career and specific job goals are components of it.

Acting on Goals

Goals are just desires until they are acted upon. To someday visit Shanghai you must first decide how to get there, fund the trip, and plan what you will do when you arrive. In a small way, those decisions can begin your action toward the goal. However, it will take greater actions to make the event happen. You will need to get a passport, purchase a ticket, make arrangements for accommodations, and perform related tasks. To enhance your trip, you will want to learn Mandarin, the official language, or Shanghainese. You probably will buy and study a book on visiting Shanghai. These are specific actions toward your stated goal.

FACT

Motivational speaker Anthony Robbins *(www.anthonyrobbins.com)* says, "A real decision is measured by the fact that you've taken a new action. If there is no action, you haven't truly decided." He also says that "action is the foundational key to all success." If you want success for yourself, your customers, your employer, and your family, you must take action on your decisions.

Your sales goals require action as well. Reaching $100,000 in annual sales is just a desire until you act upon it: Learn what it takes to make it happen, make specific plans, and acquire the skills you need to get there. You must take action on your desires to make them goals. You must *set your goals*.

Set Your Goals

A goal can be a physical objective (such as Shanghai), a financial one, a personal objective, or other aspiration. To be a true goal it must meet three criteria. It must be specific, measurable, and time-targeted.

For example, a goal of earning $100,000 in sales commissions in the coming year is specific, measurable, and set in time. It's a goal—if you take the action required to initiate it. You arrange your workday to see more prospective customers. You upgrade your selling skills to match those of people who sell that much in a year. You take actions appropriate to the goal you've set.

Your goal also must be realistic. That's where some goals fall apart. If this is your first year in sales and it looks like $50,000 in commissions is a more realistic number, setting a goal of $100,000 will discourage and frustrate you. Your goal, instead, could be to increase your sales level by 10 or 20 percent, a more modest goal. That doesn't mean you can't modify the goal later and even surpass it. It does mean that your frustration will be less.

The time component of goals also is important. There are long-term, short-term, and project goals. Each has its own set of requirements. In addition, you will have personal goals that parallel or supersede your sales goals.

Long-Term Goals

Long-term goals vary in length. They can take six months, a year, five years, or more to achieve. In most careers, a long-term goal is three to five years. Your employer plans business in long-term ranges like this. Rarely in business are long-term goals over five years in duration.

Your long-term career goals will be less specific than other goals. They are intended to guide you. For example, your long-term sales career goal may be to become a sales manager within five years. There are no financial specifics in this goal because it is difficult to project five years ahead in many volatile business environments. Even so, such a long-term goal can help you focus your short-term and other goals better because you have a long-range plan.

Short-Term Goals

Short-term goals typically have a duration of a year or less. If your long-term goal is to be a sales manager within five years, your short-term objective may be to become the top salesperson in your department or company within one year. Or it may be to enhance your formal education with courses that can help you in your management role.

Short-term goals can be more specific, such as a goal of earning commissions of $100,000 in the coming year. The goal can be even more specific, detailing how many new customers you will need, or how you expect to achieve the goal. Successful goals are both specific and measurable.

Project Goals

As you continue your sales career, you may be involved in various projects. They may be longer or shorter term, though most will be less than a year. However, the term length of projects often is defined by a specific result rather than a date. For example, the goal of a project may be to find an appropriate location for the latest in a chain of stores. There may be a vague time measurement, but, in truth, the project isn't complete until the goal is achieved.

If your sales job involves projects, setting goals is a little different because the criterion is an event or a decision rather than a date. The definition of "success" must be more measurable than a dollar amount. If finding a store location is the project, the criteria must include specifics about territory, market, costs, profitability, and other factors. Project goals require more specifics.

Personal Goals

In addition to your career goals, you will develop personal goals. For most people, they are vague: to be happy or to be rich. As you're learning in your sales career, goals must be specific and attainable, whether the goals are business or personal. You may develop a long-term personal goal of funding your children's college education within five years. Or it may be to travel to China for a least one month in the next two years. You can have personal projects, too, such as building a personal aircraft before you retire. Learning the craft of selling doesn't only benefit your professional life. It also can teach you how to set and reach personal goals, develop better communication skills, and enhance relationships through listening.

Prioritize Goals

Goals are wonderful tools for organizing your career and your life. However, you soon will have an excess of goals. Some will guide your long- and short-term sales, others will direct your business and personal projects. What can you do to make sure that you are working on the most important goals? You can prioritize them.

A *priority* is something that is prior to another. The priority can be based on time sequence, such as dressing before you leave for the office, or it can be set by relative importance to your long-term goals, such as getting additional training before getting a promotion. In your life, there often will be conflicts due to lack of time. That is, you have fourteen business and personal activities for a Tuesday, but you know you can't get to them all. Which ones should you tackle first? What about the others? Making those decisions is *prioritizing*, following a list of tasks in order of importance.

Goals require that you get rid of conflicts. You cannot have the goals of spending all your time at work and all of your time playing golf. They aren't compatible, or attainable—unless you're a golf pro. Instead, you must analyze what compromises you can make in each goal to satisfy the other. If the potential conflicts aren't evident, they will soon become so. Proactively eliminating or reducing conflicts among goals can help you prioritize them.

How can you prioritize the goals of your career? By determining their relative value to you. Is earning $100,000 more important than serving as many customers as possible? Is advancing your education more important than spending an extra hour on the phone each day? These can be tough questions, especially as you mix in goals from other aspects of your life.

Many professionals begin with their life's goals and make sure that career goals fit within them, rather than the other way around. If your life goal is to nourish and enjoy relationships with your family, obviously this will conflict with the time requirements of your career's long- and short-term goals. You must establish a balance.

One effective exercise is to list your personal and professional goals, determine what the requirements are, and then analyze how each is important to your life goal. From this you can develop a list of goals in order of importance. Prioritizing isn't easy, nor is it an exact science. Your priorities today will surely be different from those of a year hence. Priorities require adjustment based on feedback (see Chapter 18). In addition, some goals and priorities will be thrust upon you by employers, family, and others. A staff cutback at work or a medical emergency at home can shuffle your priorities in a moment. Therefore use goals as guidelines for planning your days, but as aspirations, not requirements.

QUESTION?

How can I ensure that my career goals support instead of subvert my life goals?
Communicate. If your life goals involve family, talk with the members, asking them to help you prioritize your time and assets. What do they need from you to meet their own goals? If they don't know, help them understand the importance of goals as well as their importance in your life. Have the same conversation with yourself. What do you need? With such an understanding, you can better prioritize your career efforts to balance your life.

Keeping Score

Imagine a baseball, football, or a golf game where no one kept score. What's the point? What would motivate the players and the fans? How would everyone know who won?

The same is true in sales. Keeping score helps you measure progress toward your goals. How you keep score depends on the specifics of the goals: prospects, customers, orders, territory, sales amount, and so on. For example, if your goal is to increase the number of new prospects you see each month, then your score card will measure prospects. If the goal is a level of income, the goal will be counted in dollars.

Measurable

As you establish goals, make sure that they are measurable. "A fantastic sales career" isn't a measurable goal. "Earning $100,000 a year in commission selling widgets" or "Becoming top salesperson in the office" are measurable goals. You will know when you arrive—just as the football player knows he's in the end zone.

Your goals can be measurable by stating them in terms of your objectives. That is, if the objective is financial, state the goal in financial terms. That makes it easier to keep score and to identify how close you are to your goal.

As you set goals, remember that various games have different ways of keeping score as well as different definitions for winning. Set your goals and keep your own score based on either the greatest number within a period (as many customers as possible in the next year) or as a set amount (dollars in sales). Just make sure that your sales goals are measurable.

In Writing

New Year's resolutions often melt before the snow does. As life moves on, it can be difficult to remember resolutions made just a few days or weeks ago. It's a good thing that they can be written down.

As you make your sales and life goals, record them somewhere. Make them as specific and measurable as possible. List them by priority. Include specific plans with them on how you expect to achieve these goals.

Also, be sure that you frequently refer to them. Post them as your computer screen saver or as the front page in your daily planning book. Remind yourself to read them daily or as appropriate.

Which goals should you be reading most frequently? The ones that most impact your daily life. That is, your goal may be to develop fifty new prospects this year, but it makes your job easier if you break it down into a bite-size goal: develop one new prospect this week. Post this goal on your weekly calendar and check it off when you've met your goal.

Commitment

Having a to-do list doesn't mean things will get done. That requires action. And action requires commitment. *Commitment* is a pledge or promise. When you commit to a relationship, you make a promise. When you commit to a goal, you make a pledge to take needed action.

One motivator for helping you develop commitment to a goal is to visualize the results of that goal. For example, if your goal is to increase your sales income this year by 25 percent over last year, imagine the benefits of doing so. Picture yourself being able to take more or better vacations, giving your family more security or better things, purchasing something you've always wanted. Use your desire to see results as motivation to make an appropriate commitment to your goals.

One other point: As your daily life begins to seem like an out-of-control roller coaster, make a fresh commitment to your life and career goals. They can be anchors that help you see the bigger plan in your life and how it relates to your daily activities. Your goals can keep you on track toward your values.

Tenacity

Tenacity is a college word for stubbornness. Actually, *tenacity* means to hold fast. When biting, a snapping turtle can be tenacious, locking its jaws on an object and not letting go. Life and careers sometimes require people to be tenacious about a goal or a dream, working around or through problems until desired results are reached.

Apply tenacity to your career and life goals. If you truly believe in them, fight for them, give them your best efforts, and don't give up until you've reached them. Once reached, like the snapping turtle, let go and move to your next goal.

Revising Goals

Life changes on a daily basis. Some of those changes can impact your goals. Should you be rigid or flexible about changing those goals as life changes?

The answer depends on the value of those goals and what type they are. Life situations may cut your available time to develop new prospects. You may need to revise your weekly goal of helping one new prospect. If the problem is longer term, you may have to even modify your goal of helping fifty new prospects this year. This is a *performance goal*.

Other goals are not tied to performance, but to knowledge. Your goal may be to better understand the technical side of widgets so that you can sell them to engineers. This is a *learning goal*. Though important, learning goals often are secondary to performance goals in sales careers.

FACT

A performance goal is one that measures performance, such as helping a specific number of customers or reaching an explicit income level. A learning goal helps you expand your knowledge, such as finishing courses for your degree or taking advanced classes in selling.

Should you be messing with your goals? Only if necessary to longer-term goals. That is, if events threaten one of your longer-term goals, consider revising specific shorter-term goals. If your goal is $100,000 in commissions this year and, due to an economic downturn, you'll need sixty new prospects in the year instead of fifty, adjust your short-term goal of one prospect a week to five a month.

Keep in mind that the function of goals is to take you to a desired destination. You may need to adjust smaller goals to meet larger ones. That's okay. In fact, it's expected. Life keeps changing, and those who adapt have the greatest opportunities to succeed.

CHAPTER 20

Selling Yourself

You are your greatest product. And you are the product that you know most about. So it's natural for you to sell yourself. In fact, as you build trust with customers you are selling your attributes of professionalism, honesty, and sincere helpfulness to others. But some people, even salespeople, have difficulty selling themselves to others. It can be a stumbling block to their careers. This chapter shows you how to sell yourself as an important product with proven services. It is an important step on the road to your success.

Selling Yourself Is Different

A professional salesperson can sell widgets all day long. With product knowledge and a keen interest in helping buyers make good choices, the salesperson can guide buyers through the selling process to solve specific problems. But when it comes to selling himself or herself, some salespeople choke up. Others oversell. What's the problem?

FACT

To be objective is to define something by observable facts. The definition is not influenced by emotions or prejudices. It means looking at yourself as an object, a physical thing. You can make objective observations about your person, your knowledge, and your skills without emotional or biased definitions. You can recognize and promote your features and benefits.

The problem is that it's easy to be objective about objects, but when you describe yourself, you are the subject *and* the object. A salesperson must be objective even when he or she is the subject. That's not an easy task for most people. It's a necessity for professional salespeople.

Know Yourself

Know thyself. This ancient aphorism suggests introspection or self-observation. It's an attempt to consider and reflect on your thoughts and feelings. Good advice.

However, you don't need to go that deep to become a better self-seller. Instead, you can consider yourself as you would a product that provides a service or benefit. You can be more objective. That task is easier than searching your soul, but it still isn't as easy as analyzing a widget. You are an intricate being that has qualities unknown in widgets: emotions. Understanding yourself *as a salesperson* requires that you analyze your skills and your goals.

Know Your Skills

If you haven't done so already, begin writing your professional sales resume. Consider what you have learned about sales from your reading and your experience. No one will read this version of your resume, so be as thorough as possible while still being objective.

Include on your personal resume knowledge, training, and experience that contributes to your selling skills. Consider the variety of your sales experiences as well as the types of products or services that you have sold. State facts in measurable terms. Write them down.

Think of yourself as a product. What are your features? What are the benefits of those features? What types of problems can your product (you) solve for others (your customers)? Include the features and benefits you have offered in prior selling or sales-related jobs. To know yourself objectively, you must know the extent and value of your skills.

Know Your Goals

Chapter 19 helped you define and establish your long- and short-term sales goals and your project goals. These goals, in part, help define you objectively. They are measurable indicators of what is important to your sales career and how you go about the process of success.

Your priorities, too, specify objective measurements of your sales goals and assets. By placing a high priority on Golden Rule Selling, you identify what is important to you and what you are striving to achieve in your professional life. Your desire is to sell as you want to be sold.

Knowing your goals also means analyzing them. How will you know if you've reached a goal if you don't use measurements? Your measurement and analysis of goals specifies who you are as a professional salesperson. Include met goals in your resume.

Be Your Friend

Some friends are subjective, looking at you in the light of their emotions. Everyone needs subjective friends; however, you also need objective ones. These are the types of friends that can be most helpful as you attempt to understand yourself and your qualities more objectively. Ask them for their opinions of you as a salesperson, a problem solver. Ask them why they believe so.

If you don't have an objective friend to help you understand this side of yourself, be your own objective friend. Attempt to remove emotions from your judgment as you consider your role as a professional salesperson. List your attributes in your self-resume. To sell yourself objectively you must first understand yourself impartially.

Selling Without Bragging

"Ice to the Inuit, the Brooklyn Bridge, I've sold it all! Yeah, I'm the greatest salesperson who ever lived!"

Why do some salespeople think that they have to elongate the truth? For many, it's compensation. They don't really believe in themselves, so they overcompensate by making statements that most buyers recognize as bragging. You're not that type of salesperson, but maybe you're concerned about sounding like you're bragging when you state your features and benefits. What can you do to maintain credibility when talking about yourself and what you sell? Be trustworthy. Make honest, accurate, and helpful statements that are true and verifiable. Earn your buyer's trust whether you are representing a product, a service, or yourself.

FACT

Bragging is boasting or talking about yourself. In its simplest form, bragging is acceptable and we all do it. However, some salespeople (and politicians) focus on talking about themselves when they should be discussing product. The difference between factual statements and bragging often is ego. As you sell, make sure that you are telling buyers what they need to hear rather than what you want to say.

Honesty

Chapter 2 offered a definition of honesty. *Honesty* is adherence to the facts, a refusal to lie, cheat, or steal. It is knowing as much as possible about the product or service that you sell—and not making things up if you don't know. It's how you want to be sold.

You someday may sell ice to the Inuit. Until then, be honest with your statements about yourself and your products. If a prospect or customer catches you in an untrue statement, your credibility and trust may end—along with the sale. Be honest in your dealings and your statements.

Accuracy

Accuracy is freedom from mistake or error. Facts are checked and presented without misleading the listener. As a professional salesperson, it is your job not only to offer information buyers need when making decisions, but also to be certain that information is accurate.

Unfortunately, facts can sometimes be adjusted by egos. Here's an example: In a race between two boats, the blue one finished before the red one. The owners of the blue boat stated the fact that it came in first. The owners of the red boat factually noted that theirs came in second—and added that the blue boat came in "next to last." Though factual, it misleads the listener. To reduce inaccuracy in selling yourself, make sure that your ego doesn't twist the facts to mislead your customers.

Helpfulness

Your job in sales is to help buyers buy. You can do so without bragging, boasting, or embellishing facts. In fact, buyers often recognize when salespeople are helpful without taking credit for it. Some will appreciate it sufficiently to recommend you to a potential buyer or to your employer. Being helpful without taking undue credit will establish you as a Golden Rule Seller.

Packaging Your Services

Just as the products and services that you sell require presentation, so do you. Whether you are selling yourself to your current employer (seeking a raise), a prospective employer (seeking a job), or to a new prospect (seeking a sale), you must package yourself as well as your products.

How can you package yourself? You can write an accurate and honest job description, develop a truthful resume, and document valuable credentials. You can help people understand the value of what you do without bragging.

Your Job Description

An accurate job description not only helps you focus on your primary tasks, it also guides others in identifying what they can expect from you. For example, "widget solution resource for industrial buyers in New England" is a focused job description that can help prospects understand what you do. It's easier to recognize the benefits of working with you than if you were to simply call yourself a "salesman."

Of course, you don't want to be misleading in your job description. Don't let your ego write the words "Greatest Salesperson on This or Any Planet." Stick with an honest, accurate, helpful job description. You'll use it in many ways, including in introductions to new prospects. You also may include it on your business cards and other promotional literature. It can help you describe yourself and guide others in defining you.

QUESTION?

Are there any widely recognized associations for salespeople?
Yes, there are. One is the National Association of Sales Professionals *(www.nasp.com)* or NASP. It has more than 50,000 individual and corporate members and offers a certification program based on sales experience, performance, education, continuing training, and professional and community service. The NASP also has standards of professional conduct and other trust-building opportunities. Other sales associations are established for specific businesses and industries.

Your Resume

Chapter 21 will help you find a variety of jobs in sales. It will cover how to develop a winning resume and cover letter as well as how to get it to the appropriate people. For now, know that packaging your services and selling yourself requires that you document your knowledge and experience in measurable terms. That's what your resume will be designed to do.

Your Credentials

Telling others, without bragging, of your features and benefits is a powerful way to sell yourself. However, it can be even more influential if it comes from others. For example, if you have earned a degree or accreditation related to what you sell, let others know. If you have customers who highly recommend you, ask for a written reference and make sure that hesitant prospects see it. Include these facts and references in your promotional literature, as appropriate. You may only be able to use recognized accreditation initials after your name (CE, CPA, CBM, PhD, etc.), but, if appropriate, these credentials can help you gain earned recognition and help sell yourself.

Building Your Track Record

As you grow and succeed in sales, you will build experience and meet measurable goals. You will be building a track record that you can point to as accomplishments. "I tripled sales levels within three years" isn't bragging; it's a verifiable fact that your employer and potential employers should know about you.

You can build your professional track record by keeping accurate records, winning sales awards, getting recommendations from clients and experts, and building your own self-confidence. These are important steps in selling yourself and building your sales career.

Keep Records

Chapter 9 showed you how to establish and maintain an effective record-keeping system. Using it, you can track prospects, customers, and sales. It can give you the specifics you need to show progress and success in your career.

Your sales records also can help motivate you as you step back periodically to see what progress you've made in selling. If you're not satisfied with the results, it can motivate you to do better—and possibly suggest where to start. Building and managing your records can guide you in your long and successful sales career.

Win Awards

Salespeople *love* awards. In most sales organizations, sales awards are handed out frequently. The purpose isn't to embarrass those who don't win, but to recognize those who do—and to motivate all salespeople.

The greatest awards for many salespeople are cash awards or bonuses. As many sales careers are measured in dollars sold or dollars earned, bonuses can motivate people to work harder. The bonus may come with a plaque or trophy for display. In any case, win as many awards as possible—especially ones that are significant to your customers, such as Top Home Seller.

Get Recommendations

As you build your sales career, you will get recommendations from your customers. Recommendations can come in letter form or as a list of people who will be advocates for you to others. If a customer strongly compliments you for your services, ask for a letter of recommendation. If needed, you can help draft the letter for them and get the customer's staff to put it on their letterhead. If they'd rather not write a letter, ask for approval to add the reference to a recommendation list that you give to prospects. Be certain that it is okay for others to call your reference and ask about your services. Few prospects actually make the call, but seeing a name on your list can influence their buying decision.

Build Confidence

Selling yourself is about more than facts. It also is an attitude of confidence. *Confidence* is a condition of self-reliance; it's a belief in your powers to stay in control of yourself and your situation. You need confidence in yourself, your product, your customers, and your goals.

Confidence is based on facts. You either have reasons to be confident or you don't. Some salespeople attempt to manufacture confidence from wishes rather than facts. They *want* to believe in themselves in all situations, but confidence requires facts to make it true.

On the positive side, most people have good reasons to be confident of their abilities to control many situations. It's not false bravado, it's the opportunity for confidence. You can believe in future success because of prior successes. You can build self-confidence.

FACT

Like to write? Consider writing an article for publications that your customers read. If published, it adds to your credentials. Be sure to send copies to customers and prospects. In addition to offering sound advice, an article makes clear that others recognize you as an expert. Don't like to write? Hire a ghostwriter or ask a promotional or technical writer in your office to assist you.

Cultivating Repeats and Referrals

One of the advantages of selling yourself well is that you will be more able to represent the products and services of others. You will develop customer trust by succeeding at solving problems for them. In addition, you will be building opportunities for repeat and referral business.

Repeat Business

You've worked hard to get and build your customer list. Often, it's an expensive proposition for you and your employer. You may spend dozens or even hundreds of hours attempting to turn a prospect into a customer, then into a top customer. Don't lose your investment.

A major rule in selling is: Lose a sale if you must, but never lose a customer. That's how you build repeat business. Be of service to your customers, even if it doesn't directly help your selling efforts. In doing so, you will discover something that all professional salespeople strive for: a business relationship of confidence. You will be trusted. You will have a distinct advantage over your competitors. You won't do anything for a sale, you'll do anything for a *customer*. That's Golden Rule Selling.

Referral Business

When the boss is happy, everyone's happy. That truism recognizes the power that bosses have over others in their business and fields of influence. If you can make the boss happy, you can use her power to reach those she influences in a positive way. How? By asking or suggesting that you get a referral to others.

As a professional salesperson, you will be paid in direct proportion to the value of the problems that you solve. If you solve small problems at the retail level, you will be paid a corresponding wage, typically less than double the minimum wage. If you solve large problems involving thousands or millions of dollars in products or services, you will be paid accordingly. In addition, you will gain confidence as you help others solve problems.

The best time to ask for a referral is when your customer is most happy with the solution you've provided. If you were able to get a thousand widgets to the customer in time for the holiday rush or to quickly get a technician out to the customer's plant to make an emergency repair, chances are good that you will get a statement of appreciation. "Thanks for your help. That saved us!" If you don't get it, coax it. "Was that helpful to you?"

You also can get referrals by making periodic calls to customers you don't see often. Maybe they are clients who automatically reorder what you sell and there is little need for you to visit them weekly. Instead, you make a weekly or monthly phone call to make sure that they still are satisfied with the products and services provided. If so, that's the time to ask for a referral.

- Thanks, Julio. Are there other buyers in your division that may benefit from my personal service?
- Mary, I'm going to call on your golfing buddy, Sarah. Can I mention that I've been serving your company for five years?
- Curt, can you recommend me to your boss? I'd like to meet with him about your company's national needs.

Make sure that the referrals you get are valuable to those who will receive them. You may need to ask a few questions of a prospect before using a referral because the prospect may not know or particularly like your reference. To measure the opportunity, you can ask the prospect something like: "Do you know Frank Jones of Allied Widgets?" Then follow through as appropriate depending on whether the prospect answers Yes, No, or comments in either direction.

Being a Problem Solver

The most important function of a salesperson is to solve problems for buyers. So it is vital that you become a professional problem solver for your customers. What the problem is and the solution offered depends on what you are selling and to whom and the buyer's ability to analyze problems. You can be a catalyst that helps buyers focus clearly on problems and discover valuable solutions.

Chapter 7 on people skills offered proven ideas for becoming a problem solver. The first step is to understand what your prospect or customer is telling you. The second is to learn how to resolve conflicts. The steps to understanding people are:

- Listen to what the person is saying.
- Read how the person is saying it.
- Relate or understand what is being communicated.
- Respond appropriately, either with further questions or possible solutions.

As needed, ask additional questions, get clarification, and make suggestions. Once possible solutions are offered, there may be conflicts or needed clarifications. To resolve conflicts:

- Get an agreement on the problem.
- Define and get an agreement on the areas of conflict or differences.
- Develop a resolution in partnership with the buyer.

As you grow your sales career, build your problem-solving skills and learn how to take confidence in your abilities as you sell yourself.

CHAPTER 21

Getting a Great Job in Sales

Sales can be one of the most rewarding careers available. Not only do you get to help others solve problems, you also can be paid well. In some positions, you can earn more than your boss—and the boss will be glad to write big checks because you are bringing in more business. So how can you get one of these great jobs in sales? This final chapter tells you where they are, how to get them, what credentials you'll need, how to develop your resume and prepare for the interview, and what to expect when you're hired. It's your ticket to a more rewarding life.

Benefits of a Sales Career

Congratulations! You've chosen or maybe even begun a career in sales. No matter where you begin, you may find that sales is a satisfying career choice for you. Unlike other jobs, a person doesn't get "stuck" in sales for very long. Either people love it and begin to grow or don't and find another job that is a better fit. Meantime, what they learn about sales can be applied in a variety of professional and personal situations throughout their lives.

There are no born salespeople. There are people who adapt to selling easier than others. However, with a sincere desire to serve and the patience to find the job that fits best, just about anyone can succeed as a salesperson.

Throughout this book you have read what it takes to succeed in sales by dealing honestly and building trust. Golden Rule Selling is a proven method of cleaning the tarnish from the title of salesperson. Sell as you want to be sold. It also can help you feel more comfortable with your new role as you understand the value of sales to all economies. Nothing happens until something is sold. The benefits of a sales career include service to others, a more flexible workday, potential income, and satisfaction.

Service

First, selling is a service. You may be offering a product or a service, but what you, as a salesperson, do is a service. Your service enriches other people's lives, both your customers' and your employers'. It also serves many others. If you sell cars, your efforts give jobs to those who make the cars and their parts, who create ads, and who work in the insurance, fuel, and travel industries. Whatever you offer for sale impacts many others in your neighborhood, your country, and around the world. You are a very necessary component of the modern economy.

Second, you are a problem solver. When you meet with a prospect, your job is to help that person identify and solve a specific problem. The dilemma may be to select the most appropriate refrigerator for the given needs and budget. Or you can assist the buyer in choosing a home, car, business, investment, or other important final decision. You do so by understanding the steps of problem solving as well as by guiding the buyer in making intelligent decisions.

Third, you can help people make their dreams come true. With a knowledge of local real estate laws, markets, and opportunities, you can assist young people in finding an affordable first home, guide older people in selecting the right house for retirement, and assist investors in choosing properties that help them reach their financial goals. Other sales jobs offer equal opportunities for guiding people in the realization of dreams. And you can do it as a Golden Rule Seller who sleeps well at night.

Flexibility

Salespeople typically aren't time-clock punchers or clock watchers. Instead, they see time as an ingredient of opportunity. The exception may be retail sales, where many salespeople begin and collect needed skills. Even so, retail sales can give employees hope for a better job that many other jobs in retailing don't. Fortunately, sales skills are portable, and what is learned at the retail level can be applied to selling most other products and services. Selling is not a dead-end job.

As you progress in your sales career, you will gain more independence. Instead of a boss standing over you and timing your lunch hour, your boss will look at one thing: results. If you're selling well, *how* you sell is less important. That doesn't mean you sell at any cost; that's not how *you* want to be sold. It does mean that you will increasingly be allowed to work how, when, and even where you want. Salespeople work for and are paid on results. Your lunch hour may be as productive as any other if you use that time to develop relationships that help others.

The challenge of flexibility is that you must increasingly become a self-manager, someone who sets the schedule, agenda, and plan. You do not rely on your boss to tell you when to go to lunch or what to do with your day—once you've proven yourself as a self-managing salesperson who delivers results. It's one of the great benefits of selling.

Rewards

Another important benefit of sales is the rewards available. Because many professional salespeople are paid based on results, they often can help write their own paycheck. That can be both good and bad, as sales slumps and economic downturns can also impact the paycheck, with little recourse except to work harder. As with time, professional sellers must learn to be self-managers of money. Many sales positions earn a base salary to cover the time for administrative duties, but these salaries typically are not a living wage.

An additional reward offered to many salespeople is the opportunity to travel. If travel is important to them or their employer, salespeople can see the world, flying first class and staying at the best hotels. However, travel can be a *requirement* of some sales jobs, making life more difficult for salespeople who prefer not to travel as much. Business travel isn't glamorous and usually allows little time for sightseeing. The workday is long, and the food is different. Travel is considered a reward for some salespeople, but not for all. Fortunately, those who enjoy travel can find sales jobs that match and those who dislike travel can stay closer to home.

Satisfaction

Another important benefit of selling is professional satisfaction. Golden Rule Sellers recognize their importance in the world economy as well as in individual lives. They find fulfillment in contributing to others. They offer their efforts as a service. It can be a significant reward.

In addition, salespeople benefit personally from the income and sense of accomplishment that their job offers.

ALERT!

One of the disadvantages of being a full-time salesperson is that you are in constant contact with a full-time salesperson: you. Salespeople have a tendency to talk themselves into buying things more readily than other consumers. They can justify the purchase of a new car; they can sell themselves. Be aware of this disadvantage as your sales income grows. Continue to be a smart buyer as your income grows.

How to Find the Best Jobs

As you've discovered, what matters most to employers is productivity. Can an employee bring to the company more than he costs? Many people are hired or fired based on the answer to this question. Some jobs aren't easily measured, so the price paid is conservative. Jobs that offer measurable results, especially higher results, are paid better.

Fortunately, sales jobs are often the most measurable and can offer the greatest ratio of cost-to-benefits. That's why many salespeople are paid so well. Employers know, for example, that an investment of $1 in a salesperson can return $5 in orders. It makes good business sense to pay productive salespeople well.

Measurable results works to your advantage. As a professional salesperson, you are offering a measurable and verifiable service that future employers can reference when considering your productivity and your pay. Measurable results also can be a problem. If your sales are low due to skill or market conditions, you may not get paid as much as you would at another job. You may be selling the wrong things or working for the wrong employer. Fortunately, there are millions of other sales opportunities awaiting your efforts and ambition.

Classifieds

The most common source of sales opportunities is newspaper classified ads. In any given issue, there may be dozens or even hundreds of job ads in the section titled SALES. They offer jobs ranging from minimum-wage canvassing to top sales positions. The trick can be sorting them out to determine which are appropriate for you.

ALERT!

Be aware that not all "sales" job ads are legitimate. Some will have you doing menial work for inconsequential commissions. Others require that you "invest" in their sales kit and training before you can start. And others are simply illegal or dishonest. Remember the adage: If it sounds too good to be true, it probably is. Don't waste your time on bogus jobs. Your selling skills are needed by people who will respect and reward you for them.

The Internet also offers thousands of sales jobs by type and location. A search for "sales" jobs may return more than five thousand listings. Before you begin your search, analyze the type of sales that you prefer, such as B2C or B2B (covered next), salary, commission, or both, and for what size company. These criteria will help you reduce the number of opportunities to those that best fit your goals. It will make the search easier.

Referrals

As you develop your career, you will get job referrals. Friends, relatives, business associates, and even customers will tell you of sales opportunities they've heard about. No matter the opportunity, hear it out. Listen to the speaker. It may or may not be what you are looking for, but it will honor the speaker if you give them your attention. And it may lead to a viable opportunity. Of course, if it is a current customer who is telling you about the opportunity, be especially careful that you don't, by your response, injure the business relationship.

If you do get a job opportunity from a connection, ask for a referral. That is, if your buddy tells you that his brother-in-law is sales manager for XYZ Widgets and needs a new salesperson, ask your buddy for a personal referral—a phone call or letter—to the sales manager. As you know, referrals can be powerful.

The Buzz

Salespeople typically are gregarious. They know everyone, hear everything, and go everywhere. Or so it seems. In your daily life—in a taxi, restaurant, store, at the office cooler—you will hear about employment opportunities. Or you may hear things on the local or national news that impact your industry, your employer, or competitor. They may be things that may bring you new job opportunities—or tell you that you'd better start looking right now.

Pay attention to the buzz. It can offer you knowledge that is invaluable in finding job opportunities. You are paid for what you know. You're also paid for *who* you know, so continue networking, listening, and asking—especially if you are looking for a better job in sales. Use your business and social contacts as a network to help you discover greater employment opportunities.

B2C or B2B

As you learned in Chapter 3, selling to individual and family consumers is called business-to-consumer (B2C) and selling to other businesses is business-to-business (B2B). There obviously is a difference in what and to whom you are selling. In addition, there is a difference in how you sell. You may discover, in your career, that you prefer one type of selling to the other. However, in fairness to your career, you should try both. You may learn that you have a preference or a gift for selling to one. But as you grow your skills and your life, the other may better fit your goals. Consider them both.

B2C

The majority of salespeople are selling B2C. And most of these are in retailing. They choose retailing because new sellers are consumers. They understand the buyer's problems and have experienced them. They are familiar with the products or services they offer. They can easily relate to their buyers—and that is a key to successful sales.

As you search for your first or tenth selling job, consider B2C. Because most things sold to consumers have smaller price tags—except homes and cars—the pay is also lower. However, learning to deal with the public at the retail level can help you develop skills to represent larger-ticket items.

As you've learned more about sales and yourself in this book and your experiences, consider whether selling B2C best fits your needs and goals. For the majority of salespeople, it does.

B2B

In most situations, B2B sales offers greater income opportunities than B2C. For this reason, many people start their careers selling to businesses. This is especially true for those who have specialized knowledge needed to make the sale. Trained engineers become sales engineers. Medical students take up pharmaceutical sales. These and similar jobs are only partially about selling; the other part is about knowledge.

Not all B2B sellers represent products. Some sell services. For example, you may discover that your forte is offering accounting services to small businesses or becoming a business broker. Consider your own interests, goals, and training as you choose between B2B and B2C, and between products and services. Your objective is to get a great sales job, one that fits you.

Where to Start

Once you've decided on the field and type of sales job, where should you start your search? Look around your current employment to determine what selling opportunities are available. Look also in your neighborhood, your community, within your network of friends and acquaintances. It's easier to start a new career where you have some familiarity. If you frequent a local hobby shop, a bookstore, a large retailer, or other sales outlet, consider whether you can meet your goals working there.

If you have specialized training, consider how you can put it to work. Maybe you have automotive repair experience or have worked in construction. Your degree may be in architecture or computer science. Use this training as credentials for your sales career. Selling requires knowledge.

Think about the products and services that you are most familiar with to identify sales employment opportunities. Look in your own community, but also look at products and services that are sold from your community to buyers in other areas. A local manufacturer may be your next employer. Now that you understand sales, consider the wide variety of markets for your selling skills.

Making the Transition

Once you've decided what selling job would be right for you, begin the transition toward it. For some, the move is simply to prepare a resume. For others, additional training or experience is required.

Maybe your career goal is to become a business broker, selling businesses to new owners. You can start from a variety of positions. You can begin working in retail and develop management skills and experience to better understand how businesses actually work. You can return to college and develop your business and accounting training to help analyze financial statements for business owners and buyers. You can apprentice to a successful business broker, learning the skills and technical information needed to represent sales. Or you may opt to become a licensed residential real estate agent and eventually transition into selling commercial real estate and businesses. You have many career paths toward an identified goal.

Preparing Your Resume

A resume is a selling document. It helps buyers (employers) understand the features and benefits of hiring you. It must clearly represent your credentials and your career goals to people with the authority to purchase them. How can you develop an effective resume?

Resumes and other employment documents have standardized components that employers want to see. In addition, there are proven formats for presenting your information. And there are focusing documents that help you target your resume toward specific jobs.

Resume Components

The components to most professional resumes are experience, credentials, references, and contact. The experience section tells employers what you've done. Credentials outline what you know or have been recognized for. References communicate what others say about you. Contact information tells how employers can communicate with you. Following are some proven tips for developing the components of your resume.

- Begin your experience component with the latest event and work backward.
- Only include experience that is relevant to the position for which you are applying.

- If you have other experience, summarize how it relates to your primary experience if it does.
- Use measurable terms: customers, dollars, percentages, etc.
- Make sure you get permission to use references before you list them.
- Offer multiple ways of contacting you including e-mail, voice, fax, and other methods. If appropriate, list days or hours that you are or are not available to discuss employment.

There are numerous books and online resources available on writing effective resumes. Make sure that the method or product that you use accurately represents you.

Chronological Resume

The chronological resume is popular, especially with people who are selling skills that don't need much elaboration. You worked at Bob's Widget Store as a retail clerk, then became a wholesale salesperson at Acme Widgets. The chronology of your jobs shows growth and increasing responsibility. Chronological resumes list your jobs and responsibilities by the dates that they occurred.

Chronological resumes are especially effective when the companies you've worked for and the positions you've had are recognizable. In addition, they can emphasize your longevity at jobs, showing that you are a stable employee. However, if you have moved from job to job, you may be better represented by a functional resume.

Functional Resume

A functional resume focuses on what you did rather than for whom. It will group your employment by functions. Here's where you've worked as a retail salesperson and here's where you worked in wholesale sales. Each entry will show progressive accomplishments, and they will be ordered to illustrate how you've grown in your sales career.

Functional resumes are useful as you develop your career in a specific trade. It also can help you show related background experience, such as your earlier work in the shipping department of Bob's Widget Store. Functional resumes are a little more difficult to write than chronological, but can be invaluable for presenting an image of professional growth across numerous opportunities that don't look as valuable if presented chronologically.

ALERT!

Lose the superlatives. Sales managers and human resource (HR) personnel are sophisticated buyers of salespeople. Don't try to sell them with phrases like "Fantastic salesperson" or "You won't be sorry." Instead, give them what other buyers want: factual and usable information. Give them specifics: "Increased sales by 45 percent in three months" or "Awarded Salesperson of the Year in a company with twenty-two offices worldwide." Sell yourself as you want to be known.

Combined Resume

For many professional positions, the chronological-functional resume format works best. It shows your growth in abilities and responsibilities. The combined resume is most effective if you have worked for fewer employers, but have risen in position. At Bob's Widget Store, you began in the shipping department, moved to retail clerk, then assistant manager.

The Cover Letter

The purpose of a resume is to earn an interview. The function of a cover letter is to get the resume read. It is a focusing tool. It bridges the gap between the employer's job description and your resume. Your resume can earn you numerous sales jobs. The cover letter will help the employer understand why you are the right candidate for their *specific* job.

There are four common elements in the typical resume:

1. Subject
2. Qualifications summary
3. Focused qualifications
4. Urge to action

For example:

- SUBJECT: Thank you for your considering my credentials as a sales manager for Acme Widgets.
- QUALIFICATIONS SUMMARY: I offer your firm five years' of progressive experience in selling to business clients. (Elaborate.)
- FOCUSED QUALIFICATIONS: Most importantly, I am a proven self-manager with experience helping other salespeople to reach their own and their employers' goals. (Elaborate.)
- URGE TO ACTION: Please contact me at your convenience to discuss your position further and to discover how I can help your business grow.

Your cover letter will be more detailed and relevant. The suggested outline can guide you in writing a focused letter that transitions between the job and you. It can help the employer buy what you are selling.

The Interview

The job interview is your opportunity to sell yourself face-to-face. There are numerous books on this important aspect of your career. This section highlights the most important things you should know about interviewing.

Prepare Yourself

Before your interview appointment, go over the job description or ad, and reread your cover letter and resume. These are the documents that your interviewer has and will base some of the interview upon. Consider what questions might come from these sources and be ready to answer them. For example, if your resume outlines your success selling widgets, be prepared to back it up with additional facts.

You also must be ready mentally and emotionally. Be focused on your interview and don't walk in thinking about the parking ticket you might get. Don't be late. Be neat and clean. Dress for success. Be confident in the outcome. Relax and enjoy this opportunity to present yourself as you learn about the opportunities. Remember that you are hiring an employer, not just she you.

Behavioral Interviews

Behavioral interviews are the most common. The interviewer will ask you a variety of open-ended questions to learn more about you as well as how you respond. Typical questions are:

- Tell me about the time when you had to make a very problematic sales decision.
- Give me an example of something innovative that you've done.
- Tell me how you've handled an irate customer.
- Give me an example of a time when you've had to walk away from a sale.
- Describe the situation when you've had to work with someone you didn't like.

These questions are intended to determine facts not presented in your resume. Be attentive to the type of questions asked, as they can help you better understand your employer. In addition, don't be afraid to ask for a clarification so that you can answer the question more accurately.

Stress Interviews

Stress interviews are used when the job requires the employee to handle stress well. This can be true in positions that interface with the public, such as sales and customer service. Your answer, often, is not as important as *how* you respond. Here are some examples:

- I'm not sure that you're responding well to me. Can you answer that question again?
- What would you do if you discovered that your boss was taking merchandise home?
- What do you think is wrong with the country today?
- How do you feel that this interview is going?

Your response should be thought out and not impulsive. In fact, the interviewer probably is trying to make you mad or upset in order to gauge your anger. As you know, anger has no place in the workplace. Be very careful that you don't take the bait.

QUESTION?

What questions can and cannot an interviewer ask?
Labor and antidiscrimination law states that employers cannot ask questions that may bias them about candidates on the basis of race, creed, religion, or gender. For the specifics of current labor laws, contact the U.S. Department of Labor *(www.dol.gov)*.

Ask Questions

Two sales are being made simultaneously at job interviews. You are selling yourself, and the interviewer should be selling the employer. That means you should be asking questions of the interviewer and others to discover what you can expect as an employee. In addition to salary and benefits, you can ask:

- How do you see me fitting into your company?
- What is the company's mission, and how is it doing toward fulfilling it?
- If hired, what opportunities for growth are available to me?
- Why should I not consider this job as my next?

You want to be sure of hiring your next employer. You want it to be a mutually profitable partnership that also fits into your long-term career and personal goals. You want your employer to give you a compelling reason to "buy."

Sales Career Success

That wasn't so difficult. Your resume and interview earned you an employment offer and you've accepted. Now what?

First, realize that finding the right job is similar to finding the right spouse. No matter how much research you do beforehand, there still are many aspects of the relationship that you don't yet understand. The key to developing a valuable relationship is understanding the power of compromise.

Compromise

To *compromise* is to mutually promise. Compromise isn't giving in; it's sharing. It's helping another reach goals as that person helps you reach yours. It's finding common grounds on which you can agree and respecting areas in which you cannot. It is a merger, a blend. It is how things are done successfully in both the business and personal worlds.

As you help your customers buy, as you help your employer sell, you will need to learn the value of compromise. No one gets his own way for very long. Uncompromising positions lead to gridlock, where nothing will get done—until there is compromise. Professional salespeople know this explicitly. They also know what is available for compromise and what is not.

Expectations

What do you expect from your sales job? What does your employer expect from you? These questions will be answered before you're hired. From that point, expectations may change, but they shouldn't do so significantly or easily. If you expect your employer to support your efforts, don't compromise that expectation. And if your employer expects you to put in a productive workday, don't compromise that expectation. Expect the best and give your best.

APPENDIX

Sales Glossary

Selling is about communications—with prospects, customers, suppliers, employers, competitors, and the public. This glossary of more than 150 business and sales terms can help you understand and be understood in the world of selling.

Account management

The process and discipline of working with accounts in order to build long-term, mutually beneficial business relationships.

Accounts payable

Money that you or your business owes to others.

Added value

The process of going the extra mile with a customer. Added value also is used to describe when products and services include additional features beyond what is generally desired by the customer at no additional cost.

Advocates

Those people in a customer's organization that a salesperson works with who support the recommendation being offered.

Agent

A person who has the authority or is empowered to represent a company or a company's products and services.

AIDA

Attention, Interest, Desire, Action.

B2B

A sales organization whose primary effort is selling to and doing business with other businesses.

B2C

A sales organization whose primary effort is selling to and doing business with consumers, or with individual users.

Base salary

The guaranteed portion of a salesperson's monetary compensation. Base salaries reward salespeople for their accumulated experience and overall selling efforts.

Benefit

The value experienced by the customer as a result of the purchase of a product or service. Salespeople who focus on communicating benefits and aligning those benefits to a customer's business objectives, increase the likelihood of gaining a sale.

Body language

The gestures, body movements, and mannerisms by which a person communicates their outlook or frame of mind.

Bonus

In sales compensation, a type of incentive payment, typically awarded when the salesperson or sales team achieves predetermined financial objectives.

Brainstorming

A methodology undertaken by a person or a team to solve a problem or to generate ideas by rapidly listing a variety of possible solutions and approaches.

Brand

A name, term, or symbol used to identify the products and services of the selling organization and to differentiate them from those of competitors.

Business cycle

A sequence of economic activities typically characterized by recessions, recovery, growth, and at times, decline.

Buyer

The person who purchases or procures the product or service you are selling. This person may also be the decision maker, but not necessarily.

Buying process

The steps a customer organization or a buyer actually takes in making a purchase for a product or service.

Buying signal

A statement or indication from a prospect or customer that suggests she or he is considering making a purchase.

Call

A visit or meeting with a customer or prospect.

Canvass

Another word for the activity of prospecting.

Cash flow

The cash or collected revenues being generated by a firm during a given period. Also considered the level of money projected to be available for other transactions after deducting expenses from income sources.

Catalyst
In sales organizations, a salesperson or sales manager who stimulates positive and creative change, and who causes a process or event to happen through both direct and indirect efforts.

Channel
The means by which an organization sells their products. A company who uses their own sales force is said to have a "direct channel." Other channels include distributors, wholesalers, retailers, agencies, etc.

C-Level Executive
An executive in the organization whose title often is preceded by the word "chief," e.g., CEO, COO, CIO, CFO, etc.

Close
The point at which the salesperson asks for a commitment to purchase the product or service being evaluated.

Closed questions
Questions that provide the customer with a choice among alternatives. Often these are brief answer, Yes-No questions.

Coach
A person who guides, helps, and teaches in order to enable a salesperson's success.

Cold call
A visit made to an organization without having the benefit of an appointment.

Commission
In sales compensation, this refers to a type of payment or revenue sharing resulting from achieving a sale or attaining a given sales level. Commissions are typically expressed as a percentage of the selling price for the product sold.

Commodity
Competing products or services that bear the same or similar characteristics.

Competitive advantage
Those areas deemed to have preferential value to a customer versus a similar competitive product.

Concerns
The issues a customer brings up when a salesperson recommends ideas or options for a customer to purchase.

Confidentiality agreements
Agreements between two parties affirming that the information exchanged during a relationship is maintained within the confines of the agreement, and not shared beyond the agreement.

Consultative selling
A selling methodology where the customer is seeking advice from the selling organization on a path forward.

Contact-management system
The use of technology to track customer contact information, activity, and history.

Conversion
The methodology used to convert a customer's use of one product or supplier to another.

Conversion ratio
A measure used in sales organizations where gaining sales is a function of taking away business from competition, this ratio is usually a measure of the number of targeted opportunities secured versus the number of opportunities pursued.

Cost-benefit analysis
The method a customer (or sales organization) follows to assess the viability of a recommendation, by examining the total amount of money, time, and resources used relative to the value being received.

Cost of goods sold
On an income statement, the cost of purchasing raw materials and manufacturing the finished goods.

Cost of sales
For sales compensation purposes, the percentage calculation of total sales generated by the sales force divided by the total compensation costs of the sales force.

Cross-selling
A methodology in selling where a customer need lends itself to a possible need for another product or service.

Customer profile
A document that outlines the critical information about a particular customer.

Customer relationship management (CRM)
The process used internally to manage customer relationships.

Decision maker
The person most responsible for deciding the outcome of a salesperson's or selling organization's proposal.

Demonstration call
A customer call involving a salesperson and a manager, where the manager's role is to teach and show the salesperson a technique or approach the salesperson wishes to improve.

Desire
A longing, a wish. Strong desire drives ambition and performance.

Direct marketing
The process of marketing directly to an end user. The most known form of direct marketing is direct mail.

Discount
A reduced amount (typically from list price) that is offered by the seller or the selling organization to encourage purchase of a product being offered.

Distributor
An indirect sales channel that markets or sells a product or service. Distributors are used by selling organizations to capitalize on the distributor's local presence and capacity to support the manufacturer.

Draw
In sales compensation, a cash advance, in anticipation of future sales performance.

E-business
Business conducted via the Internet.

Economic benefit
The financial value of your product or service. This is tied closely to the term ROI, or Return on Investment.

Elevator speech
Sales slang for a short, thirty-second overview of who your company is, what it does, and what you do, with the intent of gaining an individual's interest to learn more and seek further discussion.

Empathy
The ability to communicate and understand someone else's situation and feelings.

Executive summary
Often considered the first page or first several pages in a major proposal, summarizing the key issues, solution, and value a customer will receive by implementing the recommendation.

Farmer
A slang term in sales referring to a salesperson whose primary job is to maintain and grow business with existing customers, versus acquiring new customers.

Feature
A characteristic of your product or service. The distinct parts of your product or service that can be described.

Focus group
A small group selected to participate in open discussions on a topic in order to solicit opinions about that topic or area.

Forecast
A salesperson or a sales manager's prediction of sales as a result of analyzing where opportunities are in the sales cycle.

Gatekeeper
Typically the person who controls access to someone you are trying to meet with.

General benefit statement

Often used in the beginning of a sales call, the general benefit statement highlights the value or benefit that may occur as a result of the salesperson's visit, or of the selling organization and the customer working together.

Goal

The end toward which a salesperson or sales organization is headed. The ability to set and execute against ambitious yet realistic goals is considered the essential foundation to a sales organization's success.

Golden Rule Selling

Selling as you want be sold. Applying what you know as a buyer to becoming a better seller.

Gross margin

The difference between the cost of goods sold and the price at which it was sold.

Guarantee

In sales compensation, a term used to denote that portion of the salesperson's compensation mix that is assured, regardless of level of performance.

Hot buttons

Those areas which, if known, can be used to position solutions to align with a decision maker's most important criteria for selection.

Inbound call

In telesales, a call that comes into the call center.

Incentives

Any form of compensation or reward made to a salesperson or sales team to influence sales results: bonuses, commissions, trips, catalog award points, etc.

Influencer

An individual who has sway over how a decision is made but is not the direct decision maker.

Inquiries

Contacts by potential buyers to find out more about what you or your organization does. When qualified, they become qualified leads.

Inside sales

Selling typically done over the phone.

Just-in-time (JIT)

The availability of goods and services as needed, as opposed to keeping stored inventory.

Key performance indicator (KPI)

A primary measure an organization uses to measure its own internal performance.

Key players

The men and women inside an account who are essential to the selling organization gaining a positive decision.

KISS

Acronym for Keep It Simple Stupid, a reminder to sales professionals that keeping things simple and making it easy to buy will tend to generate greater results in the long term.

Lead

An opportunity that surfaces for your product or service. The opportunity may surface via response to advertisements, referrals from your network, or through your own initiatives in a market.

Lead conversion

The process of converting leads into viable business opportunities.

Leave-behind

A sample or piece of written material about your product or service that you leave with a customer during or at the end of a call.

Level of influence

The degree of influence an individual has on the decision-making process.

Leverage

An action a salesperson may take to position the exclusive advantage of a product or service.

Loss leader

A product or service that is discounted significantly from list price and used, typically for a limited period, to influence purchase behavior of other products.

Manufacturer's representative (rep)

An independent salesperson who represents your organization and noncompeting products.

Margin

The difference between the cost of a product and its selling price, expressed as a percentage or dollars-per-unit.

Marketing

The process followed by organizations to satisfy the needs, wants, and demands of their customers through the application and promotion of products and services that satisfy those customer requirements.

Market penetration

Your ability to enter and gain share in a specified market, generally measured in percentage terms.

Market share

An organization's portion of the total market, typically expressed as a percentage.

Markup

The amount added to the cost price of a product or service to determine its selling price.

Maximum

In sales compensation, this refers to the maximum a salesperson can earn in a given period.

Mission statement

An organization's purpose for being. Mission statements typically communicate what an organization values.

Mix

In sales compensation, mix refers to the various elements of the compensation plan, often expressed as percentages of the targeted total compensation.

Needs

That which is required or wanted by a customer. The ability of a sales professional to service viable, "must address" needs (versus wants) leads to greater sales success.

Needs analysis

The process of formally evaluating a customer's needs and requirements.

Networking

The process of developing and maintaining alliances externally and internally with a wide variety of contacts who can provide information, insight, help, and access to others.

Niche market

A unique segment of the market a selling organization is targeted toward. This unique segment, if served well, can provide areas of distinctive competitive value.

Objection

A term often used in sales when a customer challenges or rejects a salesperson's idea or suggestion, or when the customer communicates issues that will prevent the sale from moving forward.

OEM

Original equipment manufacturer.

Open-ended questions

Questions that encourage the customer to respond freely. They include questions of what, why, and how that require more information from the customer than a simple yes or no answer.

Opening statement

The words used to initiate a conversation with a customer or prospect. Superior salespeople plan their opening statements carefully, as they can often set the tone for the remaining portion of the sales call.

Opportunity

A situation, condition, or circumstance where you have the potential to meet a customer's business requirements.

Outbound call
A call made by a telesalesperson to a prospect for your product or service.

Outside sales
Selling primarily from the field, or outside of the organization's primary place of business.

Performance-based pay
In sales compensation, this term refers to the philosophy of paying incentives based on achieving predetermined levels of performance.

Potential
A salesperson's assessment, in dollars, units, and/or relationship, of doing business with a particular customer.

Precall plan
The salesperson's written description of the objectives for the call, the key questions that will be asked during the call, and the strategy that will be taken in order to move the sales cycle forward.

Pricing practices
The methods and strategies an organization uses to price their products and services in the marketplace.

Probability
The likelihood that a given event will occur.

Problem analysis
The process of examining the symptoms, conditions, and possible causes of a problem in order to define alternatives for a possible resolution.

Process
A series of steps bringing about a desired result.

Pro forma
Based on a given set of assumptions. In sales, it is used to describe a hypothetical income statement for a customer.

Project management
The science and discipline of planning, organizing, overseeing, managing, and tracking projects in an organization.

Proposal
An offer that is made, both verbally and in written form, between the selling organization and the customer organization in order to initiate business activity.

Prospect
A potential buyer or customer for your products and/or services.

Prospecting
The process of searching for and finding qualified customers for your product or service.

Qualify
To assess whether or not a customer or an opportunity represents a potential fit for your product or service.

Quota
A quantifiable goal or series of objectives that reflect what a salesperson must achieve in sales during the upcoming financial period.

Rainmaker
A sales slang term given to the most impressive, prodigious, consistent, high-producing salesperson or salespeople in a selling organization.

Referral
A customer's direction or recommendation to another party, internal or external, that may benefit from your product or service.

Relational Selling
A selling methodology where the customer values most the relationship with the salesperson or the sales organization.

Retention
The keeping of consumers or organizations as customers.

Request for proposal (RFP)
A document used by customers to assess respondents' solutions to specified needs.

Return on investment (ROI)
The amount, expressed as a percentage, earned by an investment.

Sales aid
A tool that supports or helps the sales professional gain an advantage.

Sales assistant
A person whose primary objective is to actively assist in the sales and servicing process, allowing sales professionals more time to find and support new business opportunities.

Sales cycle
The set of steps an organization believes is needed to make a sale.

Sales philosophy
An organization's point of view on how selling should occur.

Sales yield
A measure used by selling organizations to track the results of selling efforts.

Segmentation
The division of a market into discrete units with similar characteristics.

Selling system
The elements of a selling organization that, looked at as a group, comprise complementary components defining how the organization sells.

Smoke screen
Sales slang for a statement a customer makes that conceals the customer's actual plans or intentions.

Solution
A summary of how a salesperson will address the customer's problem or opportunity.

Stall
To avoid making a decision and, in essence, put the sales process on hold.

Strategic account manager (SAM)
The relationship manager who oversees and is responsible for strategizing, managing, and fulfilling expectations of selling and customer organizations.

Strategic selling
A selling methodology considered by some to represent the most complex type of sale due to either the number of people who are typically involved in the sales process or the nature and scope of the relationship.

Strategy
The planning of the use of all the resources available to a company or a salesperson to achieve a stated goal or purpose.

Suspect
A prospect that has not been qualified yet.

Synergy
The state in a sales organization when all parties involved feel that there is greater value in the collaboration with each other than in the individual contributions.

Target account
An account a salesperson or the sales organization has selected to focus effort and resources on.

Target market
The set of customers or organizations that you deem most viable for your product or service.

Team selling
The process of selling as a team. This term might mean many things to different people. When team selling truly occurs, there are predefined roles and tactics on the part of the sales team to acquire a given piece of business.

Telesales
The process of selling over the phone. This typically refers to calls made by inside salespeople from outbound call centers.

Territory design
The process that sales managers engage in to allocate territories in order to ensure that potential exists and to balance opportunities among their sales team members.

Testimonial

A verbal or written expression of the value a customer received by having used or purchased your product, service, or overall solution.

Test market

The process of evaluating the appeal of a product or service by selecting cities, customers, and locations in which to introduce the product or service and monitor its receptivity by the intended users.

Tool kit

A term used by salespeople to describe the various tools they use to make a sale.

Transactional selling

A selling methodology where the customer already knows precisely what he or she wants.

Value

The relative worth, utility, importance, or financial benefit that is assigned by a buyer to the product or service an organization sells.

Vertical market

A market characterized by certain unique characteristics.

White paper

A document, typically less than twelve pages in length, that describes your organization's point of view in areas that may be of interest to the customer.

Wholesaler

Sales channel typically engaged in the sale of goods in large quantities for resale.

Word-of-mouth

A powerful method of selling products by creating interest, desire, or incentives for current users to promote the use of your product and service to others.

Index

THE EVERYTHING SERIES!

BUSINESS & PERSONAL FINANCE

Everything® Accounting Book
Everything® Budgeting Book, 2nd Ed.
Everything® Business Planning Book
Everything® Coaching and Mentoring Book, 2nd Ed.
Everything® Fundraising Book
Everything® Get Out of Debt Book
Everything® Grant Writing Book, 2nd Ed.
Everything® Guide to Buying Foreclosures
Everything® Guide to Fundraising, $15.95
Everything® Guide to Mortgages
Everything® Guide to Personal Finance for Single Mothers
Everything® Home-Based Business Book, 2nd Ed.
Everything® Homebuying Book, 3rd Ed., $15.95
Everything® Homeselling Book, 2nd Ed.
Everything® Human Resource Management Book
Everything® Improve Your Credit Book
Everything® Investing Book, 2nd Ed.
Everything® Landlording Book
Everything® Leadership Book, 2nd Ed.
Everything® Managing People Book, 2nd Ed.
Everything® Negotiating Book
Everything® Online Auctions Book
Everything® Online Business Book
Everything® Personal Finance Book
Everything® Personal Finance in Your 20s & 30s Book, 2nd Ed.
Everything® Personal Finance in Your 40s & 50s Book, $15.95
Everything® Project Management Book, 2nd Ed.
Everything® Real Estate Investing Book
Everything® Retirement Planning Book
Everything® Robert's Rules Book, $7.95
Everything® Selling Book
Everything® Start Your Own Business Book, 2nd Ed.
Everything® Wills & Estate Planning Book

COOKING

Everything® Barbecue Cookbook
Everything® Bartender's Book, 2nd Ed., $9.95
Everything® Calorie Counting Cookbook
Everything® Cheese Book
Everything® Chinese Cookbook
Everything® Classic Recipes Book
Everything® Cocktail Parties & Drinks Book
Everything® College Cookbook
Everything® Cooking for Baby and Toddler Book
Everything® Diabetes Cookbook
Everything® Easy Gourmet Cookbook
Everything® Fondue Cookbook
Everything® Food Allergy Cookbook, $15.95
Everything® Fondue Party Book
Everything® Gluten-Free Cookbook
Everything® Glycemic Index Cookbook
Everything® Grilling Cookbook
Everything® Healthy Cooking for Parties Book, $15.95
Everything® Holiday Cookbook
Everything® Indian Cookbook
Everything® Lactose-Free Cookbook
Everything® Low-Cholesterol Cookbook

Everything® Low-Fat High-Flavor Cookbook, 2nd Ed., $15.95
Everything® Low-Salt Cookbook
Everything® Meals for a Month Cookbook
Everything® Meals on a Budget Cookbook
Everything® Mediterranean Cookbook
Everything® Mexican Cookbook
Everything® No Trans Fat Cookbook
Everything® One-Pot Cookbook, 2nd Ed., $15.95
Everything® Organic Cooking for Baby & Toddler Book, $15.95
Everything® Pizza Cookbook
Everything® Quick Meals Cookbook, 2nd Ed., $15.95
Everything® Slow Cooker Cookbook
Everything® Slow Cooking for a Crowd Cookbook
Everything® Soup Cookbook
Everything® Stir-Fry Cookbook
Everything® Sugar-Free Cookbook
Everything® Tapas and Small Plates Cookbook
Everything® Tex-Mex Cookbook
Everything® Thai Cookbook
Everything® Vegetarian Cookbook
Everything® Whole-Grain, High-Fiber Cookbook
Everything® Wild Game Cookbook
Everything® Wine Book, 2nd Ed.

GAMES

Everything® 15-Minute Sudoku Book, $9.95
Everything® 30-Minute Sudoku Book, $9.95
Everything® Bible Crosswords Book, $9.95
Everything® Blackjack Strategy Book
Everything® Brain Strain Book, $9.95
Everything® Bridge Book
Everything® Card Games Book
Everything® Card Tricks Book, $9.95
Everything® Casino Gambling Book, 2nd Ed.
Everything® Chess Basics Book
Everything® Christmas Crosswords Book, $9.95
Everything® Craps Strategy Book
Everything® Crossword and Puzzle Book
Everything® Crosswords and Puzzles for Quote Lovers Book, $9.95
Everything® Crossword Challenge Book
Everything® Crosswords for the Beach Book, $9.95
Everything® Cryptic Crosswords Book, $9.95
Everything® Cryptograms Book, $9.95
Everything® Easy Crosswords Book
Everything® Easy Kakuro Book, $9.95
Everything® Easy Large-Print Crosswords Book
Everything® Games Book, 2nd Ed.
Everything® Giant Book of Crosswords
Everything® Giant Sudoku Book, $9.95
Everything® Giant Word Search Book
Everything® Kakuro Challenge Book, $9.95
Everything® Large-Print Crossword Challenge Book
Everything® Large-Print Crosswords Book
Everything® Large-Print Travel Crosswords Book
Everything® Lateral Thinking Puzzles Book, $9.95
Everything® Literary Crosswords Book, $9.95
Everything® Mazes Book
Everything® Memory Booster Puzzles Book, $9.95

Everything® Movie Crosswords Book, $9.95
Everything® Music Crosswords Book, $9.95
Everything® Online Poker Book
Everything® Pencil Puzzles Book, $9.95
Everything® Poker Strategy Book
Everything® Pool & Billiards Book
Everything® Puzzles for Commuters Book, $9.95
Everything® Puzzles for Dog Lovers Book, $9.95
Everything® Sports Crosswords Book, $9.95
Everything® Test Your IQ Book, $9.95
Everything® Texas Hold 'Em Book, $9.95
Everything® Travel Crosswords Book, $9.95
Everything® Travel Mazes Book, $9.95
Everything® Travel Word Search Book, $9.95
Everything® TV Crosswords Book, $9.95
Everything® Word Games Challenge Book
Everything® Word Scramble Book
Everything® Word Search Book

HEALTH

Everything® Alzheimer's Book
Everything® Diabetes Book
Everything® First Aid Book, $9.95
Everything® Green Living Book
Everything® Health Guide to Addiction and Recovery
Everything® Health Guide to Adult Bipolar Disorder
Everything® Health Guide to Arthritis
Everything® Health Guide to Controlling Anxiety
Everything® Health Guide to Depression
Everything® Health Guide to Diabetes, 2nd Ed.
Everything® Health Guide to Fibromyalgia
Everything® Health Guide to Menopause, 2nd Ed.
Everything® Health Guide to Migraines
Everything® Health Guide to Multiple Sclerosis
Everything® Health Guide to OCD
Everything® Health Guide to PMS
Everything® Health Guide to Postpartum Care
Everything® Health Guide to Thyroid Disease
Everything® Hypnosis Book
Everything® Low Cholesterol Book
Everything® Menopause Book
Everything® Nutrition Book
Everything® Reflexology Book
Everything® Stress Management Book
Everything® Superfoods Book, $15.95

HISTORY

Everything® American Government Book
Everything® American History Book, 2nd Ed.
Everything® American Revolution Book, $15.95
Everything® Civil War Book
Everything® Freemasons Book
Everything® Irish History & Heritage Book
Everything® World War II Book, 2nd Ed.

HOBBIES

Everything® Candlemaking Book
Everything® Cartooning Book
Everything® Coin Collecting Book
Everything® Digital Photography Book, 2nd Ed.

Everything® Drawing Book
Everything® Family Tree Book, 2nd Ed.
Everything® Guide to Online Genealogy, $15.95
Everything® Knitting Book
Everything® Knots Book
Everything® Photography Book
Everything® Quilting Book
Everything® Sewing Book
Everything® Soapmaking Book, 2nd Ed.
Everything® Woodworking Book

HOME IMPROVEMENT

Everything® Feng Shui Book
Everything® Feng Shui Decluttering Book, $9.95
Everything® Fix-It Book
Everything® Green Living Book
Everything® Home Decorating Book
Everything® Home Storage Solutions Book
Everything® Homebuilding Book
Everything® Organize Your Home Book, 2nd Ed.

KIDS' BOOKS

All titles are $7.95

Everything® Fairy Tales Book, $14.95
Everything® Kids' Animal Puzzle & Activity Book
Everything® Kids' Astronomy Book
Everything® Kids' Baseball Book, 5th Ed.
Everything® Kids' Bible Trivia Book
Everything® Kids' Bugs Book
Everything® Kids' Cars and Trucks Puzzle and Activity Book
Everything® Kids' Christmas Puzzle & Activity Book
Everything® Kids' Connect the Dots
        Puzzle and Activity Book
Everything® Kids' Cookbook, 2nd Ed.
Everything® Kids' Crazy Puzzles Book
Everything® Kids' Dinosaurs Book
Everything® Kids' Dragons Puzzle and Activity Book
Everything® Kids' Environment Book $7.95
Everything® Kids' Fairies Puzzle and Activity Book
Everything® Kids' First Spanish Puzzle and Activity Book
Everything® Kids' Football Book
Everything® Kids' Geography Book
Everything® Kids' Gross Cookbook
Everything® Kids' Gross Hidden Pictures Book
Everything® Kids' Gross Jokes Book
Everything® Kids' Gross Mazes Book
Everything® Kids' Gross Puzzle & Activity Book
Everything® Kids' Halloween Puzzle & Activity Book
Everything® Kids' Hanukkah Puzzle and Activity Book
Everything® Kids' Hidden Pictures Book
Everything® Kids' Horses Book
Everything® Kids' Joke Book
Everything® Kids' Knock Knock Book
Everything® Kids' Learning French Book
Everything® Kids' Learning Spanish Book
Everything® Kids' Magical Science Experiments Book
Everything® Kids' Math Puzzles Book
Everything® Kids' Mazes Book
Everything® Kids' Money Book, 2nd Ed.
**Everything® Kids' Mummies, Pharaoh's, and Pyramids
        Puzzle and Activity Book**
Everything® Kids' Nature Book
Everything® Kids' Pirates Puzzle and Activity Book
Everything® Kids' Presidents Book
Everything® Kids' Princess Puzzle and Activity Book
Everything® Kids' Puzzle Book

Everything® Kids' Racecars Puzzle and Activity Book
Everything® Kids' Riddles & Brain Teasers Book
Everything® Kids' Science Experiments Book
Everything® Kids' Sharks Book
Everything® Kids' Soccer Book
Everything® Kids' Spelling Book
Everything® Kids' Spies Puzzle and Activity Book
Everything® Kids' States Book
Everything® Kids' Travel Activity Book
Everything® Kids' Word Search Puzzle and Activity Book

LANGUAGE

Everything® Conversational Japanese Book with CD, $19.95
Everything® French Grammar Book
Everything® French Phrase Book, $9.95
Everything® French Verb Book, $9.95
Everything® German Phrase Book, $9.95
Everything® German Practice Book with CD, $19.95
Everything® Inglés Book
Everything® Intermediate Spanish Book with CD, $19.95
Everything® Italian Phrase Book, $9.95
Everything® Italian Practice Book with CD, $19.95
Everything® Learning Brazilian Portuguese Book with CD, $19.95
Everything® Learning French Book with CD, 2nd Ed., $19.95
Everything® Learning German Book
Everything® Learning Italian Book
Everything® Learning Latin Book
Everything® Learning Russian Book with CD, $19.95
Everything® Learning Spanish Book
Everything® Learning Spanish Book with CD, 2nd Ed., $19.95
Everything® Russian Practice Book with CD, $19.95
Everything® Sign Language Book, $15.95
Everything® Spanish Grammar Book
Everything® Spanish Phrase Book, $9.95
Everything® Spanish Practice Book with CD, $19.95
Everything® Spanish Verb Book, $9.95
Everything® Speaking Mandarin Chinese Book with CD, $19.95

MUSIC

Everything® Bass Guitar Book with CD, $19.95
Everything® Drums Book with CD, $19.95
Everything® Guitar Book with CD, 2nd Ed., $19.95
Everything® Guitar Chords Book with CD, $19.95
Everything® Guitar Scales Book with CD, $19.95
Everything® Harmonica Book with CD, $15.95
Everything® Home Recording Book
Everything® Music Theory Book with CD, $19.95
Everything® Reading Music Book with CD, $19.95
Everything® Rock & Blues Guitar Book with CD, $19.95
Everything® Rock & Blues Piano Book with CD, $19.95
Everything® Rock Drums Book with CD, $19.95
Everything® Singing Book with CD, $19.95
Everything® Songwriting Book

NEW AGE

Everything® Astrology Book, 2nd Ed.
Everything® Birthday Personology Book
Everything® Celtic Wisdom Book, $15.95
Everything® Dreams Book, 2nd Ed.
Everything® Law of Attraction Book, $15.95
Everything® Love Signs Book, $9.95
Everything® Love Spells Book, $9.95
Everything® Palmistry Book
Everything® Psychic Book
Everything® Reiki Book

Everything® Sex Signs Book, $9.95
Everything® Spells & Charms Book, 2nd Ed.
Everything® Tarot Book, 2nd Ed.
Everything® Toltec Wisdom Book
Everything® Wicca & Witchcraft Book, 2nd Ed.

PARENTING

Everything® Baby Names Book, 2nd Ed.
Everything® Baby Shower Book, 2nd Ed.
Everything® Baby Sign Language Book with DVD
Everything® Baby's First Year Book
Everything® Birthing Book
Everything® Breastfeeding Book
Everything® Father-to-Be Book
Everything® Father's First Year Book
Everything® Get Ready for Baby Book, 2nd Ed.
Everything® Get Your Baby to Sleep Book, $9.95
Everything® Getting Pregnant Book
Everything® Guide to Pregnancy Over 35
Everything® Guide to Raising a One-Year-Old
Everything® Guide to Raising a Two-Year-Old
Everything® Guide to Raising Adolescent Boys
Everything® Guide to Raising Adolescent Girls
Everything® Mother's First Year Book
Everything® Parent's Guide to Childhood Illnesses
Everything® Parent's Guide to Children and Divorce
Everything® Parent's Guide to Children with ADD/ADHD
Everything® Parent's Guide to Children with Asperger's
        Syndrome
Everything® Parent's Guide to Children with Anxiety
Everything® Parent's Guide to Children with Asthma
Everything® Parent's Guide to Children with Autism
Everything® Parent's Guide to Children with Bipolar Disorder
Everything® Parent's Guide to Children with Depression
Everything® Parent's Guide to Children with Dyslexia
Everything® Parent's Guide to Children with Juvenile Diabetes
Everything® Parent's Guide to Children with OCD
Everything® Parent's Guide to Positive Discipline
Everything® Parent's Guide to Raising Boys
Everything® Parent's Guide to Raising Girls
Everything® Parent's Guide to Raising Siblings
**Everything® Parent's Guide to Raising Your
        Adopted Child**
Everything® Parent's Guide to Sensory Integration Disorder
Everything® Parent's Guide to Tantrums
Everything® Parent's Guide to the Strong-Willed Child
Everything® Parenting a Teenager Book
Everything® Potty Training Book, $9.95
Everything® Pregnancy Book, 3rd Ed.
Everything® Pregnancy Fitness Book
Everything® Pregnancy Nutrition Book
Everything® Pregnancy Organizer, 2nd Ed., $16.95
Everything® Toddler Activities Book
Everything® Toddler Book
Everything® Tween Book
Everything® Twins, Triplets, and More Book

PETS

Everything® Aquarium Book
Everything® Boxer Book
Everything® Cat Book, 2nd Ed.
Everything® Chihuahua Book
Everything® Cooking for Dogs Book
Everything® Dachshund Book
Everything® Dog Book, 2nd Ed.
Everything® Dog Grooming Book

Everything® Dog Obedience Book
Everything® Dog Owner's Organizer, $16.95
Everything® Dog Training and Tricks Book
Everything® German Shepherd Book
Everything® Golden Retriever Book
Everything® Horse Book, 2nd Ed., $15.95
Everything® Horse Care Book
Everything® Horseback Riding Book
Everything® Labrador Retriever Book
Everything® Poodle Book
Everything® Pug Book
Everything® Puppy Book
Everything® Small Dogs Book
Everything® Tropical Fish Book
Everything® Yorkshire Terrier Book

REFERENCE

Everything® American Presidents Book
Everything® Blogging Book
Everything® Build Your Vocabulary Book, $9.95
Everything® Car Care Book
Everything® Classical Mythology Book
Everything® Da Vinci Book
Everything® Einstein Book
Everything® Enneagram Book
Everything® Etiquette Book, 2nd Ed.
Everything® Family Christmas Book, $15.95
Everything® Guide to C. S. Lewis & Narnia
Everything® Guide to Divorce, 2nd Ed., $15.95
Everything® Guide to Edgar Allan Poe
Everything® Guide to Understanding Philosophy
Everything® Inventions and Patents Book
Everything® Jacqueline Kennedy Onassis Book
Everything® John F. Kennedy Book
Everything® Mafia Book
Everything® Martin Luther King Jr. Book
Everything® Pirates Book
Everything® Private Investigation Book
Everything® Psychology Book
Everything® Public Speaking Book, $9.95
Everything® Shakespeare Book, 2nd Ed.

RELIGION

Everything® Angels Book
Everything® Bible Book
Everything® Bible Study Book with CD, $19.95
Everything® Buddhism Book
Everything® Catholicism Book
Everything® Christianity Book
Everything® Gnostic Gospels Book
Everything® Hinduism Book, $15.95
Everything® History of the Bible Book
Everything® Jesus Book
Everything® Jewish History & Heritage Book
Everything® Judaism Book
Everything® Kabbalah Book
Everything® Koran Book
Everything® Mary Book
Everything® Mary Magdalene Book
Everything® Prayer Book

Everything® Saints Book, 2nd Ed.
Everything® Torah Book
Everything® Understanding Islam Book
Everything® Women of the Bible Book
Everything® World's Religions Book

SCHOOL & CAREERS

Everything® Career Tests Book
Everything® College Major Test Book
Everything® College Survival Book, 2nd Ed.
Everything® Cover Letter Book, 2nd Ed.
Everything® Filmmaking Book
Everything® Get-a-Job Book, 2nd Ed.
Everything® Guide to Being a Paralegal
Everything® Guide to Being a Personal Trainer
Everything® Guide to Being a Real Estate Agent
Everything® Guide to Being a Sales Rep
Everything® Guide to Being an Event Planner
Everything® Guide to Careers in Health Care
Everything® Guide to Careers in Law Enforcement
Everything® Guide to Government Jobs
Everything® Guide to Starting and Running a Catering
       Business
Everything® Guide to Starting and Running a Restaurant
Everything® Guide to Starting and Running
       a Retail Store
Everything® Job Interview Book, 2nd Ed.
Everything® New Nurse Book
Everything® New Teacher Book
Everything® Paying for College Book
Everything® Practice Interview Book
Everything® Resume Book, 3rd Ed.
Everything® Study Book

SELF-HELP

Everything® Body Language Book
Everything® Dating Book, 2nd Ed.
Everything® Great Sex Book
Everything® Guide to Caring for Aging Parents,
       $15.95
Everything® Self-Esteem Book
Everything® Self-Hypnosis Book, $9.95
Everything® Tantric Sex Book

SPORTS & FITNESS

Everything® Easy Fitness Book
Everything® Fishing Book
Everything® Guide to Weight Training, $15.95
Everything® Krav Maga for Fitness Book
Everything® Running Book, 2nd Ed.
Everything® Triathlon Training Book, $15.95

TRAVEL

Everything® Family Guide to Coastal Florida
Everything® Family Guide to Cruise Vacations
Everything® Family Guide to Hawaii
Everything® Family Guide to Las Vegas, 2nd Ed.
Everything® Family Guide to Mexico
Everything® Family Guide to New England, 2nd Ed.

Everything® Family Guide to New York City, 3rd Ed.
Everything® Family Guide to Northern California
       and Lake Tahoe
Everything® Family Guide to RV Travel & Campgrounds
Everything® Family Guide to the Caribbean
Everything® Family Guide to the Disneyland® Resort, California
       Adventure®, Universal Studios®, and the Anaheim
       Area, 2nd Ed.
Everything® Family Guide to the Walt Disney World Resort®,
       Universal Studios®, and Greater Orlando, 5th Ed.
Everything® Family Guide to Timeshares
Everything® Family Guide to Washington D.C., 2nd Ed.

WEDDINGS

Everything® Bachelorette Party Book, $9.95
Everything® Bridesmaid Book, $9.95
Everything® Destination Wedding Book
Everything® Father of the Bride Book, $9.95
Everything® Green Wedding Book, $15.95
Everything® Groom Book, $9.95
Everything® Jewish Wedding Book, 2nd Ed., $15.95
Everything® Mother of the Bride Book, $9.95
Everything® Outdoor Wedding Book
Everything® Wedding Book, 3rd Ed.
Everything® Wedding Checklist, $9.95
Everything® Wedding Etiquette Book, $9.95
Everything® Wedding Organizer, 2nd Ed., $16.95
Everything® Wedding Shower Book, $9.95
Everything® Wedding Vows Book, 3rd Ed., $9.95
Everything® Wedding Workout Book
Everything® Weddings on a Budget Book, 2nd Ed., $9.95

WRITING

Everything® Creative Writing Book
Everything® Get Published Book, 2nd Ed.
Everything® Grammar and Style Book, 2nd Ed.
Everything® Guide to Magazine Writing
Everything® Guide to Writing a Book Proposal
Everything® Guide to Writing a Novel
Everything® Guide to Writing Children's Books
Everything® Guide to Writing Copy
Everything® Guide to Writing Graphic Novels
Everything® Guide to Writing Research Papers
Everything® Guide to Writing a Romance Novel, $15.95
Everything® Improve Your Writing Book, 2nd Ed.
Everything® Writing Poetry Book